Complete
English
Language

for **Cambridge International**
AS & A Level

Second Edition

Dr Julian Pattison
Duncan Williams

OXFORD
UNIVERSITY PRESS

Great Clarendon Street, Oxford, OX2 6DP, United Kingdom

Oxford University Press is a department of the University of Oxford. It furthers the University's objective of excellence in research, scholarship, and education by publishing worldwide. Oxford is a registered trade mark of Oxford University Press in the UK and in certain other countries

© Oxford University Press 2019

The moral rights of the authors have been asserted.

The publisher would like to acknowledge the contributions of Tina Bali to this title.

First published in 2019

ISBN 978 0 19 844576 0

Printed in Great Britain by Bell and Bain Ltd. Glasgow

Acknowledgements

Photo credits:

MIX
Paper from responsible sources
FSC® C007785

Cover: Virinaflora/Shutterstock; **p14**: Barry Barnes/Shutterstock; **p18**: The Granger Collection/Alamy Stock Photo; **p23**: Everett Collection Inc/Alamy Stock Photo; **p24**: Steve Collender/Shutterstock; **p33 (TR)**: Niday Picture Library/Alamy Stock Photo; **p33 (BR)**: Universal Images Gtoup/Getty Images; **p37**: Unknown/Alamy Stock Photo; **p42**: United Archives GmbH/Alamy Stock Photo; **p46**: PACIFIC PRESS/Alamy Stock Photo; **p51**: Shutterstock; **p54**: Benjamin Clapp/Shutterstock; **p57**: Library of Congress Prints and Photographs Division ; **p58**: Kathy deWitt/Alamy Stock Photo; **p59**: Colines/Alamy Stock Photo; **p65**: ober-art / Shutterstock; **p66**: Associated Newspapers/Daily Mail/REX/Shutterstock; **p68**: Reg Innell/Toronto Star/Getty Images; **p81**: Nicram Sabod/Shutterstock; **p86**: Better Stock/Shutterstock; **p88**: Mark reinstein/Shutterstock; **p109**: Aleem Zahid Khan/Shutterstock; **p111**: Jeff Morgan 02/Alamy Stock Photo; **p114**: Common Sense Media; **p115**: Moviestore collection Ltd/Alamy Stock Photo; **p124**: Denis Makarenko/Shutterstock; **p125**: Shutterstock; **p135 (T)**: kontur-vi/Shutterstock; **p135 (B)**: REDPIXEL.PL/Shutterstock; p 143: DILBERT ©1994 Scott Adams. Used By permission of ANDREWS MCMEEL SYNDICATION; p 147: By permission of the British Library/C.59.e.11; **p162**: Photobac/Shutterstock; **p163**: Harris, Sidney/Cartoonstock; **p167**: Phattana Stock/Shutterstock; **p191**: Speak Good English Movement; **p195 (T)**: JohnnyGreig/iStockphoto; **p195 (M)**: HAGENS WORLD PHOTOGRAPHY/Moment/Getty Images; **p195 (R)**: Glow Asia RF/Alamy Stock Photo; **p201**: Geraint Lewis/Alamy Stock Photo; **p206**: Morgan, Ron/Cartoon Stock; **p223**: Betsy Streeter/Cartoon Stock; **p235**: Abadonian/Getty Images.

Artwork by Q2A Media Services Pvt. Ltd. and Aptara.

The authors and publisher are grateful for permission to reprint the following copyright material:

John Adams: excerpts from *The Adams Papers: Papers of John Adams, Volumes IX-X*, edited by Gregg L. Lint, Joanna M. Revelas, and Richard Alan, Cambridge, Mass.: The Belknap Press of Harvard University Press, Copyright © 1996 by the Massachusetts Historical Society, reprinted by permission of Harvard University Press.

Chimamanda Ngozi Adichie: excerpt from *Americanah*, © 2013 Chimamanda Ngozi Adichie reprinted by permission of HarperCollins Publishers Ltd., Alfred A. Knopf, an imprint of the Knopf Doubleday Publishing Group, a division of Random House LLC, and Vintage Canada/Alfred A. Knopf Canada, a division of Penguin Random House Canada Limited, all rights reserved.

Chimamanda Ngozi Adichie: excerpt from *Half of a Yellow Sun*, Copyright © 2006 by Chimamanda Ngozi Adichie, reprinted by permission of Alfred A. Knopf, an imprint of the Knopf Doubleday Publishing Group, a division of Penguin Random House LLC, and HarperCollins Publishers Ltd, all rights reserved.

Alzheimer's Research UK: quotations (Expert 3, Rebecca Wood, and Expert 4) regarding side-effects of commonly-prescribed drugs, reprinted by permission.

Margaret Atwood: excerpt from *The Handmaid's Tale* published by Jonathan Cape, © 1985, 1986 by O. W. Toad, Ltd., reprinted by permission of The Random House Group Ltd., Houghton Mifflin Harcourt Company, Emblem/McClelland & Stewart, a division of Penguin Random House Canada Limited, and Curtis Brown Group Limited, all rights reserved.

Lillian Beckwith: excerpt from *The Loud Halo*, Copyright © The Beneficiaries of the Literary Estate of Lillian Beckwith 1964, reprinted by permission of Curtis Brown Group Ltd, London on behalf of the Literary Estate of Lillian Beckwith.

Tim Berners-Lee: excerpt from pp. 1-2 from *Weaving the Web*, Copyright © 1999, 2000 by Tim Berners-Lee, reprinted by permission of HarperCollins Publishers.

Douglas Biber, Susan Conrad, Geoffrey Leech: excerpt from *Longman Student Grammar of Spoken and Written English*, Pearson Education Limited, © Pearson Education Limited 2002, reprinted by permission.

Katherine Boo: from *Behind the Beautiful Forevers: Life, Death, and Hope in a Mumbai Undercity*, Copyright © 2012 by Katherine Boo, reprinted by permission of Random House, an imprint and division of Penguin Random House LLC, Granta Books, and Scribe Publications Pty Ltd., all rights reserved.

Raymond Carver: 'The Father' from *Will You Please Be Quiet, Please?*, (1976), Copyright © Raymond Carver, Copyright ©Tess Gallagher, 1993, reprinted by permission of The Random House Group Limited and The Wylie Agency (UK) Limited.

Eleanor Catton: excerpt from *The Luminaries*, Copyright © 2013, 2014 Eleanor Catton, reprinted by permission of Emblem/McClelland & Stewart, a division of Penguin Random House Canada Limited, Little, Brown and Co., an imprint of Hachette Book Group, Inc., Granta Books, and United Agents on behalf of the Author, all rights reserved.

Raymond Chandler: excerpt from *The Big Sleep*, (Penguin Books, 2011), Copyright © 1939 by Raymond Chandler and renewed 1967 by Helga Greene, Executrix of the Estate of Raymond Chandler, reprinted by permission of Alfred A. Knopf, an imprint of the Knopf Doubleday Publishing Group, a division of Random House LLC, and Rogers, Coleridge and White Literary Agency, all rights reserved.

Prof. Tim Chico: short quotation (Expert 2) regarding side-effects of commonly-prescribed drugs, reprinted by permission.

Common Sense Media: excerpt from 'Dancing with the Stars: Juniors' by Emily Ashby, and Common Sense Media Logo, reprinted by permission of Common Sense Media.

Bernard Comrie: excerpt from 'Language and Thought', Linguistic Society of America, (linguistic.org), reprinted by permission.

David Crystal: excerpt from *How Language Works*, © 2005 by David Crystal, reprinted by permission of Penguin Books Ltd.

William Dalrymple: excerpt from *The Age of Kali*, © 1998, William Dalrymple, reprinted by permission of HarperCollins Publishers Ltd.

Debrett's London: excerpt from www.debretts.com, reprinted by permission of Debrett's Limited.

European Parliament: excerpt from report 'Gender-Neutral Language in the European Parliament' (© European Parliament 2018), reprinted by permission.

Department for Education and Skills: excerpt from report 'Birth to Three Matters: A Review of the Literature' by Tricia David, Kathy Goouch, Sacha Powell, and Lesley Abbott, © Queen's Printer 2003, public sector information licensed under the Open Government Licence v3.0 (http://www.nationalarchives.gov.uk/doc/open-government-licence).

William Faulkner: excerpt from *The Sound and the Fury*, published by Chatto & Windus © Copyright 1929 and renewed 1957 by William Faulkner, reprinted by permission of Random House, an imprint and division of Penguin Random House LLC, and W. W. Norton & Company, Inc., all rights reserved.

Janet Frame: excerpt from *To the Is-land*, Copyright ©1982, The Janet Frame Literary Trust, used by permission of The Wylie Agency (UK) Limited.

Erving Goffman: excerpt from *The Presentation of Self in Everyday Life*, copyright © 1959 by Erving Goffman. reprinted by permission of Penguin Books UK Limited and Doubleday, an imprint of the Knopf Doubleday Publishing Group, a division of Penguin Random House LLC, all rights reserved.

David Graddol: excerpts from 'Global English' 28 July 2005, from https://www.open.edu/openlearn/history-the-arts/culture/english-language/global-english, © The Open University, reprinted by permission of The Open University.

Claire Le Guern: article 'When the mermaids cry: The great plastic tide' written by Claire Le Guern, Coastal Care's General Director - Contributor – Author, http://coastalcare.org/2009/11/plastic-pollution/, © SAF - Coastalcare.org sole property, reprinted by permission of Coastal Care.

Mark Haddon: excerpt from *The Curious Incident of the Dog in the Night-Time: A Novel*, published by Jonathan Cape, Copyright © 2003 by Mark Haddon, reprinted by permission of Doubleday, an imprint of the Knopf Doubleday Publishing Group, a division of Penguin Random House LLC, and The Random House Group Limited, all rights reserved.

Mohsin Hamid: excerpt from *The Reluctant Fundamentalist*, Copyright © 2007 by Mohsin Hamid, reprinted by permission of Houghton Mifflin Harcourt Publishing Company and Penguin Books (UK), all rights reserved.

Ernest Hemingway: from *In Our Time*, Copyright © 1925, 1930 by Charles Scribner's Sons, Copyright renewed 1953, 1958 by Ernest Hemingway, reprinted with the permission of Scribner Publishing Group.

Prof. Simon Horobin: excerpt from article 'What will the English language be like in 100 years?' written in 2015 by Simon Horobin, Professor of English Language and Literature at the University of Oxford, published in The Conversation (theconversation.com), reprinted by permission.

Continued on back page

Contents

Contents

Answers to activities in this book and other supporting material can be found on your free support website. Access the support website here:

www.oxfordsecondary.com/9780198445760

AS LEVEL

Introduction to AS Level English Language

This chapter will:

→ help you to identify your readiness for the course, your strengths and weaknesses
→ outline what the course involves
→ describe the skills you need
→ give you an outline of how you will be assessed.

Getting started

This book is not a traditional textbook because it can't possibly include examples of all the different sorts of speech and writing that you will need to be familiar with in order to tackle the examinations at the end of the course. Rather, it is a companion to help you along the way.

As you read, the book will introduce you to a wide variety of key words that you will need in order to analyse texts that are given to you at that point or that you find for yourself. These key words will be printed in **bold** type the first time you encounter them and will be defined. You need to learn these words and their definitions. There is a glossary of all the key words at the end of the book. Throughout this book, the word '**text**' is taken to mean any communication in the English language, either written or spoken.

Because of my background (middle-aged, British, teacher), you will find some rather British turns of phrase and perhaps some slightly British humour (and spelling) in this book. All of this could be edited to make things more language-neutral, but I want you to have some picture of me as a real person – I am trying to build up a relationship with you through the way that I write. I want you to trust my judgements about the subject and, as we are going to be companions for a number of weeks, I'd like you to think we might be friends. In other words, I am constructing a personality on paper and, of course, one of the things about English as a global language is that you have to get used to adapting yourself to the variety in the language as you listen and read. That's the colour of the language, its diversity, its spice, and also the central concern of what is to follow.

Am I ready?

Let's start with some words of congratulation …

If you are reading this book, then you have already done the hardest part of the course!

You may not be a virtuoso violinist or a world-class soccer player, but in terms of language skills you are already an expert. Since you were a baby you have been trying to make an impression on the world, and one of the most obvious ways in which you will have done this is by learning to talk.

From the age of about five you will have been talking in your first language (it doesn't have to be English) with great fluency, making only occasional errors. That's quite a trick, particularly because you will have gained these skills without having been anywhere near a textbook.

Not only had you learned to talk by that stage, but you had a sound grasp of how to put the language together in a wide variety of ways. In other words, you had managed to internalise the rules of English, or your first language, with no great difficulty. This is probably the cleverest thing you will ever do – it's certainly one of the most useful.

In his book *The Language Instinct*, Steven Pinker, the experimental psychologist, puts it like this:

> 'Language is a complex, specialized skill, which develops in the child spontaneously without conscious effort or formal instruction ... People know how to talk in more or less the sense that spiders know how to spin webs. Web-spinning was not invented by some unsung spider genius and does not depend on having had the right education or on having an aptitude for architecture or the construction trades. Rather, spiders spin webs because they have spider brains, which give them the urge to spin and the competence to succeed.'

Elsewhere, Pinker notes that a first-language English speaker will have a strong sense of how words work together, even if he or she has never put together a particular phrase before. Even when sentences appear to be nonsense you are able to speculate about meaning: 'The mups glorped spodily', will create a picture in your mind, even though you have no experience of three of the words, because you will have immediately fitted them into sentence patterns that you recognise.

This suggests that we learn language from principles, that there is such a thing as universal grammar, and that learning a first language is not done simply by repeating examples that we have heard. We know instinctively that 'Mo nailed posters to the wall' sounds reasonable, while 'Mo nailed the wall with posters', is somehow wrong. Without going into the detail of Pinker's argument we can be confident that 'Amy poured water into the glass' is a workable sentence, whereas 'Amy poured the glass with water' is not, even though it makes grammatical sense and in textbook terms is an exact equivalent of 'Dad loaded the car with luggage'.

By now, you have a vocabulary of many thousands of words and you can conjure any of them at a moment's notice in order to make an impression on other people. What's more, you can put them together in an infinite number of combinations in order to express your needs and desires to a wide variety of people in different situations.

With a moment's reflection, you can see how skilful you are in this subject. Compare this with learning an additional language, with its grammar books and exercises and the errors that you make in quite simple communications, both spoken and written. Somewhere along the way you have managed to accomplish something extraordinary with your first language, seemingly without effort.

Slightly more problematic, perhaps, is your relationship with reading and writing because you probably haven't given them the thousands of hours of practice that you have unconsciously put into listening and speaking. Nonetheless, you probably have little memory of a stage before you could read, where words were just a jumble on the page, and you quite possibly have little memory of your first efforts at handwriting, though your parents may have kept some examples of your faltering first attempts.

That's not right!

By the time you were five, you would have found virtually all of the sentences below strange to say; you would have felt instinctively that they weren't quite right.

- Mummy goed out.
- Sammy jump over wall.
- I bigged it.
- It goed round and round.
- I willn't do it.
- He got two arm.
- I see Daddy bike.
- Mine is the bestest.
- Me don't want to do it.
- The mans bettern't do that.

Bearing in mind that small children construct grammatical rules without a textbook, why might the speakers of each of these utterances assume that what thehy say is correct?

On sunday I went to the parck with my bruver and my frend. We plad crickit then we went home to have a loley. Then we went back to the parck and plad rawdus with my frend. ✓ Good

↑ **Figure 1.1** Humble beginnings

By now, you may have written more on a computer (or a mobile phone or tablet) than on paper and may even find the business of shaping letters by hand quite hard work. In other words, you are a typical 21st-century user of your mother tongue.

What's involved?

Having reached a high level of competence with a language, it is possible to start thinking much more explicitly about how texts are constructed in order to create meaning. All texts contain elements of content, and that's always attached to issues of how the text can be shaped for maximum effect. If you fall off the back of a boat, it's obvious that you would probably shout 'Help!' in the brief seconds you had before you hit the ocean, rather than phrasing the request more formally as 'I wonder if someone would offer me assistance'. In other words, situations shape texts. The process of discussing how texts create meaning is called **discourse analysis.** You will be looking at a vast range of different sorts of texts during your studies. At the same time you will also be producing your own texts in a variety of styles, and reflecting upon the choices that you make as a speaker or a writer. You will also enlarge your technical vocabulary for critical analysis.

Activity 1.1

Test your current competence with the following **verbs** followed by **prepositions** in the list below. Write down a definition for each one.

- knock in, knock out, knock down, knock round, knock through
- break in, break down, break through, break up.

The chances are that you will be able to see that each of the phrases means something different. You will be able to define most, if not all, of them.

Non-native speakers have to learn each one individually and then to realise that in British English 'knock off' can mean both to steal and to stop work.

Phrases like these demonstrate a language at work at its most idiomatic and colloquial, where a native speaker will understand automatically, and a second-language speaker will either have to nod wisely or find a dictionary.

There are four main areas of expertise that you will be developing:

1. a critical and informed response to texts in a range of forms, styles and contexts
2. the interdependent skills of reading, analysis and research
3. effective, creative, accurate and appropriate communication
4. a firm foundation for further study of language (in use) and **linguistics** (the scientific study of language and its structure).

During the course you will be asked to engage with a wide variety of different sorts of texts, and you will need to be sure that you have read examples of the following different **genres** (types of writing):

advertisements   brochures   leaflets   editorials   news stories

articles   reviews   blogs   investigative journalism   letters

podcasts   biographies and autobiographies   travel writing   diaries   essays

scripted speech   narrative writing   descriptive writing

What skills do I need?

You will need to be able to demonstrate that you can:

- respond to a range of different types of writing, produced for a variety of different readers
- communicate effectively.

You will do this when you:

- sustain accurate and fluent writing
- produce informed responses, whether by writing originally or in imitation, and by writing critical responses to others' writing
- demonstrate an understanding of form, style, context and audience
- demonstrate knowledge and understanding of both what you have read and of texts that you produce yourself.
- use your wider knowledge of texts and text types in order to respond to the demands of the examination questions.

How will I be assessed?

At AS Level, the assessment will take the form of **two** written examinations.

Paper 1 Reading (50 marks) lasts 2 hours and 15 minutes.

The paper has two sections, Section A: Directed response and Section B: Text analysis. There will be two questions, one in each section. Both are compulsory.

Section A: Directed response, Question 1 (25 marks in total) asks you to read a text of approximately 550–750 words and then:

(a) Produce a short piece of your own writing (150– 200 words) that uses information from the original, but adapts it to fit a specific form, purpose and audience. (10 marks)

(b) Compare your writing in 1(a) with that of the original, identifying, analysing and comparing characteristic features of the texts and relating these to their purpose, audience and contexts. (15 marks)

Section B: Text analysis, Question 2 (25 marks in total) asks you to read another text of approximately 550–750 words and then:

Write a stylistic, organised analysis of the text, commenting on its form, structure and language and identifying characteristic features of the text relating to meaning, context and audience.

Paper 2 Writing (50 marks) lasts 2 hours.

The paper has two sections, Section A: Shorter writing and reflective commentary, and Section B: Extended writing.

You will answer one compulsory question in Section A, but have a choice of three questions in Section B from which you will choose one.

Section A: Shorter writing and reflective commentary, Question 1 (25 marks in total) asks you to:

(a) Write a response of no more than 400 words in a particular genre, choosing vocabulary, style and structure to fit a specific form, purpose and audience. (15 marks)

(b) Write a reflective commentary on your writing in 1(a), drawing attention to how your linguistic choices helped you to fulfil the task. (10 marks)

Section B: Extended writing, Question 2 (25 marks in total) asks you to write a sustained piece of 600–900 words, expressing your idea clearly, coherently and accurately, using an appropriate range of language and in a manner appropriate to the form, purpose and audience. You can choose from **one** of the following categories:

- imaginative/descriptive writing
- discursive/argumentative writing
- review/critical writing.

The text type you may be required to create depends on the category; see page 8 for a list of some of the text type possibilities.

The big picture

Every time you come across a text or are asked to create one, you need to think about the circumstances of its production and its effectiveness.

Let's start by thinking about the process of creating a text.

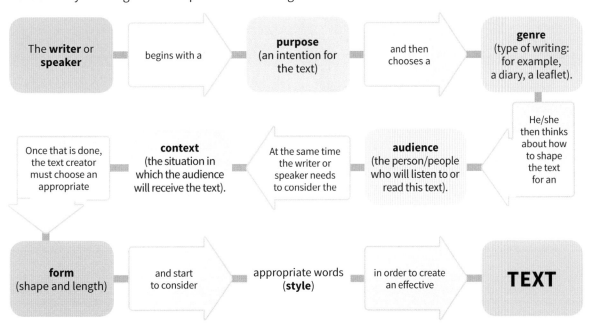

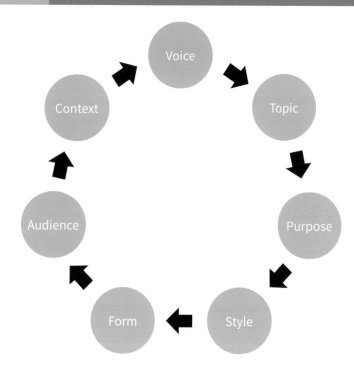

By looking at the various stages of text production, you are starting to engage with the construction of texts. You will have noticed that although this is a course in English language, we have thus far avoided any mention of things like grammar. That's not because they are unimportant, but because the primary function of the analysis you will be expected to do focuses on patterns of language and the social and cultural contexts in which it is used. Of course, you will need to be able to analyse in detail, but you need to keep the bigger picture in mind as you encounter texts. Your main focus, therefore, is on language **in use**. So as you read, speak or listen, you need to be constantly asking yourself the following questions.

- What is this text trying to do? (**Purpose**)
- Who is it trying to communicate these ideas to? (**Audience**)
- Where will this text appear? (**Context**)
- What does it look or sound like? (**Form/structure**)

And of course all of these things exist side by side in a piece of writing. The model isn't quite a straight line. Perhaps it's more like the diagram on the left.

You can go deeper by starting to consider the relationship between the social and cultural contexts in which a text is produced. For example, if you think about greeting a friend at school or college with a casual 'Hi, how are you?', both of you know that your friend is not being invited to give a full account of his or her health, mood and relationships. You both have a common understanding of this sort of exchange, and you obey the rules. This sort of understanding between people is known as **pragmatics**. It means that you don't have to explain absolutely everything to a listener or a reader before you can start communicating with each other.

Here's a silly example. If you travel by train to London from the north of England, you get to Euston station and discover a sign on the escalator to the underground trains that says 'Suitcases must be carried on the escalator'. Having located a suitcase and picked it up, you then journey on to Charing Cross, where a new message creates further difficulties. By now, 'Suitcases and heavy shopping must be carried on the escalator'. It's clear what the sign means (if you happen to have a suitcase or heavy shopping with you at the time, you should carry them on the escalator), but there is an assumption about the word *must* that may not be shared by all members of the audience for the text. But to go looking for a suitcase and some shopping would be perverse – it is fairly obvious from the context what the language is intended to mean. Context is everything here.

For our purposes, it is important to recognise that words can be differently interpreted. For example, when Abraham Lincoln was shot by John Wilkes Booth on 14 April 1865, he didn't die instantly and some of Booth's friends claimed that it wasn't Booth who killed Lincoln: it was the incompetent doctors who tried to save him that really killed him. Booth simply fired the gun.

At times, when trying to compress a story into only a few words, newspaper headline writers produce statements that can be read in two ways, often with comic effect. Without meaning to, they give completely the wrong impression.

RED TAPE HOLDS UP NEW BRIDGE

Nurse critical after operation

KIDS MAKE NUTRITIOUS SNACKS

HERSHEY BARS PROTEST

Squad helps dog bite victim

Drunk gets nine months in violin case

END TO FREE SCHOOL LOOMS

Stolen painting found by tree

Miners refuse to work after death

PRINCESS DIANA DRESSES TO BE AUCTIONED

LACK OF BRAINS HINDERS RESEARCH

Teenager held over shredder

↑ **Figure 1.2** How effective is this sign?

Activity 1.2

Try to explain why these headlines are open to different interpretations. Then pick one of them and write a brief (200-word) article that takes the unintended story as a serious piece of news.

Activity 1.3

Have a look at the sign in Figure 1.2. In what way does it not quite achieve the effect intended by the writer?

Activity 1.4

1. Copy and complete the following table with examples of the different types of language you might hear or use. Think about how you present yourself in terms of language in this range of different situations.

Where?	Examples of different uses of language	Constraints/rules
home and family		informal need to maintain order and discipline affection family-agreed codes and 'in' jokes
school and teachers		more formal structured/pre-meditated in terms of lesson content
soccer, Saturday afternoon	limited topics	very informal lower threshold for 'bad' language 'male' dominated

2. Add a few more scenarios from your own experience to the ones given in the left-hand column and then complete the rows.

Activity 1.5

Another way of thinking about this is to consider different influences on your own language that determine the ways in which you speak. You should try to think about six or seven different aspects of your own language use.

Factor	Use of language with examples
education	
gender	

You can apply the same ideas to yourself in terms of your written work too.

Working with your own experience

Whenever we produce texts, we are saying something about our relationships with each other. As soon as you start to talk or write, an audience or reader will start to make judgements about the words used, your accent, your level of education, the complexity of the way you express yourself, and your world view. You construct yourself (in part at least) through your use of language.

By now, you will have learned to write and speak in a variety of styles, and you will be acutely aware that an essay in school written for your teacher is very different to the sort of piece that you might produce by text message, where emoticons and abbreviations are acceptable, or in an email, where you will probably be rather more informal. You are on your way to recognising yourself as part of a **language community** – a group of people who demonstrate belonging and gain their identity from their language choices. More correctly, you will be identifying yourself as part of a number of communities, all of which share much in common (the vastness of the same language) but have subtle differences between them.

Spend a few minutes now on Activity 1.6. You will quickly establish that, although there are many variations of colour, shape, material and expense, people tend to wear shoes on their feet and hats on their heads. In other words, the function remains the same, even though the costume is different. The same is true of words in a sentence. Different types of words (verbs, nouns, etc.) perform different grammatical functions, but a writer or speaker's choice of particular examples ('exclaimed' rather than 'said', for example), gives a different impression to a reader or listener. In terms of both writing and clothing, we can define this separation as **style**. Understanding this difference, and being clear about it, will be crucial to your success in this course.

Activity 1.6

People often stake out their claims to belong to a group through what they wear. See if you can identify a number of different youth fashions, and then discuss the differences in style between them.

Conclusion

We have established a number of things in this opening chapter.

- You know what is involved in the course.
- You are aware of your own linguistic history and current competence in the language.
- You have started to think about yourself as a producer and consumer of texts.
- We have recognised that the main purpose of the course is to examine language in use.
- We have established some very broad outlines of terminology that you will need to develop as we move forwards.

This chapter will:

→ introduce you to the vocabulary that you need to know in order to be able to analyse texts

→ demonstrate these terms in action

→ make you aware of how thinking about writing by other people can help you reflect upon the thinking process and choices that you make in your own writing

→ give you a firm grounding in some of the concepts involved in discourse analysis.

Genre and context

One way in which we start to understand any text that we encounter is by trying to relate it to other similar texts that we have seen before. We immediately start to think about characteristics of this text that are familiar to us. Consider, for example, the warning sign in Figure 2.1. The information given is quite simple: CAUTION TRIP HAZARD. But someone needed to design this for particular effect. In other words, even the shortest of texts have genre constraints and considerations to be borne in mind.

So how did this notice come into being? The person who created this sign probably (even if unconsciously) went through the following process:

↑ **Figure 2.1** How effective is this sign?

author	the person in charge of public safety
audience	ordinary people, hence both words and cartoon
purpose	to warn people of the hazard
situation	a public place
physical form	a bright sign, big writing
constraints/rules	no need for salutations etc.
content	brief
level of formality/register	formal
style	directly addresses the other person
written language	doesn't need to be in sentences: emojis/cartoons could be used. Words need to be straightforward and easy to understand
structure	none required, but probably short, simple sentences or phrases or single words; needs absolute clarity

The notice would be much less effective if it said:

Notice to users: Members of the public are advised that there is some risk of tripping up in this area.

Any good piece of writing does what it needs to do: nothing more, nothing less.

The left-hand column of the table on page 14 gives you a list of terms that are useful for the analysis of any text that you come across, and you should get in the habit of reading texts with them in mind. The important point to recognise is that, almost unconsciously, you make a large number of decisions about any text you either produce or try to interpret. This is **genre classification**, and it is a key factor in being able to make sense of a text. In very formal terms, this sort of text identification is known as **corpus linguistics**, the linking of a text to the 'body' of other texts with which it shares central characteristics.

There are, of course, instances of writers playing tricks with genre, using an established form in order to manipulate a reader. William Carlos Williams wrote the following: 'This is just to say I have eaten the plums that were in the icebox and which you were probably saving for breakfast Forgive me they were delicious so sweet and so cold'. At first it seems like a casual note, in part because of its lack of punctuation. But once you know that Williams was a famous poet, it changes things considerably.

Activity 2.1

Try comparing the version above with the way that the poem appears in Williams's *Collected Poems* (below). You will need to think about the layout, the use of capital letters and the fact that it is typeset, not hand-written.

THIS IS JUST TO SAY

I have eaten
the plums
that were in
the icebox

and which
you were probably
saving
for breakfast

Forgive me
they were delicious
so sweet
and so cold

All of a sudden, you have to start applying the rules of genre that you know as poetry, not the rules for casual notes stuck to the fridge, and so you have to ask rather different questions of the text from those you might have originally had in mind.

As you can see, context and audience make a difference to your interpretation of a text. For example, the sentence 'You have a green light' is ambiguous. Without knowing the **context** (the identity of the speaker/writer, his or her intent, the **situation**) it is difficult to infer the meaning with confidence. It could mean:

- that you have a green light while driving your car and can move on
- that you can go ahead with a project (a metaphorical meaning)
- that your body has a green glow
- that you possess a light bulb that is tinted green.

This is an example where context gives the clue, of pragmatics in action.

Activity 2.2

Select three or four texts from a variety of sources and see if you can apply the rules of genre classification to them. Remember that the texts can be quite short.

In classifying these texts, you are demonstrating some of the fundamental skills you need for this course: you are responding to a number of forms, styles and contexts and thinking about the audience that they are directed towards. You could, of course, also apply these ideas to an evening's viewing on the television – the conventions for news broadcasts are, for example, entirely different from those of a cookery programme.

As you work, it will be clear that you are applying a series of rules in order to place the texts. They will probably be something like this:

- obvious features of form and shape – formal letters or a utility bill might be examples of this

- particular subject matter – a detective story focuses on finding out who committed the crime while a **biography** focuses on detailing the life of its subject, usually chronologically

- the writer's attitudes or the expected response from a reader – a travel brochure is based on the reasonable understanding that the reader agrees with the writer that taking a holiday to an exotic spot is a worthwhile thing to do

- expectations over time – if you have experienced James Bond or Bollywood movies, you know what to expect when one comes on the television. In other words, you have a **prototype** (a pre-formulated model) in mind as you read, watch or listen.

It will also be clear that, as with the Williams poem, there is no such thing as a fixed number of sorts of texts and that 'genre' is often a flexible term. Genres can be very wide: when you categorise the natural world, vultures, albatrosses and chickens all belong to the family of birds, even though each is obviously and very significantly different from the others. Similarly there are vast numbers of different types of experience categorised as 'smartphone apps.'

Activity 2.3

Here are some text openings. Identify the genre of each of them.

- Make wonderful plans to do new things in your life during the next 10 days while Jupiter aspects Pluto …

- Once upon a time …

- First, chop the onion …

- He's placing the ball. I think he's the man hoping to strike it, but first he's having a word with the captain …

- The manhunt extended across more than one hundred light years and eight centuries …

- Set on the tip of the peninsula, the hotel's grounds take in the sea, Samana village, and a tropical cliché worth of palm trees …

Write one of these openings down and then pass it on to another student. The other student should then write a further sentence in the same genre, fold over the paper so the next writer can't see your initial contribution and then pass it on again. Do this five or six times and then read out the result. See if the genre is still in place by the end.

Now you should assess how far the texts you have produced follow the rules for the particular genre.

Voice and point of view

Every text you come across, unless it is mechanically generated (a bus ticket, for example), will create a relationship with the audience. It does this in part by establishing a **voice**, a personality that comes through as you read or listen. Before we go into the detail, it's important to understand that there are two fundamental ways of creating a voice in a piece of writing. The first is when you aim to tell things from your own point of view, using the word '*I*'. This is called **first-person narrative**. You can also tell things in a rather more objective way, **third-person narrative**, where everything seems to be seen as a camera might take a picture, without prejudice and simply reporting what is seen. Both may involve you in talking about **point of view**, the stance that the narrator is taking in relation to the information he or she wants to tell you.

You can, incidentally, also write using the second person, using 'you', which is what this book is doing by talking to you directly on paper.

First-person narrative

With first-person narrative, the advantage is that the writing has a sense of immediacy – the reader gets involved with the person that is talking to them right from the beginning. Even a few words are enough to draw you in: 'I come from Des Moines. Somebody had to', the opening to Bill Bryson's book *The Lost Continent: Travels in Small Town America*, leads you into thinking that you are listening to someone who has a good sense of humour. Think too about the opening of Herman Melville's 900-page **novel** *Moby Dick*, where we are invited into an immediate and close relationship with the narrator with the words 'Call me Ishmael.'

Look at the opening of the novel *The Adventures of Huckleberry Finn* by American writer Mark Twain and have a go at Activity 2.4.

Activity 2.4

What sort of person is talking to you here? What can you work out about Huck from the way in which he addresses you?

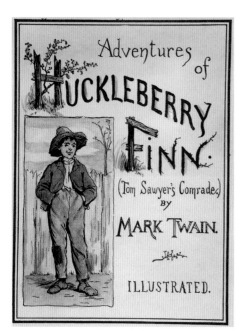

↑ **Figure 2.2** The first edition cover of *The Adventures of Huckleberry Finn*

Text type: prose narrative, fiction, USA

You don't know about me without you have read a book by the name of *The Adventures of Tom Sawyer*; but that ain't no matter. That book was made by Mr. Mark Twain, and he told the truth, mainly. There was things which he stretched, but mainly he told the truth. That is nothing. I never seen anybody but lied one time or another, without it was Aunt Polly, or the widow, or maybe Mary. Aunt Polly – Tom's Aunt Polly, she is – and Mary, and the Widow Douglas is all told about in that book, which is mostly a true book, with some stretchers, as I said before.

Now the way that the book winds up is this: Tom and me found the money that the robbers hid in the cave, and it made us rich. We got six thousand dollars apiece – all gold. It was an awful sight of money when it was piled up. Well, Judge Thatcher he took it and put it out at interest, and it fetched us a dollar a day apiece all the year round – more than a body could tell what to do with. The Widow Douglas she took me for her son, and allowed she would sivilize me; but it was rough living in the house all the time, considering how dismal regular and decent the widow was in all her ways; and so when I couldn't stand it no longer I lit out. I got into my old rags and my sugar-hogshead again, and was free and satisfied. But Tom Sawyer he hunted me up and said he was going to start a band of robbers, and I might join if I would go back to the widow and be respectable. So I went back.

The Adventures of Huckleberry Finn by Mark Twain

Reflecting on language data

You might recognise that there is quite a subtle mixture of first-person and second-person narrative going on here, and that the writer is aiming for a very particular effect from this. A further point to note, of course, is that Huck is a fictional creation – his voice has been created by Mark Twain – but Twain tries hard to give the reader the impression that the narrator is quite simple, speaks truthfully and is not very educated. Although the book is a novel, it has disguised its genre to give you the impression that it is an **autobiography** (someone's life directly written or spoken from their own experience). The text is a written text, but it's clear that Huck thinks that he is talking directly to you from the page, almost as though this is a transcript of a live interview. Fairly obviously, as the speaker is involved in the action, his point of view is **subjective** and may be biased or slanted in order to present himself in a particular way.

Here are two more examples for you to talk about.

Text type: prose narrative, fiction, USA

In my younger and more vulnerable years my father gave me some advice that I've been turning over in my mind ever since.

"Whenever you feel like criticizing anyone," he told me, "just remember that all the people in this world haven't had the advantages that you've had."

He didn't say any more, but we've always been unusually communicative in a reserved way, and I understood that he meant a great deal more than that. In consequence, I'm inclined to reserve all judgments, a habit that has opened up many curious natures to me and also made me the victim of not a few veteran bores. The abnormal mind is quick to detect and attach itself to this quality when it appears in a normal person, and so it came about that in college I was unjustly accused of being a politician, because I was privy to the secret griefs of wild, unknown men. Most of the confidences were unsought – frequently I have feigned sleep, preoccupation, or a hostile levity when I realized by some unmistakable sign that an intimate revelation was quivering on the horizon; for the intimate revelations of young men, or at least the terms in which they express them, are usually plagiaristic and marred by obvious suppressions. Reserving judgments is a matter of infinite hope. I am still a little afraid of missing something if I forget that, as my father snobbishly suggested, and I snobbishly repeat, a sense of the fundamental decencies is parcelled out unequally at birth. And, after boasting this way of my tolerance, I come to the admission that it has a limit. Conduct may be founded on the hard rock or the wet marshes, but after a certain point I don't care what it's founded on. When I came back from the East last autumn I felt that I wanted the world to be in uniform and at a sort of moral attention forever; I wanted no more riotous excursions with privileged glimpses into the human heart.

The Great Gatsby by F. Scott Fitzgerald

Text type: prose narrative, fiction, UK

It was 7 minutes after midnight. The dog was lying on the grass in front of Mrs Shears' house. Its eyes were closed. It looked as if it was running on its side, the way dogs run when they think they are chasing a cat in a dream. But the dog was not running or asleep. The dog was dead. There was a garden fork sticking out of the dog. The points of the fork must have gone all the way through the dog and into the ground because the fork had not fallen over. I decided the dog was probably killed with the fork because I could not see any other wounds in the dog and I do not think you would stick a garden fork into a dog after it had died for some other reason, like cancer for example, or a road accident. But I could not be certain about this.

> I went through Mrs Shears' gate, closing it behind me. I walked onto her lawn and knelt beside the dog. I put my hand on the muzzle of the dog. It was still warm.
>
> The dog was called Wellington. It belonged to Mrs Shears who was our friend. She lived on the opposite side of the road, two houses to the left.
>
> *The Curious Incident of the Dog in the Night-Time* by Mark Haddon

You will have noticed that as you read you are hard at work trying to make sense of the voice, to work out whether the speaker is old or young, rich or poor, clever or stupid – the list could go on. And, of course, you have to decide if you want to listen to this voice, whether you trust and like it or not. If you write in the first person, you need to be very aware that readers are conjuring up a picture of you in their minds. The advantage of the voice here is that we are allowed direct access into the thoughts of the person writing. The disadvantage is that we have no means of knowing what other people might think about the events that are being described or whether the narrator is telling the truth.

Third-person narrative

As we have seen, first-person narrative offers you intimacy with the speaker or writer's voice. You can demonstrate this easily by contrasting Haddon's narrator in *The Curious Incident of the Dog in the Night-Time* to the opening of Charles Dickens's novel *A Tale of Two Cities*, below.

> **Text type: prose narrative, fiction, UK**
>
> It was the best of times, it was the worst of times, it was the age of wisdom, it was the age of foolishness, it was the epoch of belief, it was the epoch of incredulity, it was the season of Light, it was the season of Darkness, it was the spring of hope, it was the winter of despair, we had everything before us, we had nothing before us, we were all going direct to Heaven, we were all going direct the other way – in short, the period was so far like the present period, that some of its noisiest authorities insisted on its being received, for good or for evil, in the superlative degree of comparison only.
>
> *A Tale of Two Cities* by Charles Dickens

Here Dickens writes as though he is **omniscient**, with an all-seeing eye, someone who is telling the story and has the right to observe events and comment on them in very serious tones. Sometimes the writer creates a voice that comments on the action **explicitly**, as here. This is called **intrusive narration**. Narrators who simply let the action unfold are **unintrusive**. If the writer seems to know everything then it can be called **unrestricted narrative**. On the other hand, sometimes writers limit themselves to **restricted narrative**, where the events unfold themselves without the writer seeming to know everything from the start. Remember, too, that writers may be trying to convey an impression of themselves as they write which may not correspond to the day-to-day characters of the writers themselves. You will also notice that a writer can choose to be **objective**, non-judgemental, about what is being said, or can offer a commentary in which they express some opinion, which then makes the writing **subjective**.

Sometimes, factual writing borrows some of the techniques of fictional writing in order to become more vivid, as can be seen in the following extract.

Activity 2.5

Focus on three aspects of Boo's style here:

- how it moves straight into the situation
- details of the story that could come from a newspaper report
- vividness of description.

Which is the most important?

Text type: prose narrative, non-fiction, India

Prologue: between roses July 17, 2008—Mumbai

Midnight was closing in, the one-legged woman was grievously burned, and the Mumbai police were coming for Abdul and his father. In a slum hut by the international airport, Abdul's parents came to a decision with an uncharacteristic economy of words. The father, a sick man, would wait inside the trash-strewn, tin-roofed shack where the family of eleven resided. He'd go quietly when arrested. Abdul, the household earner, was the one who had to flee.

Abdul's opinion of this plan had not been solicited, typically. Already he was mule-brained with panic. He was sixteen years old, or maybe nineteen—his parents were hopeless with dates. Allah, in His impenetrable wisdom, had cut him small and jumpy. A coward: Abdul said it of himself. He knew nothing about eluding policemen. What he knew about, mainly, was trash. For nearly all the waking hours of nearly all the years he could remember, he'd been buying and selling to recyclers the things that richer people threw away.

Now Abdul grasped the need to disappear, but beyond that his imagination flagged. He took off running, then came back home. The only place he could think to hide was in his garbage.

He cracked the door of the family hut and looked out. His home sat midway down a row of hand-built, spatchcock dwellings; the lop-sided shed where he stowed his trash was just next door. To reach this shed unseen would deprive his neighbors of the pleasure of turning him in to the police.

He didn't like the moon, though: full and stupid bright, illuminating a dusty open lot in front of his home. Across the lot were the shacks of two dozen other families, and Abdul feared he wasn't the only person peering out from behind the cover of a plywood door. Some people in this slum wished his family ill because of the old Hindu–Muslim resentments.

Others resented his family for the modern reason, economic envy. Doing waste work that many Indians found contemptible, Abdul had lifted his large family above subsistence.

The open lot was quiet, at least—freakishly so. A kind of beach-front for a vast pool of sewage that marked the slum's eastern border, the place was bedlam most nights: people fighting, cooking, flirting, bathing, tending goats, playing cricket, waiting for water at a public tap … The pressures that built up in crowded huts on narrow slum lanes had only this place, the maidan, to escape. But after the fight, and the burning of the woman called the One Leg, people had retreated to their huts.

Now, among the … water buffalo … there seemed to be just one watchful presence: a small, unspookable boy from Nepal. He was sitting, arms around knees, in a spangly blue haze by the sewage lake—the reflected neon signage of a luxury hotel across the water. Abdul didn't mind if the Nepali boy saw him go into hiding. This kid, Adarsh, was no spy for the police. He just liked to stay out late, to avoid his mother and her nightly rages.

It was as safe a moment as Abdul was going to get. He bolted for the trash shed and closed the door behind him.

Inside was carbon-black, frantic with rats, and yet relieving. His storeroom—120 square feet, piled high to a leaky roof with the things in this world Abdul knew how to handle. Empty water … bottles, mildewed newspapers …, wadded aluminum foil, umbrellas stripped to the ribs by monsoons, broken shoe-laces, yellowed Q-tips, snarled cassette tape, torn plastic casings that once held imitation Barbies. Somewhere in the darkness, there was a Berbee or Barbie itself, maimed in one of the experiments to which children who had many toys seemed to subject those toys no longer favored.

Behind the Beautiful Forevers by Katherine Boo

Another technique that a third-person writer can use is to give you partial insight into what one of the characters or participants is thinking, or how he or she is responding to a situation. The voice is external, but we are seeing the situation through the eyes of a character. The opening of Chimamanda Ngozi Adichie's novel *Half of A Yellow Sun*, set during the civil war in Nigeria, offers a fine example.

Text type: prose narrative, fiction, Nigeria

Master was a little crazy; he had spent too many years reading books overseas, talked to himself in his office, did not always return greetings, and had too much hair. Ugwu's aunty said this in a low voice as they walked on the path. "But he is a good man," she added. "And as long as you work well, you will eat well. You will even eat meat every day." She stopped to spit; the saliva left her mouth with a sucking sound and landed on the grass.

Ugwu did not believe that anybody, not even this master he was going to live with, ate meat every day. He did not disagree with his aunty, though, because he was too choked with expectation, too busy imagining his new life away from the village. They had been walking for a while now, since they got off the lorry at the motor park, and the afternoon sun burned the back of his neck. But he did not mind. He was prepared to walk hours more in even hotter sun. He had never seen anything like the streets that appeared after they went past the university gates, streets so smooth and tarred that he itched to lay his cheek down on them. He would never be able to describe to his sister Anulika how the bungalows here were painted the colour of the sky and sat side by side like polite well-dressed men, how the hedges separating them were trimmed so flat on top that they looked like tables wrapped with leaves.

His aunty walked faster, her slippers making slap-slap sounds that echoed in the silent street. Ugwu wondered if she, too, could feel the coal tar getting hotter underneath, through her thin soles. They went past a sign, ODIM STREET, and Ugwu mouthed street, as he did whenever he saw an English word that was not too long. He smelled something sweet, heady, as they walked into a compound, and was sure it came from the white flowers clustered on the bushes at the entrance. The bushes were shaped like slender hills. The lawn glistened. Butterflies hovered above.

"I told Master you will learn everything fast, osiso-osiso," his aunty said. Ugwu nodded attentively although she had already told him this many times, as often as she told him the story of how his good fortune came about: While she was sweeping the corridor in the mathematics department a week ago, she heard Master say that he needed a houseboy to do his cleaning, and she immediately said she could help, speaking before his typist or office messenger could offer to bring someone.

"I will learn fast, Aunty," Ugwu said. He was staring at the car in the garage; a strip of metal ran around its blue body like a necklace.

"Remember, what you will answer whenever he calls you is Yes, sah!"

"Yes, sah!" Ugwu repeated.

They were standing before the glass door. Ugwu held back from reaching out to touch the cement wall, to see how different it would feel from the mud walls of his mother's hut that still bore the faint patterns of moulding fingers. For a brief moment, he wished he were back there now, in his mother's hut, under the dim coolness of the thatch roof; or in his aunty's hut, the only one in the village with a corrugated iron roof.

Half of a Yellow Sun by Chimamanda Ngozi Adichie

Activity 2.6

What do you learn about Ugwu from the passage? How do you learn it?

Speeches

We have looked at genre and voice and can now think about how they combine in political speeches.

Here is the ending of John F. Kennedy's inaugural address given on 20 January 1961 on becoming President of the United States of America.

Text type: scripted spoken, USA

So let us begin anew – remembering on both sides that civility is not a sign of weakness, and sincerity is always subject to proof. Let us never negotiate out of fear, but let us never fear to negotiate.

Let both sides explore what problems unite us instead of belaboring those problems which divide us. Let both sides, for the first time, formulate serious and precise proposals for the inspection and control of arms, and bring the absolute power to destroy other nations under the absolute control of all nations. Let both sides seek to invoke the wonders of science instead of its terrors. Together let us explore the stars, conquer the deserts, eradicate disease, tap the ocean depths, and encourage the arts and commerce. Let both sides unite to heed, in all corners of the earth, the command of Isaiah – to "undo the heavy burdens, and [to] let the oppressed go free." And, if a beachhead of cooperation may push back the jungle of suspicion, let both sides join in creating a new endeavor – not a new balance of power, but a new world of law – where the strong are just, and the weak secure, and the peace preserved. All this will not be finished in the first one hundred days. Nor will it be finished in the first one thousand days; nor in the life of this Administration; nor even perhaps in our lifetime on this planet. But let us begin. In your hands, my fellow citizens, more than mine, will rest the final success or failure of our course. Since this country was founded, each generation of Americans has been summoned to give testimony to its national loyalty. The graves of young Americans who answered the call to service surround the globe. Now the trumpet summons us again – not as a call to bear arms, though arms we need – not as a call to battle, though embattled we are – but a call to bear the burden of a long twilight struggle, year in and year out, "rejoicing in hope; patient in tribulation," a struggle against the common enemies of man: tyranny, poverty, disease, and war itself.

↑ **Figure 2.3** John F. Kennedy

Can we forge against these enemies a grand and global alliance, North and South, East and West, that can assure a more fruitful life for all mankind? Will you join in that historic effort?

In the long history of the world, only a few generations have been granted the role of defending freedom in its hour of maximum danger. I do not shrink from this responsibility – I welcome it. I do not believe that any of us would exchange places with any other people or any other generation. The energy, the faith, the devotion which we bring to this endeavor will light our country and all who serve it. And the glow from that fire can truly light the world. And so, my fellow Americans, ask not what your country can do for you; ask what you can do for your country. My fellow citizens of the world, ask not what America will do for you, but what together we can do for the freedom of man.

Finally, whether you are citizens of America or citizens of the world, ask of us here the same high standards of strength and sacrifice which we ask of you. With a good conscience our only sure reward, with history the final judge of our deeds, let us go forth to lead the land we love, asking His blessing and His help, but knowing that here on earth God's work must truly be our own.

John F. Kennedy's inaugural address

Activity 2.7

What picture does Kennedy aim to give of his new administration?

Now look at the Gettysburg Address, given by Abraham Lincoln towards the end of the American Civil War at the inauguration of the American National Cemetery (1863).

Text type: scripted spoken, USA

Four score and seven years ago our fathers brought forth on this continent, a new nation, conceived in Liberty, and dedicated to the proposition that all men are created equal.

Now we are engaged in a great civil war, testing whether that nation, or any nation so conceived and so dedicated, can long endure. We are met on a great battlefield of that war. We have come to dedicate a portion of that field, as a final resting place for those who here gave their lives that that nation might live. It is altogether fitting and proper that we should do this.

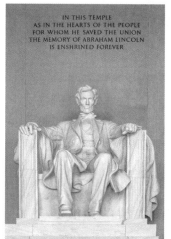

↑ **Figure 2.4** Lincoln Memorial in Washington D.C.

But, in a larger sense, we cannot dedicate—we cannot consecrate—we cannot hallow—this ground. The brave men, living and dead, who struggled here, have consecrated it, far above our poor power to add or detract. The world will little note, nor long remember what we say here, but it can never forget what they did here. It is for us the living, rather, to be dedicated here to the unfinished work which they who fought here have thus far so nobly advanced. It is rather for us to be here dedicated to the great task remaining before us—that from these honored dead we take increased devotion to that cause for which they gave the last full measure of devotion—that we here highly resolve that these dead shall not have died in vain—that this nation, under God, shall have a new birth of freedom—and that government of the people, by the people, for the people, shall not perish from the earth.

Gettysburg Address by Abraham Lincoln

Activity 2.8

When Kennedy was preparing his speech, he got his speechwriters to study Lincoln's words carefully. What connections in terms of style and strategy can you make between the two pieces?

It might help you to see the similarities by using the table that you used to determine the genre of a text (see page 14).

You will probably find that you have identified some of the following:

- **emotive** language, designed to stir your emotions
- bold, simple statements
- **rhetorical questions** – 'Will you join in that historic effort?'; you, the listener, are not being invited to reply out loud, so it is a question where the answer is already understood
- inclusive **pronouns** (we, our)
- **metaphor** ('can we *forge* against our enemies …')
- **alliteration**
- repetition/parallels
- understatement
- **irony**
- escalation in **tone** (the relationship between diction, **sentence structure**, etc.)
- **colloquial** or **idiomatic** language – language that makes you feel that the speaker is talking directly to you and using expressions that are quite informal or local, and turns of phrase that are understood by first-language speakers but cannot be easily defined by looking up the individual words ('brush with death', for example)
- **allusions** – references to other texts: politicians are particularly fond of the Bible because it makes them sound like prophets)
- **discourse markers**, terms such as *but* and *now* that move the argument forward and link paragraphs

Almost certainly, you will have considered the following areas:

- context – cultural, social and historical
- ideas and issues
- values
- structure
- style and language features
- rhetorical devices.

What's very clear is that both of them are trying to conjure up a presidential voice to match the seriousness of the occasion.

Activity 2.9

See if you can apply the same principles to the following speech given by the Australian Prime Minister, The Hon. P.J. Keating, in 1993 on the burial of his country's Unknown Soldier, a symbol of all who die in battle but whose bodies, if recovered, are never identified.

Text type: scripted spoken, Australia

We do not know this Australian's name and we never will. We do not know his rank or his battalion. We do not know where he was born, or precisely how and when he died. We do not know where in Australia he had made his home or when he left it for the battlefields of Europe. We do not know his age or his circumstances – whether he was from the city or the bush; what occupation he left to become a soldier; what religion, if he had a religion; if he was married or single. We do not know who loved him or whom he loved. If he had children we do not know who they are. His family is lost to us as he was lost to them. We will never know who this Australian was.

Yet he has always been among those we have honoured. We know that he was one of the 45,000 Australians who died on the Western Front. One of the 416,000 Australians who volunteered for service in the First World War. One of the 324,000 Australians who served overseas in that war, and one of the 60,000 Australians who died on foreign soil. One of the 100,000 Australians who have died in wars this century.

He is all of them. And he is one of us.

This Australia and the Australia he knew are like foreign countries. The tide of events since he died has been so dramatic, so vast and all-consuming, a world has been created beyond the reach of his imagination.

He may have been one of those who believed that the Great War would be an adventure too grand to miss. He may have felt that he would never live down the shame of not going. But the chances are that he went for no other reason than that he believed it was his duty – the duty he owed his country and his King.

Because the Great War was a mad, brutal, awful struggle distinguished more often than not by military and political incompetence; because the waste of human life was so terrible that some said victory was scarcely discernible from defeat; and because the war which was supposed to end all wars in fact sowed the seeds of a second, even more terrible, war – we might think that this Unknown Soldier died in vain.

But, in honouring our war dead as we always have, we declare that this is not true.

For out of the war came a lesson which transcended the horror and tragedy and the inexcusable folly.

It was a lesson about ordinary people – and the lesson was that they were not ordinary.

On all sides they were the heroes of that war: not the generals and the politicians, but the soldiers and sailors and nurses – those who taught us to endure hardship, show courage, to be bold as well as resilient, to believe in ourselves, to stick together.

The Unknown Australian Soldier we inter today was one of those who by his deeds proved that real nobility and grandeur belongs not to empires and nations but to the people on whom they, in the last resort, always depend.

That is surely at the heart of the ANZAC story, the Australian legend which emerged from the war. It is a legend not of sweeping military victories so much as triumphs against the odds, of courage and ingenuity in adversity. It is a legend of free and independent spirits whose discipline derived less from military formalities and customs than from the bonds of mateship and the demands of necessity.

It is a democratic tradition, the tradition in which Australians have gone to war ever since.

This Unknown Australian is not interred here to glorify war over peace; or to assert a soldier's character above a civilian's; or one race or one nation or one religion above another; or men above women; or the war in which he fought and died above any other war; or one generation above any that has or will come later.

The Unknown Soldier honours the memory of all those men and women who laid down their lives for Australia.

His tomb is a reminder of what we have lost in war and what we have gained.

We have lost more than 100,000 lives, and with them all their love of this country and all their hope and energy.

We have gained a legend: a story of bravery and sacrifice and with it a deeper faith in ourselves and our democracy, and a deeper understanding of what it means to be Australian.

It is not too much to hope, therefore, that this Unknown Australian soldier might continue to serve his country – he might enshrine a nation's love of peace and remind us that in the sacrifice of the men and women whose names are recorded here, there is faith enough for all of us.

Prime Minister P. J. Keating speaking at the burial of Australia's Unknown Soldier

Structure, form and cohesion

One of the things to look out for in a piece of writing is its structure, the shaping of the writing. This can also be called form. An obvious example of this lies in jokes. Although they may seem rather trivial examples of texts, you still have to learn the rules in order to be able to tell them effectively. And, as the audience for a joke, you need to know when to laugh.

Example 1

Knock knock

Who's there?

Howie

Howie who?

I'm fine, how are you?

Example 2

An Englishman, Irishman, Welshman and Scotsman are captured while fighting abroad, and the leader of the captors says, "We're going to line you up in front of a firing squad and shoot you all in turn. But first, you each can make a final wish."

The Englishman responds, "I'd like to hear 'God Save The Queen' just one more time to remind me of the old country, sung by the London All Boys Choir. With morris dancers dancing to the tune."

The Irishman replies, "I'd like to hear 'Danny Boy' just one more time to remind me of the old country, with Riverdance dancers skipping gaily to the tune."

The Welshman answers, "I'd like to hear 'Men Of Harlech' just one more time to remind me of the old country, sung by the Cardiff Male Voice Choir."

The Scotsman says quickly, "I'd like to be shot first."

Example 3

Will you remember me in a week?

Yes

Will you remember me in a month?

Yes

Will you remember me in a year?

Yes.

Knock knock

Who's there?

Forgotten me already?

Activity 2.10

Make a list of jokes and try to establish the rules that make them work.

Reflecting on structure, form and cohesion

In the second example, a rule of jokes is being deliberately broken (it's almost always three people because three allows the situation to be set up, confirmed and then changed). In this case, there have to be three speakers first in order to establish firmly what a nightmare the Scotsman will face if he has to put up with the others' last wishes. It's no accident that Goldilocks has to deal with three bears in the children's story.

Rhetoric and spoken language

Since ancient times, public speakers have been aware that words need to be particularly and specifically shaped for maximum effect. Modern politicians, like their Roman predecessors, are very fond of building a sentence with the same pattern of repetition in sets of three (technically called a **tricolon**). It helps them escalate the tone of a speech, and is a clue that they are expecting a round of applause or a cheer. Take for instance the excerpts below from Barack Obama's election victory speech in Chicago, November 2008.

> 'It's been a long time coming. But tonight, because of what we did on this day, in this election, at this defining moment, change has come to America.'

The tone is escalated still further by the repetition of combinations of words, as below with 'who still' (technically called **anaphora**).

> 'If there is anyone out there who still doubts that America is a place where all things are possible, who still wonders if the dream of our founders is alive in our time, who still questions the power of our democracy, tonight is your answer.'

In both cases Obama implies a question through his **rhetoric** and then answers it for himself – **epiphora** – in order to elicit a response from his audience.

Cohesion

In your own writing you will need to develop a strong sense of the rules, conventions and structures of a variety of different sorts of writing. It's perhaps best to see the issue in terms of playing a sport. If there is no net in a tennis game or no lines on a soccer pitch, then some of the challenge of the game disappears and it's much less fun for the spectators. Similarly, you wouldn't expect to buy a house or a boat unless you were convinced that it had a coherent design and structure, suited for the purpose you have in mind.

One way of doing this is to make sure that everything fits together logically. It may be, however, that the patterns are not immediately apparent. That doesn't necessarily make the text less effective: it just means that the reader or writer has to work harder to make sense of the structure, and the process of reading is more strenuous. As we saw earlier in this section, you have to be taught the rules of a joke before you can begin to appreciate the fun.

The business of linking words into phrases, sentences, paragraphs, and then into a whole text is called **cohesion**. A number of principles can be suggested, some of them to do with content, some to do with language.

To be cohesive a text often demonstrates:

- explicit links with what has gone before, connected by relationships of time, result or contrast: 'I went early. However, Ali stayed for dinner with our friends.'
- features that can't be interpreted without some reference to what has gone before. This is called **co-reference**. It can look backwards (**anaphoric reference**): 'The rioters approached. They seemed angry.' Here the word *they* can't be understood without the word *rioters* from the previous sentence. The reference can also look forward (**cataphoric reference**): 'Listen to this: there's going to be a new James Bond film.'
- **ellipsis**, there is no need to re-explain something that is commonly understood. We saw this as pragmatics earlier on: 'What time does the match start?' (There is no need to specify which match.)
- repetition: 'The doctor arrived. The doctor was cross.'
- relationships between word families (**lexical relationship**): 'The *boats* steamed into harbour. At the front was a *battleship*.'
- comparison: 'My homework was *terrible*. Hers was *worse*.'

These are tricks you can use in your own writing. However, you need to be careful not to use these devices without careful thought. The following sentence, dreamed up by the linguist Nils-Erik Enkvist (quoted by David Crystal), is cohesive to the point of excess but nonsense nonetheless:

> 'A week has seven days. Every day I feed my cat. Cats have four legs. The cat is on the mat. Mat has three letters.'

Activity 2.11

1. Here's a recipe that has been jumbled up. Using both your understanding of textual coherence, your understanding of food preparation, and, of course, your common sense, try to put it into the right order.

Text type: instructional, UK

3 rounded tablespoons of mayonnaise. Place in a large mixing basin and add the scrubbed and coarsely grated carrots, the apples, peeled, quartered and coarsely grated, and the scrubbed and finely shredded celery. 4–5 tablespoons oil and vinegar dressing. ½ a white cabbage heart. Meanwhile, in a small basin, thin down the mayonnaise with the cream.

Rinse the cabbage leaves under cold water and remove any outer damaged leaves. 1–2 sticks celery. Leave to chill for 15–20 minutes. 4 tablespoons of single cream. Pour over the salad and toss well to mix before serving. Cut in half, cut away the core, and then shred the cabbage finely. 2 dessert apples. Coleslaw. Toss the salad with 4–5 tablespoons oil and vinegar dressing. 2–3 new young carrots. Time taken 30–60 minutes.

2. Now examine the recipe using the cohesion terminology you have learned in order to discuss its structure.

Reflecting on Activity 2.11

With luck, you will have established quickly that it's best to have the ingredients first, followed by a coherent account of the process that needs to be undertaken.

Things get slightly more complicated when you are dealing with a piece of imaginative writing. Ernest Hemingway was known for being able to condense a lot of meaning in a story into very few words. Here's one of his stories. It is printed complete but in the wrong order.

Text type: prose narrative, fiction, USA

1 All the shutters of the hospital were nailed shut.

2 When they fired the first volley he was sitting down in the water with his head on his knees.

3 There were pools of water in the courtyard.

4 They tried to hold him up against the wall but he sat down in a puddle of water.

5 One of the ministers was sick with typhoid.

6 Two soldiers carried him downstairs and out into the rain.

7 There were wet dead leaves on the paving of the courtyard.

8 Finally the officer told the soldiers it was no good trying to make him stand up.

9 They shot the six cabinet ministers at half past six in the morning against the wall of the hospital.

10 It rained hard.

11 The other five stood very quietly against the wall.

In Our Time by Ernest Hemingway

Activity 2.12

Work with a partner to reconstruct Hemingway's original story. Try to explain why you decide on a particular order, both in terms of the logic of the story and of the various cohesion clues that the story contains.

Reflecting on Activity 2.12

What you will certainly notice by the time you agree on your final version is that you have made decisions about the structure of the narrative that also have implications for its meaning. If you clustered all the references to weather at the beginning, you were emphasising the atmosphere. If you used sentence 9 as the opening, you probably wanted to place the political implications of the narration firmly in the foreground of the reader's thinking. You might also have wanted the shock value of the immediacy of sentence 9.

Answers to activities in this book are available online at www.oxfordsecondary.co.uk/9780198445760. Here you can find the actual order in which Hemingway wrote the narrative.

What this tells us is that writers are not simply committed to telling stories in chronological order. Matters of theme, character or atmosphere may be just as important. Take, for instance, the opening of Donna Tartt's *The Goldfinch*.

Activity 2.13

Compare your version with Hemingway's original. What different effects might your version have on a reader?

Text type: prose narrative, fiction, USA

While I was still in Amsterdam, I dreamed about my mother for the first time in years. I'd been shut up in my hotel for more than a week, afraid to telephone anybody or go out; and my heart scrambled and floundered at even the most innocent noises: elevator bell, rattle of the minibar car, even church clocks tolling the hour, de Westertoren, Krijtberg, a dark edge to the clangor, an inwrought fairy-tale sense of doom. By day I sat on the foot of the bed straining to puzzle out the Dutch-language news on television (which was hopeless, since I knew not a word of Dutch) and when I gave up, I sat by the window staring out at the canal with my camel's-hair coat thrown over my clothes – for I'd left New York in a hurry and the things I'd brought weren't warm enough, even indoors.

Outside, all was activity and cheer. It was Christmas, lights twinkling on the canal bridges at night; red-cheeked *dames en heren*, scarves flying in the icy wind, clattered down the cobblestones with Christmas trees lashed to the backs of their bicycles. In the afternoons, an amateur band played Christmas carols that hung tinny and fragile in the winter air.

Chaotic room-service trays; too many cigarettes; lukewarm vodka from duty free. During those restless, shut-up days, I got to know every inch of the room as a prisoner comes to know his cell.

The Goldfinch by Donna Tartt

Tartt's intention is to introduce you to the narrator. His jumpiness about 'innocent noises' and his admission that he'd 'left New York in a hurry' suggest that there is a mystery involved that has a 'dark edge' and is associated with his 'fairy-tale sense of doom'. The contrast between the picturesque jollity of what's going on in the streets and the claustrophobic atmosphere of the hotel room (compared to a 'cell'), with the inside and outside paragraphs alternating, suggests feelings of guilt, particularly when we hear of his upset at not being able to understand the news. It's going to take another 700 or so pages for us to find out how he got into the situation – but plainly the writer (Tartt, not the narrator) has decided that we can know about what happened at the end before we know the beginning of the tale. It's a crafty trick to get a reader involved.

Here's another opening to a novel, set during the New Zealand gold rush of 1866.

Text type: prose narrative, fiction, New Zealand

In which a stranger arrives in Hokitika; a secret council is disturbed; Walter Moody conceals his most recent memory; and Thomas Balfour begins to tell a story.

The twelve men congregated in the smoking room of the Crown Hotel gave the impression of a party accidentally met. From the variety of their comportment and dress – frock coats, tailcoats, Norfolk jackets with buttons of horn, yellow moleskin, cambric, and twill – they might have been twelve strangers on a railway car, each bound for a separate quarter of a city that possessed fog and tides enough to divide them; indeed, the studied isolation of each man as he pored over his paper, or leaned forward to tap his ashes into the grate, or placed the splay of his hand upon the baize to take his shot at billiards, conspired to form the very type of bodily silence that occurs late in the evening, on a public railway – deadened here not by the slur and clunk of the coaches, but by the fat clatter of the rain.

Such was the perception of Mr. Walter Moody, from where he stood in the doorway with his hand upon the frame. He was innocent of having disturbed any kind of private conference, for the speakers had ceased when they heard his tread in the passage; by the time he opened the door, each of the twelve men had resumed his occupation (rather haphazardly, on the part of the billiard players, for they had forgotten their places) with such a careful show of absorption that no one even glanced up when he stepped into the room.

The strictness and uniformity with which the men ignored him might have aroused Mr. Moody's interest, had he been himself in body and temperament. As it was, he was queasy and disturbed. He had known the voyage to West Canterbury would be fatal at worst, an endless rolling trough of white water and spume that ended on the shattered graveyard of the Hokitika bar …

The Luminaries by Eleanor Catton

Activity 2.14

Try to write a paragraph (use the one on *The Goldfinch* as a model for tone) that analyses the structure of this passage and the hints that it is giving you about what is to follow. Pay particular attention to:

- changing perspective (don't forget about the paragraph in italics)

- how the scene's atmosphere is created (clothes, location, weather, for example)

- the historical detail that puts the narrative into a particular period

- contrasts between the 'stranger' as an observer and the twelve men already in the smoking room. What do you make of him being named very formally as Mr. Walter Moody, for example?

Lexis and diction

These terms are often used to describe exactly the same thing. **Lexis** deals with the study of words; a lexicographer is someone who compiles dictionaries.

The origin of dictionaries

Dr Johnson completed the first proper dictionary of English in 1755. It took him nine years to complete, and he chose his words from printed, respectable sources, mostly literary. It's not surprising then that he defined his own job jokingly as: "Lexicographer: a writer of dictionaries, a harmless drudge, that busies himself in tracing the original, and detailing the signification of words."

The first full American dictionary, *An American Dictionary of the English Language*, was published by Noah Webster in 1828. For both Johnson and Webster, writing a dictionary was a means of guiding people towards correct and tasteful use of the language.

These days, dictionaries reflect the language in use and do their best to keep up to date, a battle they are destined to lose. By the time you read this you will able to look up the words *dumbphone*, *selfie*, *single-use* and *flexitarian* in a good dictionary – they may even be part of your own vocabulary. Other trendy words, on the other hand (*slacktivism*, 2014, *plogging*, 2018), may have already been consigned to the linguistic graveyard.

The standard dictionary of British English is the *Oxford English Dictionary*, which you could see as being like a bridge that needs to be painted all the time. No sooner has the job been finished than the first end is ready for a fresh coat. By the time you buy a dictionary it's already out of date.

↑ **Figure 2.5** Dr Johnson and Noah Webster

Activity 2.15

Choose a subject area that you know well and put together a lexicon of terms related to it, ranging from the formal to the colloquial. You could choose sport or perhaps an abstract quality such as courage or intelligence.

Think, too, about the hundreds of different ways you have of saying 'no', ranging from the apologetic ('if it was up to me') to the evasive ('let's talk about it later') to the highly informal ('you must be joking'; 'fat chance').

Obviously, with every text you encounter you need to think about the word choices that a writer, also called a text producer, makes, and this often gives you important clues about the writer's attitudes and values, as well as the genre and voice that are being created.

We all carry around in our heads lists of suitable words for talking about different things. There is, for example, a large vocabulary of words for talking about food or drink. This is called a mental **lexicon**.

Sometimes there are high incidences of language related to the same topic in a piece of writing. For example, you would expect a newspaper article about soccer to be loaded with terminology that is relevant to the game ('goals', 'referee' and so on). This can help you to establish the genre of a text. The grouping together of words from one specific area is called a **semantic field** or a **lexical field**. If you want to comment on this when writing about a text, you need to do more than notice a clustering of words. You need to comment too on the level of formality or informality and its significance for the piece as a whole. In doing so, you are also identifying the tone and the **mood** of the writing.

More interesting is the fact that all of us put these words into mental hierarchies and orders, ranging from the very **formal** to the informal. Think, for example, of words we might use for someone misbehaving. Depending on the seriousness of what they have done, their actions might be 'immoral' and they might have 'transgressed' or been guilty of 'misconduct'. On the other hand, less serious wrongdoing could be described as 'naughtiness', 'shenanigans', 'mischief', 'high jinks', 'daftness', 'monkey business' or 'horse-play'. In one way, all these words are synonymous (they mean the same thing), but in another way, the choice of words from this semantic field conveys a distinct attitude and awareness of **register**.

With each different audience, the choice of words is different. Informal use of language is often called 'colloquial', and it is often very specific to language communities.

Classifying words

The table below details what are formally called **parts of speech**, referred to by more modern linguists as **word class**. You will be familiar with all of them already.

nouns	Abstract nouns focus on states of mind, concepts and ideas such as *courage* or *progress*. (Think back to the opening of *A Tale of Two Cities*.)
	Concrete nouns describe solid events, characters and places: *kitchen* and *kettle* are examples.
adjectives	These are words that describe nouns: for example, the *black* cat.
verbs	Stative verbs (*to think*, *to believe*) indicate a writer's desire to describe states of mind.
	Dynamic verbs (*to watch*, *to eat*) place emphasis on actions or things that are happening.

adverbs	These are words used to describe verbs: for example, she was walking *slowly*.
prepositions	These words describe the place of an object: for example, *in*, *up* and *with*
interjections	These are interruptions or exclamations in speech or writing: for example, *yes*, *wow* and *awesome*.
conjunctions	These words are used to join words and clauses: examples are *and*, *however*, *when* and *but*.
pronouns	These take the place of a noun to avoid repetition: 'The puppy is very naughty. *He's* only five weeks old.' There are also possessive pronouns: 'The puppy likes *his* walk in the afternoon.'
modifiers	These are the adjectives (applied to nouns) and adverbs (applied to verbs) that add to descriptions and help to shape a reader's response to a text. If there are lots of them, the text could be described as highly modified and quite ornate. If there are not very many, then a text might be thought of as quite cold or sterile.

Activity 2.16

Just to remind you about the various functions of these parts of speech, you could play Mad Libs. You simply take a piece of text, remove the relevant parts of speech and then ask someone else for words that will fit in, without sharing the original. You will find the results bizarre, funny or just plain ridiculous.

Here's an example. Fill in the spaces.

"….." (exclamation), he said ….. (adverb) as he jumped into his convertible …. (noun) and …. (verb) off with his …. (adjective) wife.

A difficulty in English is that words slip in and out of their various classes depending on their use in the sentence.

Using the word *round*, David Crystal gives the following useful examples of word conversion according to context:

- in the sentence *Mary bought a big round table*, it serves as an adjective, like *red*, *big*, *ugly* and many more
- in the sentence *The car skidded round the corner*, it functions as a preposition, like *into*, *past*, *near* and many more
- in the sentence *The yacht will round the buoy soon*, it functions as a verb, like *pass*, *reach*, *hit* and many more
- in the sentence *We walked round to the shop*, it functions as an adverb, like *quickly*, *happily*, *regularly*, along with many more
- in the sentence *It's your round*, it functions as a noun like *turn*, *chance*, *decision* and many more. (Examples taken from *How Language Works* by David Crystal.)

Word conversion often works to help us fill in a gap in the language. When people started to want to look things up on an internet search engine, it was natural that if the search engine was called Google, then 'to google' must be a verb.

Words can be broken down into bits (slow/slowly). You do not need to do this but you should know that this element of language study is called **morphology** and that individual elements of words are called **morphemes**.

Style, register and tone

When you think about words in texts you also need to think about how to characterise them. You could do this by using a series of adjectives such as:

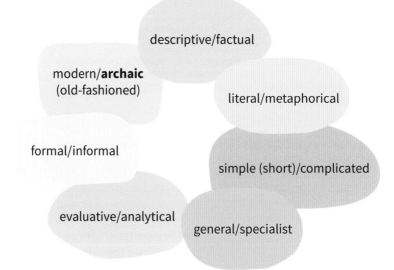

descriptive/factual

modern/**archaic**
(old-fashioned)

literal/metaphorical

formal/informal

simple (short)/complicated

evaluative/analytical

general/specialist

The focus needs to be on the way language is chosen for particular situations. Think about the language used in the legal world, between a mother and her baby, in a biology research lab, in a news report or on a sports field. Text producers need to be acutely aware of the register of language that is appropriate (often seen in terms of levels of formality or informality) for the current situation and for the genre they are attempting to produce.

A police report, for example, records details of a crime as objectively as possible.

Case Number:	**VT 05/04/19/3462**
Incident:	**Vehicle Theft**
Reporting Officer:	**Constable Ranjit Singh**
Date of Report:	**05 April 2019**

At about 10.40 hours on 5th April 2019, I met with Ms. Vanessa Price at 61 South Chorley Drive regarding a vehicle theft. Ms. Price said she parked her car by a parking meter outside Chorley Leisure Centre at about 09:45 hours and went into a nearby shop to return a faulty torch she had purchased the previous day. She said that when she returned to the leisure centre at about 10.00 hours, she discovered her car was missing.

Ms. Price described her car as a white, 2017 Mitsubishi Eclipse Cross with a glass roof. The car registration number is KM67 UHT. She estimated the value of the car at £18,500 and said there were no distinguishing marks on the bodywork.

Ms. Price told me she locked the car, but she does not have the keys. She now believes she may have left the keys in the boot lock after removing the faulty torch from the boot. Ms. Price said she gave no-one permission to take her car.

I conducted a survey of the crime scene but found no items of evidence. I saw no broken glass in the area, and there were no items to retrieve or photograph.

I obtained a sworn statement from Ms. Price and provided her with the case number and Information Leaflet 99/07 ("What to do when your car is stolen"). I entered the vehicle into the station database as a stolen vehicle. I also searched the area but was unable to find the vehicle.

Reflecting on the source

This is written very formally, with no **contractions** such as *can't* or *didn't* and without colloquial words or idioms (the car was *stolen*, not *pinched* or *nicked*). There is no attempt to be stylish or to vary the sentence structure. The writer is careful to be impersonal, and does not introduce either Ms Price's thoughts and feelings or his own. Dates, times and details are recorded as precisely as possible.

Activity 2.17

We can explore this by taking a text and transforming it into another genre. With the police text as your model, rewrite this traditional British nursery rhyme using a tone and register that would be suitable for a crime report:

Little Miss Muffet
Sat on a tuffet
Eating her curds and whey;
Along came a spider
Who sat down beside her
And frightened Miss Muffet away.

You can distinguish between different registers or styles by characterising them as outlined in the table below.

↑ **Figure 2.6** The eponymous victim of *Little Miss Muffet*

Register/style	Typical features
ultra-colloquial	■ often street language used by the young with new words, or older words adapted to mean something new ■ non-standard pronunciation (*gonna*, *innit*) ■ non-standard grammar, with some function words (*of* or *to*) missed out ■ sometimes called **vernacular** language
colloquial	■ words that belong to private rather than public life, often with idiomatic expressions ■ the language used between friends and family ■ when spoken, allows hesitations, pauses and imprecise expression; grammatical rules not always followed ■ often described as 'conversational'
modified formal	■ plain words and expressions where a choice to be more formal is made, so *child* not *kid*, *dismiss* not *fire*, *why* not *how come* ■ will prefer to talk about real things rather than abstract terms ■ some abbreviations or contractions (*can't*, *won't*) both in speech and writing ■ will flow easily and is the normal language of the working world and will normally obey the rules for 'standard' English
formal	■ may use a lot of abstract nouns; this is the language of scholarly discussion ■ one-word, precise terms rather than short phrases (*discover* not *find out*) ■ complex or varied grammar ■ the passive voice (for scientific papers, for example) ■ when written, conforms carefully with the conventions of 'standard' English ■ no colloquial language or slang unless it is explicitly drawn attention to for a specific purpose

| ultra-formal | ■ formal address ('Ladies and gentlemen')
■ archaic forms of language (long words, often derived from Latin), grammar and syntax ('Please be seated') |

↑ Adapted from *Grammar, Structure and Style* by Shirley Russell

All of these can, of course, be used in either speech or writing, but the vernacular is often hard to understand when written, while the ultra-formal is most often reserved for formal spoken occasions or legal documents. It is worth noting too that, particularly in speech, people often move between different registers with great fluency, and that the boundaries between them are often very fluid. As we noted earlier, your own spoken language will vary considerably depending on whether you are at home with your family, with your friends, or contributing in class. This adaptation of language levels and register to different circumstances and situations is called **code-switching**.

Skilled writers often play with levels of register and tone to create meaning. In the next passage, Sathnam Sanghera, a British Asian writer, is helping his parents pack (or rather unpack to avoid excess baggage charges) in preparation for their forthcoming trip to the Punjab to see family.

Activity 2.18

Look closely at the passage and then discuss Sanghera's presentation of himself and his relationship with his parents.

Text type: autobiography, UK

With Mum gone, my editing became more brutal. Two of the three prayer books went. The teabags and Rice Krispies went. But then, underneath the cereal boxes, I came across something more surreal than even the coconuts: two 2kg boxes of East End vegetable margarine – "made with 100% vegetable oil, no animal fat". Incredible. Mum had allocated a fifth of her allotted luggage weight on her flight from Birmingham to Amritsar with a five hour stop in the […] metropolis of Tashkent to … margarine.

I laughed, made a mental note to tell Laura about it later, and tried to think of a possible explanation. Maybe she was planning to make chapattis along the journey to my father's village? Perhaps there was some superstition relating to margarine? I flicked through my mental database of Punjabi folklore.

It was good luck to mutter "*Waheguru*" before you embarked on any task.

It was bad luck to wash your hair on a Saturday or a Tuesday.

It was bad luck to look at the moon.

It was bad luck to sneeze when setting off on a journey (a nightmare when you have allergies, like I do).

It was bad luck to step on money.

It was bad luck to leave one shoe resting on another.

It was bad luck to point your feet at a picture of a guru or a prayer book.

It was bad luck to spill milk.

It was good luck to scoop up the placenta of a cat that had just given birth.

It was bad luck for a nephew or niece to be in the same room as an uncle from their mother's side of the family in a thunderstorm.

No. I couldn't remember anything margarine-related …

But picking out the boxes with the intention of storming into the living room and remonstrating, I found they were lighter than I'd expected. They rattled too. Phew. Mum was using the boxes as containers. She hadn't lost the plot completely. I opened one and found it contained medication. Mum's herbal pills for her migraines; non-herbal pills for her arthritis; antidepressants; vitamin supplements; paracetamol. The second one was heavier and contained five boxes of tablets. The brands emblazoned across them meant nothing to me. But the name on them did. Jagdit Singh. Dad.

I thought this peculiar because my father is rarely ill. He has diabetes, but the condition is managed well. I had a fuzzy memory of him once being prescribed sleeping pills. But I thought that was a temporary thing. Indeed, I couldn't remember a single time that he'd complained of feeling sick. Couldn't recall him ever having a lie down during the day, for that matter. Ferreting around the box for a clue, I found an envelope addressed 'TO WHOM IT MAY CONCERN.' I was a 'to whom it concerned', so I opened it. It was a note from Dad's GP, Dr Dutta.

> This patient has been registered on my panel since 1969 and was re-registered in 1993. In fact, he is known to me from 1969. He suffers from paranoid schizophrenia. (He is often confused and cannot communicate facts and his wife has to assist him.) He is on regular treatment of injection and tablets (which he often forgets), and his wife has to keep an eye on his medication. He also suffers from diabetes for which he is having regular check-ups and treatment. He is visiting his family in India and he is going for a short visit.

Blinking at the words, I thought: … *Schizophrenia*.

And then: *Christ*. That's what my sister Puli must have too.

The Boy with the Topknot by Sathnam Sanghera

Reflecting on Activity 2.18

You will have noticed that the writer maintains a detached, ironic humouring of his parents (think about his use of the word *remonstrating*, for example) in order to increase the shock value of the doctor's formal letter, a complete change of tone, register and genre, that reports in a detached, clinical manner. As the tone changes, so too does the seriousness of the piece, with the writer suddenly realising that he has to re-discover his family relationships in completely different terms.

As we have seen, word choice often creates the tone of a piece of writing, but you can take your analysis still further by looking at a text and describing it in terms of the frequency of different word classes. Such analysis will often help you to recognise some of the genre characteristics of a text. You will quickly discover the following:

- conversation has a very high density of verbs
- news reporting and other sorts of informative writing tend to have a high density of nouns because they are content-driven
- because adjectives are linked to nouns, texts with a high frequency of nouns tend also to have high levels of adjectives; so informative writing will have high densities of both nouns and adjectives
- as adverbs are linked to verbs and typically describe situations relating to actions, processes and states, there will tend to be more of them in conversation and fiction
- literary writing, particularly when describing, has a high density of both adjectives and adverbs.

Adapted from the *Longman Student Grammar of Spoken and Written English*

Activity 2.19

Read the following text. Using the points above, try to make a statement about the genre type. How would it read without the adjectives and adverbs?

Text type: prose narrative, drama, UK

It is spring, moonless night in the small town, starless and bible-black, the cobblestones silent and the hunched, courters'-and-rabbits' wood limping invisible down to the sloeblack, slow, black, crowblack, fishing boat-bobbing sea.

Under Milk Wood by Dylan Thomas

You might remember that in Chapter 1 of this book, we thought about style in terms of clothes. Let's go back to that comparison. On occasion, it is expected that we will wear suits – a job interview might require this. At other times – a beach party, for example – jeans and a T-shirt will be perfectly acceptable, and to turn up in a suit would embarrass other people or make someone look ridiculous. So there are matters of appropriateness at stake. It would be sensible to say that the register and lexical field (or general expectation) of one sort of event would be the suit, while the register of the other would be jeans and a T-shirt, the tone of one formal, the other informal.

But it's more complex than that. There are many different variations within the 'suit' register (colour and cut being just two) and there are many variations possible for jeans – skinny, boot cut, hipster, etc. Any written text can be seen in the same way. There are appropriate registers for each genre, but at the same time there can be variations in layout, vocabulary choice and sentence structure. In any text, there will be a lexis associated with the subject matter (think of a newspaper report of a soccer match) but the style may be very different.

Activity 2.20

(a) Choose a few examples of writing from the same register and try to determine what the common elements are. Then examine the variations that are acceptable as the style of each piece. You could make use of the film reviews in Chapter 5.

(b) Go back to the extract by Katherine Boo (page 21) and examine it again in terms of register, taking particular note of the ways that it mixes the registers of a newspaper report with those of fictional narrative.

Grammar

Let's start with a definition. **Grammar** is a term that covers two aspects of language:

- the structure of individual words and their function
- the arrangement of these words within a sentence (this can also be called **syntax**).

When most people think about grammar, they have in their minds rather dusty books that publishers produce for foreign language teaching. There is also a slight fear that discussions about grammar are full of pitfalls, where people are simply just waiting for you to make a mistake (often called a **solecism**). A certain type of person will wait for an error and take pleasure in pointing out that you have got something wrong. These people are called **prescriptivists** (although they probably don't know it) because they are very keen on the rules. They will be keen to tell you that you should never begin a sentence with *and* or *but*. But they will never clearly explain (see this sentence) why this is such a bad thing. They will tell you that you should never end a sentence with a **preposition** (a word like *up* or *down*) and would presumably prefer Churchill's joke sentence "These are things up with which we will not put" to the more natural sounding "These are things we won't put up with."

Most of these rules come from an 18th-century desire for the English language to behave like Latin (which, of course, it doesn't). So teachers may still encourage students not to split **infinitives** (the root of a verb in English, for example, *to split*), even though the model is faulty because in Latin infinitives (*facere*, *amare*) can't be split as they consist of only one word. But the prescription goes on.

The most famous split infinitive comes from the TV and film series *Star Trek*, in a voice-over we always hear:

> 'Space: the final frontier. These are the voyages of the starship *Enterprise*. Its five-year mission: to explore strange worlds, to seek out new life and new civilisations, to boldly go where no man has gone before.'

Boldly to go? To go boldly? Not quite such an exciting mission, is it?

So for our purposes, prescription is not the way forward. You need to see yourself as a **descriptive** grammarian, someone who describes what is actually going on in a text. However, you will also need some sense of the general rules for the language, without too much detail – a map of the territory.

David Crystal suggests in *How Language Works* that of the 3,500 features of English grammar, only about 1% of them are ever the focus of grammatical prescriptivism.

Activity 2.21

Try re-writing the following sentence without the split infinitive, and you will see how the 'rule' falls at the first fence – it leads you into ugly, unclear writing.

> I expect our output to more than double next year.

Slippery language

We can all agree that the word *everyone* is not plural: 'Everyone is here so let's start,' said the tour guide (singular verb). Watch how it transforms itself. 'As we are moving into the dust-free area, everyone should leave his or her coat here,' she continued. Suddenly it starts to feel wrong: there may be women in the audience, so *his* won't do for everyone, but to put *his or her* in the sentence sounds ugly. So the chances are that suddenly *everyone* becomes plural. 'Everyone should leave their coats here' sounds much better. Here is language adapting itself for the needs of the times as we don't have non-gender pronouns (we are stuck with *him/her*, *his/hers*), although there have been attempts to use *she/he* in writing.

The point is that there is something called grammatical correctness, but a native speaker or writer will always adapt to what sounds right, rather than to what is formally correct. At any time, too, there are also pressures for change on a language, as the example above shows. And, of course, if you are learning any language as a second language, this is one of the things that make it so hard.

But then there are some who always want to find fault, although they would never, of course, argue that they 'can't get no satisfaction' (as the Rolling Stones do) over these matters because that's a double negative and must be avoided at all costs. This is despite the fact it has a perfectly respectable history in the language from Chaucer onwards as an intensifier: 'I couldn't not buy that dress in the sales – it was a bargain.'

If I say, 'I would of loved one of them apples what you did bought yesterday,' you would understand what I had said. Nonetheless, you would be aware that I had not communicated my thoughts in a pleasing or particularly clear, effective way. If, on the other hand, I had come up with the linguist Chomsky's demonstration phrase, 'Colourless green ideas sleep furiously,' you would have been confident that this is a sentence, a coherent unit of sense with a verb that tells you when the events happened, even though the sentence makes no sense.

You could test this by rearranging the words: 'Furiously sleep ideas green colourless'. Intuitively, however, you knew that the first of these sentences was better than the second, and this shows that our understanding of grammar exists independent of any sense of meaning.

In many other languages, sentences are constructed by changing the beginnings or endings of words to give readers a clear sense of their function in a sentence. In Latin, 'Caesarem occidit Brutus' and 'Brutus Caesarem occidit' both mean that Brutus killed Caesar. We don't have that choice in English. In English grammar, word order is central.

Activity 2.22

Examine the position of the word *only* in these three sentences. Can you identify a difference in meaning between them?

- I only put on my shoes when she asks.
- I put on my shoes only when she asks.
- Only I put on my shoes when she asks.

The Simpsons and the English language

You may have wondered how a new word comes into the language. Often, English finds a need for a word and simply borrows it from another language (*pizza* and *bungalow* are good examples). These are called **loanwords**. At other times, it works by association – a little thing on a desk that scurries around as it points to bits of the screen looks something like a mouse, so a mouse it is.

To actually make a word stick in the language is quite hard. In 1996, the writers of the television show *The Simpsons* had a go. In the episode 'Lisa the Iconoclast', they came up with the words *cromulent* and *embiggen*, words that sound as though they should exist. The high school principal says of Homer's audition for the job of Springfield town crier: "He's embiggened that role with his cromulent performance." *Cromulent*, which means fine or acceptable, hasn't really taken off, but by 2013 *embiggen* was starting to have a life of its own in science papers in relation to string theory (don't ask!) and also with tablet computers where you can stretch or enlarge a picture with your fingers. Perhaps its time has come.

↑ **Figure 2.7** The perfectly *cromulent* Simpsons family

When words are put together, the rules that govern them are usually called grammar. In technical terms, the whole business of word order is more properly called the **syntactic structure** or **syntactic rules** of a sentence. Some of you will have come across 'syntax errors' when trying to program a computer. When that happens, the computer can't read what you are trying to say and stubbornly refuses to let you move to the next stage. With a less exacting reader or listener in a 'real' language you can, of course, simply carry on, but at times syntax errors mean that others have to struggle to work out what you mean.

Sentence structure

The fundamental structure of a sentence is quite straightforward.

The most basic form is the **simple sentence**. You need one verb and you need to demonstrate **tense** (*when* something happened) and **number** (how many people were doing the thing).

> The elephant ate grass.

You can add to this in all kinds of ways, but as long as it only has one verb, it is a simple sentence.

> The grey elephant slowly ate green grass, old leaves and apples.

We have increased the amount of detail by expanding some ideas into phrases (it's now a grey elephant), but added nothing to the fundamentals of the sentence.

You could, of course, add another clause (a group of words with another verb with tense and number), although the elephant remains the central focus.

> The elephant ate grass and wandered off into the forest.

The presence of two verbs turns this into a **compound sentence** with different clauses bound together by linking words (**conjunctions**) such as *and* or *but*. It could easily be two sentences.

Much of the time we want to say something slightly more complicated, so we need to add more verbs.

> The elephant ate apples that had been left by the visitors.

'Had been' adds another verb, but the elephant is still the main subject of the sentence. We could miss out the bit about the visitors. This means that we have started to work on **subordination**, noting that some bits of a sentence support the main meaning but cannot exist without the **main clause**: 'had been left by the visitors' has both tense and number, but there is something missing so it can't stand as a sentence on its own.

Morphemes (words constructed out of bits that create various meanings, e.g. (sad/sadly/sadness)

create **phrases** (units of meaning without verbs with tense and number).

They, in turn, build into **clauses** (groups of words organised around a verb).

Clauses are then used to build **sentences**.

Exam tip

In your own writing

Joining contrasting statements? Words like *although*, *however*, *but*, *though* and *nevertheless* are useful here.

Single- and multi-clause sentences

Simple sentences are sometimes referred to as 'single-clause sentences', while compound and complex sentences may be called 'multi-clause sentences'. The use of 'simple', 'compound' and 'complex', however, is more appropriate at AS and A Level.

Exam tip

In your own writing

It's worth having a record of the major words that you use to begin subordinating clauses.

after	if	that	where
although	in order that	though	whereas
as	once	unless	wherever
because	provided that	until	whether
before	rather than	whatever	while
even if	since	when	
even though	so that	whenever	

If a sentence has **subordinate clauses** (underlined) then it can be described as a **complex sentence**:

> The elephant, <u>which was getting rather old</u>, ate green grass, and old leaves, and the apples <u>that had been left by the visitors</u>.

And then, of course, you can add another main clause if you like and you will have come up with a **compound-complex sentence**. Here the subordinate clauses are underlined; and the second main clause is in italics.

> The elephant, <u>which was getting rather old</u>, ate green grass, old leaves and the apples <u>that had been left by visitors</u>, *and wandered into the forest*.

Once you start to see how the different elements of sentences build up, then you can start to be more confident about your own writing. Using only simple sentences can be rather jerky, although that in its own way can create an effect on a reader. So an ability to write a variety of types of sentence is an important skill to have: it will make your writing more engaging and interesting to read.

You should remember the introductory phrase or clause too as a means of getting you into the substance of a sentence.

Exam tip

The most important point is, of course, that you should be clear in your writing. At times you may feel that your sentences need to be complicated because you want to say something quite complex. Often, that's precisely the moment when you need to stop and sort out your thoughts into smaller units.

- When Tom got up, he put on his brown suit.
- Although he didn't like his suit, Tom felt he ought to wear it for the interview.
- As he was walking towards the bus stop, he had a terrible thought.
- Unfortunately, he had mistaken the day of the interview.
- Over coffee, he told his girlfriend what had happened.

You can get yourself into a real mess with grammatical discussions, so it's often best not to try. However, you can often make points about the length of sentences or about syntactic variations without having to use the technical terms. Think, for example, about how the words placed in an unusual order may change your view of their content, the context or the speaker.

- With this ring, I thee wed. (Church of England wedding service)
- When nine hundred years old you reach, look as good you will not.
  (Yoda, *Star Wars Episode VI: Return of the Jedi* – COURTESY OF LUCASFILM LTD. LLC)

Verbs and tenses

As with so many aspects of this course, noting the effect of a language choice is more important than being able to analyse it in precise detail. So there is no need to get caught up in a discussion of the complexities of describing the various tenses in English (and there are many of them). However, you will mainly come across writing in two tenses: the present and the past.

The present tense

There are fundamentally two variations on this.

You can write in the **simple present tense**.

> She wants to be an astronaut.

You can also use the **present continuous tense**.

> He is walking to the shops.

In this next extract, Hilary Mantel, a contemporary novelist, uses the present tense to bring alive an episode from history – Cardinal Wolsey's fall from grace during the reign of Henry VIII. The narrator is Thomas Cromwell, Wolsey's adviser; Cavendish is Wolsey's personal attendant.

Activity 2.23

What, in your view, does Mantel achieve by writing predominantly in the present tense in the following passage? What is the effect on the reader?

Text type: prose narrative, fiction, UK

The cardinal dismounts under the shadow of old Bishop Wayneflete's keep, surmounted by octagonal towers. The gateway is set into a defensive wall topped with a walkway; stern enough at first sight but the whole thing is built of brick, ornamented and prettily inlaid. 'You couldn't fortify it,' he says. Cavendish is silent. 'George, you're supposed to say, "But the need could never arise."'

The cardinal's not used the place since he built Hampton Court. They've sent messages ahead, but has anything been done? Make my lord comfortable, he says, and goes straight down to the kitchens. At Hampton Court, the kitchens have running water; here, nothing's running but the cooks' noses. Cavendish is right. In fact it is worse than he thinks. The larders are impoverished and such supplies as they have show signs of ill-keeping and plunder. There are weevils in the flour. There are mouse-droppings where the pastry should be rolled. It is nearly Martinmas, and they have not even thought of salting their beef. The batterie de cuisine is an insult, and the stockpot is mildewed. There are a number of small boys sitting by the hearth, and, for cash down, they can be induced into scouring and scrubbing, children take readily to novelty, and the idea of cleaning, it seems, is novel to them.

My lord, he says, needs to eat and drink *now*; and he needs to eat and drink for … how long we don't know. This kitchen must be put in order for the winter ahead. He finds someone who can write, and dictates his orders. His eyes are fixed on the kitchen clerk.

Wolf Hall by Hilary Mantel

Reflecting on Activity 2.23

With this technique you are right in the middle of the action and the drama of Cardinal Wolsey's flight from London is described as though a camera is scanning across the scene. We see the events through the eyes of Thomas Cromwell as though he is a camera lens. At the same time, we are aware that the camera is not neutral as we are aware of his preoccupations and concerns. This is not first-person narrative (see page 17) but it shares some of its characteristics – what Cromwell says, for example, is not given speech marks.

In recent years in British English, teenagers have adopted the habit of talking in the present tense about things that happened in the past. This isn't wrong and it does give a listener a sense of being intimately involved, but to older ears it comes across as rather too immediate.

> 'So I'm walking down the street and my friend comes up to me. And she says "I want to go to the cinema." So I say "What shall we go and see?" So she says…'

Other writers and speakers mix present and future tenses to give a sense of vision, hope and expectation for the future, as Emma Watson, the actor and UN Women Goodwill ambassador, does here in a speech delivered to the United Nations in 2014. Notice the importance and effect of the repeated use of the first-person pronoun 'I', and the use of other pronouns in the speech ('we' and 'you') to create a sense of inclusion.

(see page 17)

Exam tip

In your own writing

It may be best to avoid present tense narration. It grabs hold of a reader's attention but is hard to sustain.

↑ **Figure 2.8** Emma Watson, UN Women Goodwill ambassador, speaking at the UN

Activity 2.24

With careful attention to your use of pronouns, write a short speech for a student audience where you argue for change in the world on an issue you feel deeply about.

Text type: scripted speech, USA

Today we are launching a campaign called "HeForShe."

I am reaching out to you because I need your help. We want to end gender inequality – and to do that we need everyone to be involved.

This is the first campaign of its kind at the UN: we want to try and galvanize as many men and boys as possible to be advocates for gender equality. And we don't just want to talk about it, but make sure it is tangible. […]

Men – I would like to take this opportunity to extend your formal invitation. Gender equality is your issue too.

Because to date, I've seen my father's role as a parent being valued less by society despite my needing his presence as a child as much as my mother's.

I've seen young men suffering from mental illness unable to ask for help for fear it would make them look less "macho" – in fact in the UK suicide is the biggest killer of men between 20–49 years of age; eclipsing road accidents, cancer and coronary heart disease. I've seen men made fragile and insecure by a distorted sense of what constitutes male success. Men don't have the benefits of equality either.

We don't often talk about men being imprisoned by gender stereotypes but I can see that that they are and that when they are free, things will change for women as a natural consequence. […]

If we stop defining each other by what we are not and start defining ourselves by what we are – we can all be freer and this is what HeForShe is about. It's about freedom.

Extract from the speech 'Gender equality is your issue too',

Emma Watson, United Nations Headquarters, New York, 20 September 2014

The past tense

The conventional way of talking about the past is to use the simple **past tense**, possibly in combination with the **imperfect tense** which is used for continuing actions in the past.

> I was walking to school one day, when a tree fell down in front of me.

Two actions have finished taking place, but the second of them, expressed in the simple past, interrupted something that was happening at the time.

The advantages of past tense narration are:

- things are already finished – you, the writer, know how things are going to turn out
- you can include comments that reflect upon the situation, as Dickens does with 'It was the best of times; it was the worst of times.'

On the whole, once you have decided on a tense for your discourse, stay with it unless there is a very good reason to change. Controlling a 'mixed' piece of writing demands great skill and you have to be very clear about the sequencing of your material.

Active versus passive voice

You will sometimes come across reference to the passive voice (note that it is a voice, not a tense). It is often used in scientific writing as it can give a sense of impartiality and can often be a genre clue.

- The results are given in Table 1.
- The volume of carbon dioxide was carefully measured.

Putting something in the passive makes the person who did the thing sound less involved and makes the receivers of the action more important by turning them into the subject of the sentence.

- The boy broke the window. (active)
- The window was broken by the boy. (passive)
- The dog chased the cat. (active)
- The cat was chased by the dog. (passive)

Without going into the technicalities, you should simply notice that in your own writing it is usually best to avoid the passive voice unless you are aiming for a very particular emphasis. In the sentence 'President Kennedy was assassinated in 1963,' for example, it is clear that the writer is making a point about Kennedy as a victim and that there has been a deliberate decision not to include the name of his assassin.

Punctuation

Some years ago, the British journalist Lynne Truss wrote the most unlikely of things – a bestselling book about punctuation called *Eats, Shoots & Leaves*. It takes its title from an old joke.

> A panda walks into a café. He orders a sandwich, eats it, then draws a gun and fires two shots in the air.

"Why?" asks the confused waiter, as the panda walks towards the exit. The panda produces a badly punctuated wildlife manual and tosses it on the table.

"I'm a panda," he says, at the door. "Look it up."

The waiter turns to the entry in the manual and, sure enough, finds an explanation.

"**Panda.** Large black-and-white bear-like mammal, native to China. Eats, shoots and leaves."

The story makes a point: punctuation is important if it helps the reader and clarifies things along the way. By inserting a comma, the whole meaning changes. The last sentence looks like a list, and therefore the words *shoots* and *leaves* convert themselves to verbs. Note, too, that we can now add to our analysis of jokes (pages 27–8) that they are normally told in the present tense.

You will already know how to write in sentences (capital letter at the start, full stop/period at the end) but it might be useful just to spend a few moments on some of those punctuation marks that perhaps seem slightly more mysterious.

Mark	Name	Definition
,	comma	Use this for separating things out in a list or for helping to demonstrate that some bits of a sentence are subordinate to others. At times, commas are vital to the sense of a sentence. Try the following without the commas. 'She took her inspiration from cooking, her family, and her dog.' 'I'd like to thank my parents, J.K. Rowling, and Dan Brown.'
–···–	dashes	You use these when you want to put an 'aside' into a sentence and make it slightly stronger than two commas. The text between the dashes could be missed out of the sentence if necessary. 'My new car – the one you can see from the window – is in need of a wash.'
:	colon	Use this to introduce a list or an example. 'There are three things you need to know: firstly …'
;	semi-colon	Use this to join two linked thoughts together. For example, 'Godzilla is a misunderstood creature; beneath his raging desire to set people on fire and eat them lies a gentle giant.' Both aspects of this are obviously important, and they are linked. Technically speaking, the semi-colon is linking independent clauses because there is a main verb with tense and number in each half. You can also use it to separate items in a complex list, where commas may not be strong enough to do the job. In effect, it acts as a super-comma, where you need commas to be doing something else in the sentence. 'I would like to thank my colleagues at our headquarters, London; the team on site in the factories in England, France, and Switzerland; and our customers around the world.'

Reflecting on punctuation

As you read texts, it is useful to reflect on how punctuation is being used. Sometimes it's just a matter of fact, a way of keeping the writing clear and unambiguous. At other times punctuation is working with other aspects of the text to create meaning and significance, and it's in these instances that you should try to comment upon its purpose and effectiveness.

Metaphorical language

During your earlier years at school you will have become very familiar with the idea that text producers often like to describe one object in terms of another in order to make it vivid to an audience. You probably won't need reminding that this can also be called **figurative** language and that it stands in opposition to **literal** language, which simply articulates facts.

In simple terms, we have four types of figurative language.

- **Simile:** 'His face was like a wedding cake that had been left out in the rain' (the word *like* shows us this comparison is a simile).

- **Metaphor:** 'He ploughed through his pile of homework' (ploughs are used in fields). In this case one thing becomes the other and there is no need to compare by saying 'like a plough through a field'.

- **Personification:** 'The sun smiled on them when they were on holiday.' This gives human attributes to something which does not have human feelings or abilities.

- **Symbolism:** particularly in literary texts, for example, apples tend to stand for innocence or temptation (as in the story of Adam and Eve) while spiders' webs are a symbol of entrapment or hard work.

However, these definitions merely help you to spot the devices, not to see how crucial metaphorical language is to virtually all communication. In your language studies you need to recognise that the mere observation of examples of figurative examples is of little importance. Rather, you need to be aware of figurative language as central to the various ways in which speakers of a language formulate a view of the world.

The difficulty is that much of the time we don't actually recognise that we are dealing with non-literal language. When people say 'to coin a phrase' they don't dwell on the idea for long enough to recognise that at one stage this idea had a link with the minting of new currency. These are called **dead metaphors**: they have been overused to the point that no one even notices their presence. They can, however, become very vivid by accident if a text producer starts to join them together incorrectly without realising that they have metaphorical significance.

This happens most often when a text producer runs together two idiomatic phrases, and they are called **mixed metaphors**.

- "I'm going to stick to my laurels."

- "We need to grasp the nettle by the horns."

- "Senator McCain suggests that somehow, you know, I'm green behind the ears." (Barack Obama, former US President, during his 2008 election campaign)

In recent years, attention has been turned more to the way that unconscious metaphors inform our world view. Lakoff and Johnson have suggested that in academic life argument is often spoken about as a journey: we 'make progress', we take it 'step-by-step', we ask if people can 'follow' what we say. At other times, we see such discourse as being a container: the argument, like a bucket, has 'holes' in it and 'leaks', and can be criticised for being empty. Sometimes, the metaphors are all to do with war: claims are 'indefensible', arguments are 'attacked', 'demolished', and can be 'shot down'.

Companies often have a mission statement and talk about having a 'vision'. Users of language like this are trying to make their daily business into something rather more mysterious than it actually is or to motivate their sales staff; they want to see their business as having the significance of a religion, not of a trade. When economists talk about money, they talk about cash flow, about it circulating in the economy, about it being the life blood of capitalism. For them, cash is injected, funds haemorrhage from a failing business. In thinking like this, they frame the whole discussion in terms of the economy being like a human body. If you see a number of metaphors, each of which builds on the same basic idea, then these are called – unsurprisingly – **extended metaphors**.

We also show a great capacity for thinking about the same thing in entirely different terms. For example, at times we see the human mind as being like a machine. My mind isn't 'operating' today, I'm a little 'rusty', I've 'run out of steam'. But at other times, the mind is like a precious vase. She's feeling 'very fragile' and has to be 'handled with care'. He was 'shattered by what happened' and went completely 'to pieces'.

Activity 2.25

Below are ten sentences that demonstrate that we often think of time as a commodity, something that can be traded, or a limited resource.

1. I don't have the time to .... you.

2. How do you .... your time these days?

3. You need to .... your time carefully when you revise.

4. I .... a lot of time on my project when I was off school.

5. I don't .... time to .... for that.

6. You don't .... your time ....

7. You're .... of time.

8. He's living on .... time.

9. This machine will .... you hours each week.

10. .... some time for your hobbies.

Insert the following words where appropriate:

put aside	have enough	use	running out	spend	give
profitably	budget	spare	lost	save	borrowed

Occasionally, you can see someone trying to come to terms with something unfamiliar by framing a metaphor. Tim Berners-Lee, the inventor of the World Wide Web, reflects on how his initial ideas moved from being modelled on the idea of an electronic reference book, towards the now familiar idea of a web.

When I first began tinkering with a software program that eventually gave rise to the idea of the World Wide Web, I named it Enquire, short for *Enquire Within upon Everything*, a musty old book of Victorian advice I noticed as a child in my parents' house outside London. With its title suggestive of magic, the book served as a portal to a world of information, everything from how to remove clothing stains to tips on investing money. Not a perfect analogy for the Web: but a primitive starting point.

What that first bit of Enquire code led me to was something much larger, a vision. The vision I have for the Web is about anything being potentially connected with anything. It is a vision that provides us with new freedom, and allows us to grow faster than we ever could when we were fettered by the hierarchical classification. It leaves the entirety of our previous ways. It leaves our previous fears for the future in addition; it brings the workings of society closer to the workings of our minds.

Unlike *Enquire Within upon Everything*, the Web that I have tried to foster is not merely a vein of information to be mined, nor is it just a reference or research tool. Despite the fact that the ubiquitous WWW and .com now fuel electronic commerce and stock markets all over the world, this is a large, but just one, part of the Web. Buying books from Amazon.com and stocks from E-trade is not all there is to the Web. Neither is the Web some idealized space where we must remove our shoes, eat only fallen fruit, and eschew commercialization.

Weaving the Web by Tim Berners-Lee

↑ **Figure 2.9** Tim Berners-Lee, the inventor of the World Wide Web

Reflecting on the source

We can see here that Berners-Lee chose to move his metaphor towards something more natural (he uses the phrase 'organic growth', for example), where there is a clear sense that everything is interconnected. The words *vein* and *mined* show he must have thought, too, about the metaphor as being one of natural resources being excavated.

Having said that, there is of course the limitation of the metaphor that a spider weaves a web, that there is one central creator at work, and a central purpose, something that is plainly no longer the case. Along the way, the vividness of the metaphor has faded and become irrelevant. But in another way it hasn't. A number of governments, recognising the power of the internet, have attempted to control it and place themselves in the position of being the spider. Early on in the history of the internet, it was spoken of as an information 'superhighway', until many with slow download speeds realised that they were stuck in the slow lane. In short, the choice of metaphor often dictates the way that we think about an aspect of the real world.

The important thing for your purposes is to recognise that many metaphors are not merely on the surface of a text, simply devices for making writing more vivid. Instead, when you examine them closely, you often get much closer to the deepest attitudes and values of a speaker or writer, to the way that their mind shapes their world. While you read, it is worth taking the time to see if you can identify metaphorical patterns emerging, rather than simply noting examples.

Spoken and written language

Although at this level our concern is mainly with written language, some of the texts you will encounter will give the impression of having some characteristics of spoken language in order to create a particular voice or tone. You have to remember, too, that speech itself is enormously varied. The distinction between everyday talk and scripted speech is, of itself, worthy of discussion.

The key differences between everyday speech and written language are outlined in the following table.

Spoken language	Written language
It usually involves more than one person and is interactive.	Although it will have an audience in mind, the presence of the audience is not needed at the moment of composition, so it can be a monologue.
It is immediate: the audience hears it as soon as it is said (although with many types of recording available it can be repeated).	There is a time lag between production and reception.
It has a loose structure which allows for rephrasing, repetition and clarification.	It is more carefully and more consciously planned.
It can be appreciated by more than one person at a time.	It is usually only read by one person at a time, at a time chosen by the reader.
It can change register easily.	It will probably stick fairly rigidly to one register and genre.
It can rely on other clues such as facial expression, tone of voice and listener feedback to aid meaning and understanding.	Once it has been written and printed, it is fixed. It is therefore the natural medium for records, tables, lists and notes.
As the speaker knows who is listening, it is suitable for expressing personal attitudes.	It cannot make too many assumptions about the reader as it may be read by wide varieties of different audiences.
It can rely quite heavily on the common understanding between speaker and listener and thus can be more vague because the context of the utterance often explains what is meant.	It can be received and interpreted at the reader's own pace.

Representing spoken language in fictional writing

You will already know about the formal conventions of presenting speech in a story such as speech marks, but the table above will have made you more aware of the problems of trying to give the impression that characters are talking spontaneously in either a novel or a script. The difficulty is that when we talk informally in real life, there is often only a loose sense of purpose, and we often pause (with an 'um' or an 'er' to fill the space), or go back on ourselves to clarify things. A lot of the time, we don't speak in full sentences either.

In contrast, when people in a novel or a soap opera talk, they are doing so in order to move the plot forward in some way, and they don't interrupt each other or talk over each other, as quite often happens in real conversation. You may have noticed, for example, that characters in soap operas never talk about what they saw on the television last night, or what they had for lunch. A popular British soap opera, *EastEnders*, is set in working-class London, and yet no one ever swears, and so its writers constantly have to work around real-life speech features that would, in fact, give their script authenticity.

What's more, speech conventions are very much dictated by the particular variety of English that you speak, as well as your education, age and social class. If you ever want to include speech in your own writing, you need to be absolutely confident that you have a grasp of the idioms and speech patterns of the speaker in order to make it sound authentic. That probably means that you should only attempt it if the character speaking comes from the same country as you and has roughly the same background, or if you know someone from the same background as your character sufficiently well that you can imitate the sorts of things that they would say.

Represented speech can also, of course, be used for local colour, as Emily Brontë does in *Wuthering Heights* with the servant Joseph by trying to represent his broad Yorkshire accent.

> "T' maisternobbut just buried, and Sabbath not o'ered, und t' sound o' t' gospel still i' yer lugs, and ye darr be laiking! Shame on ye! sit ye down, ill childer! there's good books eneugh if ye'll read 'em: sit ye down, and think o' yersowls!"

This could be translated as:

> "The master just recently buried, and the Sabbath not over, and the sound of the gospel still in your ears, and you dare be larking about [having fun]! Shame on you! Sit down, bad children! There are good books enough if you'll read them: sit down, and think of your souls!"

The next extract offers the clever trick of being able to address itself to 'you' by including an audience for the speaker as a character in the book. Writing where there is only one speaker can be called a **monologue**. The writer, Mohsin Hamid, carefully sets up his narrator (note that it is a character in the novel, not Hamid himself) in what could be a casual meeting in a café in Lahore. This allows him to build a narrative voice that borrows much from natural speech. Read the extract and attempt the questions in Activity 2.27.

Text type: prose narrative, fiction, Pakistan

Excuse me, Sir, but may I be of assistance? Ah, I see I have alarmed you. Do not be frightened by my beard: I am a lover of America. I noticed that you were looking for something; more than looking, in fact you seemed to be on a mission, and since I am both a native of this city and a speaker of your language, I thought I might offer you my services.

How did I know you were American? No, not by the color of your skin; we have a range of complexions in this country, and yours occurs often among the people of our northwest frontier. Nor was it your dress that gave you away; a European tourist could as easily have purchased in Des Moines your suit, with its single vent, and your button-down shirt. True, your hair, short-cropped and your expansive chest – the chest, I would say, of a man who bench-presses regularly, and maxes out

→

Activity 2.26

Make a brief transcript (around 200 words will do) of a soap opera or TV series familiar to you and discuss the various factors that make you aware that the characters are not speaking spontaneously.

Exam tip

A word of warning: don't ever try to represent speech in a story unless you are absolutely confident that the speaker will sound authentic. It's always dangerous to write about characters who speak in a markedly different way from the way that you yourself speak.

well above two-twenty-five – are typical of a certain type of American; but then again, sportsmen and soldiers of all nationalities tend to look alike. Instead, it was your bearing that allowed me to identify you, and I do not mean that as an insult, for I see your face has hardened, but merely as an observation.

Come, tell me, what were you looking for? Surely, at this time of day, only one thing could have brought you to the district of Old Anarkali – named, as you may be aware, after a courtesan immured for loving a prince – and that is the quest for the perfect cup of tea. Have I guessed correctly? Then allow me, sir, to suggest my favorite among these many establishments. Yes, this is the one. Its metal chairs are no better upholstered, its wooden tables are equally rough, and it is, like the others, open to the sky. But the quality of its tea, I assure you, is unparalleled.

You prefer that seat, with your back so close to the wall? Very well, although you will benefit less from the intermittent breeze, which, when it does blow, makes these warm afternoons more pleasant. And will you not remove your jacket? So formal! Now that is not typical of Americans, at least not in my experience. And my experience is substantial: I spent four and a half years in your country. Where? I worked in New York, and before that attended college in New Jersey. Yes, you are right: it was Princeton! Quite a guess, I must say.

What did I think of Princeton? Well, the answer to that question requires a story. When I first arrived, I looked around me at the Gothic buildings – younger, I later learned, than many of the mosques of this city, but made through acid treatment and ingenious stonemasonry to look older – and thought, *This is a dream come true.* Princeton inspired in me the feeling that my life was a film in which I was the star and everything was possible. *I have access to this beautiful campus*, I thought, *to professors who are titans in their fields and fellow students who are philosopher-kings in the making.*

The Reluctant Fundamentalist by Mohsin Hamid

↑ **Figure 2.10** The Gothic architecture of Princeton University

Activity 2.27

- What impression do you get of the narrator here? How, precisely, does he speak? What are his most pressing concerns?

- How does Hamid create the character of the American? Start by thinking about how it is clear that, although the American does speak, the narrator chooses not to report it directly.

Another variant of this is to allow a story to develop with some authorial intervention but let the speech itself move the narrative forward, as in this extract from a novel. Elisabeth, the central character, is attempting to renew her passport.

Text type: prose narrative, fiction, UK

Now he's comparing the photograph inside the old passport with the new sheet of booth shots Elisabeth has brought with her.

Recognizable, he says. Just. (Shoulders.) And that's just the change from twenty two to thirty two. Wait till you see the difference when you come back in here for a new passport in ten years' time. (Shoulders.)

He checks the numbers she's written on the form against the ones in the outdated passport.

Going travelling? he says.

Probably, Elisabeth says. Just in case.

Where you thinking of going? he says.

Lots of places, I expect, Elisabeth says. Who knows. World. Oyster.

Seriously allergic, the man says. Don't even say the word. If I die this afternoon, I'll know who to tell them to blame.

Shoulders. Up, down.

Then he puts the booth photographs down in front of him. He screws his mouth over to one side. He shakes his head.

What? Elisabeth says.

No, I think it's all right, he says. The hair. It has to be completely out of your eyes.

It *is* completely out of my eyes, Elisabeth says. It's nowhere near my eyes.

It also can't be anywhere near your face, the man says.

It's on my head, Elisabeth says. That's where it grows. And my face is also attached to my head.

Witticism, the man says, will make not a jot of difference to the stipulations which mean you can, in the end, be issued a passport, which you will need before you are permitted to go anywhere not in this island realm. In other words. Will get you. Nowhere.

Right, Elisabeth says. Thanks.

I think it's all right, the man says.

Good, Elisabeth says.

Wait, the man says. Wait a minute. Just a.

He gets up off his chair and ducks down behind the divide. He comes back up with a cardboard box. In it are various pairs of scissors, rubbers, a stapler, paperclips and a rolled-up measuring tape. He takes the tape in his hands and unrolls the first centimetres of it. He places the tape against one of the images of Elisabeth on the booth sheet.

Yes, he says.

Yes? Elisabeth says.

I thought so, he says. 24 millimetres. As I thought.

Good, Elisabeth says.

Not good, the man says. I'm afraid not good at all. Your face is the wrong size.

How can my face be a wrong size? Elisabeth says.

You didn't follow the instructions about filling the facial frame, that's if the photobooth you used is fitted with passport instructions, the man says. Of course, it's possible the booth you used wasn't passport-instruction-fitted. But that doesn't help here either way I'm afraid.

What size is my face meant to be? Elisabeth says.

The correct size for a face in the photograph submitted, the man says, is between 29 millimetres and 34 millimetres. Yours falls short by 5 millimetres.

Why does my face need to be a certain size? Elisabeth says.

Because it's what is stipulated, the man says.

Is it for facial recognition technology? Elisabeth says.

The man looks her full in the face for the first time.

Autumn by Ali Smith

Activity 2.28

- What effect does Smith achieve by shaping an audience's reaction almost entirely from what the characters say?
- How does she create an impression of the characters?
- What are the effects of not putting speech marks around the utterances?
- Why does Smith not characterise the speech with adverbs ('*she said angrily/wittily etc.*')?
- What is the effect of all the simple sentences?
- What is the effect of the narrator's interventions?
- How would you describe the tone and register of the story?

Conclusion

We have come a long way and it's time to think about what you now know.

You should have a much larger range of terminology and concepts, a more varied set of tools, for describing language and its effects. You now have a strong sense of the main ideas that are central to formal discourse analysis which:

- focuses on language beyond the simple analysis of word, clause, phrase or sentence
- looks at patterns of language in texts and considers the links between the language and the social and cultural contexts in which it is used
- recognises that the use of language presents different views of the world and different understandings and perceptions
- examines the relationship between the participants – speaker/listener or reader/writer
- considers how language creates and influences identities and relationships
- examines how views of the world and identities are constructed through different varieties of discourse and linguistic techniques.

You are now ready to start thinking about how you might apply all of this in an examination.

Language issues

3

This chapter will:

→ look at some of the wider issues raised by language study

→ consider the language of advertising

→ explore ways in which language can unconsciously convey attitudes and values, particularly in relation to gender

→ consider language change and variation with reference to English, the internet and electronic communication

→ consider the conventions and functions of diaries, autobiographies and biographies.

We have already noted that language doesn't exist in a vacuum – it is shaped and modified by the society that uses it from day to day. The study of this shaping of language is called **sociolinguistics**. Broadly speaking, it aims to examine ways in which cultural values, expectations and contexts influence how language is used. You have already seen aspects of this at work, identifying yourself as part of a speech community and recognising that you constantly practise code switching (adapting your language to fit the situation you find yourself in). Your work on register in the last chapter will have given you some awareness of how ethnicity, religion, status, gender, education and country of origin all influence the way that someone uses a language.

Advertising

One of the most potent uses of language is to persuade people and advertisers do this as their profession. Over the years, they have honed their skills in order to persuade you to buy certain products. These days, advertisements that simply give you information about where a product comes from (see Figure 3.1) are rare.

On the whole, adverts need to have an emotional appeal; they appeal to your needs or your fears. Most commonly they focus on your need to:

- have something new
- be accepted
- not be ignored
- change old things
- be secure
- become attractive.

Alternatively they can focus on your fear of:

- accidents
- death
- being avoided
- getting sick
- getting old.

Some advertisements have it both ways, combining your desire for something new with your fear that you might be thought less of because you don't have the latest trainers, or that your friends might be avoiding you because you don't use the right shampoo. You are often being sold a 'lifestyle' rather than the product itself, and advertisers work hard to appeal to your pre-existing attitudes and values in order to make you want what they have to sell. Therefore, advertisements work on the basis of **presupposition**, an understanding of what an audience brings with it to the text. For example, hair is thought to be more glamorous if shiny; holidays to unfamiliar places are thought to be prestigious and desirable.

↑ **Figure 3.1** A relatively straightforward advert for the Ranger Naturalist Service in Lassen Volcanic National Park, 1938

Activity 3.1

Gather a range of advertisements and discuss the various ways in which they are framed to appeal to you. You should examine:

- presuppositions
- foregrounded elements in terms of attitudes and values
- backgrounded elements
- ways in which images work with words to create an impression and to hold your attention.

↑ **Figure 3.2** How effective is this slogan?

Linguists have increasingly turned to exploring the attitudes and values (often called **ideologies**) of texts in recent years. In their analyses, they talk about how the text is presented and the angle or perspective the writer or speaker is working from. This is called **framing** (in the same way that you might 'frame' an argument in an essay), a useful term to use when discussing a wide range of texts. Texts also emphasise some concepts or issues while playing down other aspects, such as price. This is called **foregrounding** and **backgrounding**. If you were trying to persuade your parents to buy you a new computer, for example, you might well foreground its importance for your studies and success at school, while carefully avoiding (backgrounding) your concealed aim, which is to play computer games for ten hours a day.

You will probably have noticed that one aspect of advertising centres on the use of 'buzz words'. These are hooks to reel you in – few people can resist reading on if the word *free* appears in big print. Often the key words are adjectives that might be applied to the product: better, crisper, less fattening, smoother, tastier, tastiest. The adjectives might be applied to the consumer after they have sampled the product too: thinner, healthier, happier.

For major companies, an image (think of the golden arches used by McDonalds or the Coca-Cola logo) is central to brand identification, but this is often linked to a brief phrase (a **slogan**) that is instantly identifiable with their product. Companies long for you to apply make-up 'because you're worth it' and to 'think different' when choosing an expensive smartphone. They want you to hit the gym and 'just do it' in your branded sports gear before enjoying a burger on your way home ('I'm lovin' it'), perhaps while driving in your car to show 'Vorsprung durch Technik'.

Activity 3.2

(a) Look again at the advertisements you chose for Activity 3.1. Your task now is to examine the language. Look for:

- use of different types of word class (adjectives may feature strongly) and register
- use of phrases (combinations of words without a verb) as opposed to full sentences
- slogans
- use and effectiveness of asking the reader/viewer a question
- relationships between the attitudes and values that are being sold and the language used.

An analysis of this type moves us beyond description of the surface features of a text. It aims to provide an explanation of why a text may be as it is and what it is aiming to do. In looking at the relationship between language, social norms and values, an analysis attempts to describe, interpret and explain the relationship between text and audience. By doing so, it also helps a reader/listener to recognise and perhaps challenge some of the hidden (**implicit**) social, political and cultural values that underlie the surface discourse.

(b) Now go back to your genre table (Chapter 2, page 14) and do an analysis of the texts you have found. You will need to look for patterns that all the texts have in common and also at ways in which there are sub-genres (car advertisements, for example) that share the major characteristics of the main genre but have distinctive features of their own.

One of the things that you may have noticed is that many advertisements – particularly for washing powder or beauty products – make assertions about the benefits of their products by saying things that cannot readily be proved.

This use of fake scientific lexis is often used to give the advertisement a formal register, and this can be combined with dubious survey evidence ('Nine out of ten cat owners that expressed a preference …'). The aim is to impress the innocent, and to suggest that a product has some particular, almost magical, properties. Cosmetics are a particular example: one, for example, claims to contain rare diamond dust particles and to have been tested on astronauts in outer space (it's good to know that they worry about their skin). Another says it has been developed after laboratory tests using a SIAscope on skin for a Spectrophotometric Intracutaneous Analysis.

Another feature you will notice in advertising hype (in other words, exaggeration) is the idea that you personally are in some way important to the company. Words like 'exclusive' feature largely, as does the implication that you are in some way privileged or a VIP. Package tours can offer you 'Hidden Spain' or 'Unknown Portugal', although if these holidays are advertised in national newspapers, the offer is hardly for something hidden or unknown, particularly if you will be going as part of a group.

Activity 3.3

Have a look at the following advertisement for a holiday in Rajasthan and then comment on the techniques that the writer has used to persuade you that this holiday would suit you. Think specifically about:

- the potential purchaser the writer has in mind and the way he or she is addressed
- the attitudes and values that are implicit (that is, not openly stated) in the writing.

Text type: advertisement, India

Royal Rajasthan On Wheels

Rajasthan is the magnificent land of numerous kingdoms, majestic forts and palaces, diverse cultures, varied landscapes and vibrant colours. Experience the land of regal splendour with Royal Rajasthan on Wheels, the contemporary royal living. The Royal Rajasthan on Wheels is the regal delight where every moment is woven together into an everlasting and immemorial experience to be lived and cherished forever. The makers of the Palace on Wheels have rekindled the charm of luxury with utmost consideration of your comfort and modern amenities at the Royal Rajasthan on Wheels. This tour is extensively planned to take you through the whispering sands of desert, the intriguing sagas of forts and palaces, and the adventurous escapades to the wilds; while you witness the luxuries on the train in a truly royal fashion. This train is newly built and designed in a contemporary royal style. You will be delighted with the magnificent interiors, sumptuous meals, expensive wines, and personalised service.

It stands on its tracks; a gleaming sealed carriage, every bit is royal. The air-conditioning works silently, creating a space where only the excitement of the history of the Rajput kingdoms permeates through, clearly captured in a contemporary mode.

In all, there are fourteen saloons, each equipped with two twin-bedded and two double-bedded chambers, with attached baths that have running hot and cold water and showers. The modern conveniences have been thoughtfully provided, sofas to sink into, strategically placed lights to read by, wonderfully appointed beds with comfortable furnishings, inbuilt wardrobes for the storage of one's clothes and bags, and huge plate glass windows to watch the countryside roll past. Outside the bedrooms, each coach also has a seating lounge where passengers can get together, just sit and watch the cities as they glide past outside the windows, or enjoy a quiet cup of tea.

Tourism Rajasthan

Activity 3.4

Write a similar advertisement for a local attraction near where you live.

Activity 3.5

How might you re-frame the following sentences in order to avoid gender bias?

1. Our group is going to need a new chairman.

2. The dinnerladies serve delicious lunches to the children.

3. The businessmen are meeting in New York next week.

4. The doorman always lets us in.

5. I want to be a policeman.

6. The air hostess brings us snacks and drinks.

Exam tip

To eliminate sexism in your own writing:

- avoid male words (chairman), preferring neutral alternatives

- avoid traditional idioms (the man in the street)

- use Ms as a neutral alternative to Mrs or Ms

- rework sentences (see page 42) where male pronouns dominate unnecessarily

- try not to use examples that only deal with one gender

- avoid consistently putting reference to males before reference to females

- choose words of equal status: if they are the men's toilets, then the ones for women are not the Ladies'

- avoid modifications that suggest a normal state that is being deviated from: 'the lady doctor,' 'the male secretary'.

Language and attitudes

Whenever we speak or write, we convey something of our own prejudices and beliefs. In recent years, much has been done to eliminate one of the most deeply embedded difficulties of the English language – its inherent bias towards a male-dominated view of the world, where the words used reflect a world where people who fight fires are by definition firemen, where people who run companies are always chairmen. Similarly, certain roles may be characterised as 'female jobs' and by extension of less value: maid, waitress. Nowadays, it's thought best to avoid sexist language and to use **gender-neutral** terms.

Here are some real examples of messages that appeared on Twitter which were sent in to a website called www.everydaysexism.com.

- 'Playing Football Manager 2013, and there is no way to stop the game referring to me as a "he".'

- 'Getting annoyed at programmes and speakers who use 'man' instead of humankind, or humanity.'

- 'Vax advert for vacuum cleaner "super power for super mums" – do dads never vacuum?'

- 'People who send letters to my work addressed to "Dear Sir": You are aware that women work in offices now, right?'

These examples demonstrate how the matter of framing, discussed above, shapes discourse. It may be unconscious on the part of the speaker or writer, but it's there all the same.

One of the key purposes of this rebalancing in terms of gender-based language is to eliminate causes for offence and to provide equality.

This re-framing of language is sometimes called political correctness, although its true goal is to provide non-judgemental, inclusive terminology. It has, at times, come in for much mockery, but that simply demonstrates that the labels we give things have enormous power over our perceptions of matters of gender, race, sexual orientation and disability. The previous sentence, for example, creates a list which might be thought to imply a rank order. That is not my aim but I am bound by the conventions of linearity in prose.

The desire for inclusive language – think back to the discussion of the word *everyone* in the last chapter – can also lead to bizarre attempts not to say the wrong thing. Consider, for example, the rather odd briefing instruction to an interview panel: 'the applicant does not have to tell us they are pregnant,' using *they* to avoid *she*. The interesting thing here, of course, is that gendered language exists on a grammatical level, whereas when in the cases of race, sexual orientation or disability the re-framing is simply a matter of lexical concern.

Language change and variation

These days English is thought of as a global language – Globish, as it's sometimes called. If you are planning to continue your studies to A Level, then you will read a lot more about this in the second part of the course. For present purposes, it's enough to observe that British English is now a minority variant of a language that is spoken as a first language by more people outside the UK than within it. It's also the second language of choice across large sections of the world. In linguistic terms, this means that although the language is still called English, the British have very little to do with its current or its future developments, in the same way as Britain invented soccer and cricket and now finds that both sports are played with great facility elsewhere. Speakers elsewhere in the world are more creative with the language, and, indeed, they are the innovators.

The history of all this must wait until another time. The central point for you now is that you need to recognise that variations of the language across the world do not make one version more or less 'correct'. Instead, it means that the language exists in a number of different forms, although there is something called **Standard English** which is the generally accepted currency for international communication in formal spoken and written situations.

One of the oldest variations is that which exists between British and American English. The Irish writer George Bernard Shaw took the view that 'England and America are two countries separated by a common language.' But it's actually more complicated than that nowadays because both British English and American English are sub-groups of the language as a whole.

One crucial distinction is, of course, that the two languages have a different lexicon. If people move to a new country, there are new things to name. A second point is that each culture chooses to name some of the same things differently. American readers may have been irritated, for example, to have cell phones described as mobile phones earlier on in this book. These are differences of vocabulary, most of which are easily translated.

American English has also tried to rationalise spelling (not always successfully or consistently): *doughnut* becomes *donut*, for example.

The curious thing is, however, that the differences have tended to remain lexical or to do with pronunciation, rather than grammatical. Of course, there are preferences between the two – 'a half-hour' (American), 'half an hour' (British), 'in the hospital' (American), 'in hospital' (British) – but these are not deep features of the language.

Increasingly, American English influences British English (it hasn't happened the other way round for a long time), with words like *get* starting to replace the word *have*: 'Can I get a coffee?' (American). To *fill out* a form is now more common in Britain than to fill one in.

One of the most interesting examples of significant difference of meaning is the American use of *gotten*, a word that doesn't exist in British English. Americans use it to mean 'obtain' – 'She's gotten a new dress', which is rather different to the British phrase, 'She's got a new dress.' 'Gotten' can also mean 'become': 'he's gotten rather set in his ways'. Oddly, *gotten* to mean simply 'have' is unacceptable in American: 'I've gotten the answer' is not acceptable. *Gotten* does allow some flexibility in expression that is not part of British English: 'they've gotten to spend some time in Florida' does not mean that they have to spend some time there; it means that they have managed to do so.

The difference between British and American English is, of course, only one of thousands of possibilities, all of which could be usefully explored using the same methods.

Activity 3.6

Allocate each of the following word pairs to British or American usage:

diaper/nappy
boot/trunk
fall/autumn
windscreen/windshield
bumper/fender
CV/résumé
cookies/biscuits
closet/wardrobe
toilet/restroom
sidewalk/pavement

English, the internet, and electronic communication

Over the last few decades, English has established itself, for the time being at least, as the language of computing. This in turn has contributed greatly to the growth of English as a global language. So it's worth considering some aspects of the pressures for change on the language that has been expanded through this new medium of communication.

Obviously, we have needed some new words because of what computers and mobile phones can do: examples of new words are *download*, *chat room*, *hyperlink* and *hashtag*. The majority of other words related to computing are simply borrowed or adapted from the current language already in existence: *menu*, *options*, *font*, *track*, *mouse*, *avatar*, *troll*, *spam*, and so on. Made-up words like *twitterati* and *twitterholic* won't last, so the actual contribution to the lexicon of the language consists of a few thousand words in relation to the million plus that already exist in English. There is little evidence that computer-specific words are passing into everyday life, or being used without any reference to computers, although a colleague of mine was once described as being in 'energy-saving mode' when having a nap at lunchtime.

A more interesting area for study is the way that computers have created new possibilities for text production. David Crystal's book *Internet Linguistics: A Student Guide*, which was published in 2011, makes it clear that genre characteristics for electronic texts are not yet fully established or developed. Perhaps they never will be, as things change so quickly that new genres appear and disappear with great rapidity.

Email

Some forms are nevertheless now sufficiently established for linguists to be able to list the characteristics typical of the genre. Let's take email as an example. In one episode of *The Simpsons*, Homer asks his friends "What's an email?" He hopes for a nice clear answer. The response he gets from Lenny is, "It's a computer thing, like, er, a letter." Carl adds helpfully, "Or a quiet phone call". In fact it's both of those and more besides. As with many electronic media, an email sits awkwardly on the edge, uncertain if it is a spoken or a written text. This sort of meeting of old styles or forms of writing with new ones is called **convergence**, particularly where speech and writing come together into a **mixed medium**, where rules from both sorts of discourse coincide.

Emails can share some aspects of speech such as informality of tone, and few people these days would set one up as a letter. Nonetheless, there are instances where the written conventions of letters, such as politeness, have remained. In Japan, for example, it is thought very rude simply to start directly with the business of an email, so there will often be comments on the weather such as 'Greetings! It has just becoming spring here in Tokyo.'

However, an email is also a formal written record of things, as a number of large companies have discovered to their cost when they have been ordered to find emails as legal evidence, despite their protestations that they have been lost, deleted, or were not meant for wider public consumption.

Debrett's, a British guide to good manners, recently published a set of guidelines.

Text type: webpage, UK

Email has replaced many traditional forms of communication, both verbal and written. The writer of an email must remember that their message may be stored permanently, and that there is no such thing as confidentiality in cyberspace.

- Delicate communications should therefore be sent by other means, and you must think carefully before hitting 'send' if the message is written in haste or when emotions are running high.

- Avoid sarcasm and subtle humour unless you know that the reader will 'get it'. If in doubt, err towards the polite and formal, particularly where you are not well acquainted with the recipient.

- Think carefully about using smiley faces, 'kisses', etc. Are these symbols really suitable for the recipient?

- Using capital letters looks like shouting and should be avoided. If you want to emphasise something, try underlining or using italics.

- Aim to stick as closely as possible to the conventions of traditional letter-writing. Close attention should be paid to spelling and grammar, and the habit of writing in lower case throughout should be avoided.

- A well thought-out subject line will ensure that the message gets the attention it deserves.

- Emails will often be printed and filed, and therefore close attention must be paid to layout. Again, treating the construction of an email just as you would a 'real' letter is the most effective approach.

- Where there is more than one recipient, list them alphabetically or, in the business environment, according to hierarchy. This applies also to the 'cc' line.

- Avoid blind copying ('bcc') where possible: instead, forward the original email on to the third party, with a short note explaining any confidentiality. Blind copying is, however, appropriate for distribution lists, for example, where all recipients must remain anonymous.

- If you send an email in error, contact the recipient immediately by telephone and ask them to ignore/delete the message.

- It is polite to reply to emails promptly – a simple acknowledgement with a promise that you will give the email your full attention at a given later point is preferable to 'sitting on' the message.

- Never use email to reply to correspondence or an invitation that was not sent by email or does not supply an email address as an RSVP option.

There is no replacement for paper and ink; in this day and age where propriety is so often sacrificed for the sake of immediacy, the truly sophisticated correspondent will put pen to paper rather than dashing off a quick email.

Activity 3.7

(a) What sort of reader/audience does Debrett's have in mind for its **netiquette** advice?

(b) Write 10 rules for email communication for people your own age. You should note that these will vary across the world, even among English speakers, particularly when traditionally there have been very formal greetings and signing off procedures in letters. Your rules need to reflect what happens where you live.

Blogs

Another example is that of blogs. Originally, they were a way for internet users to share their journeying around the web, a track of sites visited that allowed the 'blogger' to leave comments. In effect, early bloggers were creating a map of points of interest on the internet: they were some of the first settlers. Nowadays, blogs have moved firmly into the area of mass communication, and there are professional bloggers who write for newspapers and magazines. This means that the rules and conventions have changed to be much more like those of magazines and newspapers. It's becoming clear, too, that blogs are no longer free from the intervention of the law, so the free-for-all of the early days of blogging is gradually becoming constrained by the rules of libel that would apply to remarks made in newspapers and magazines. Many blogs are also really advertisements, written to give you the impression that comments are being offered independently when they are, in fact, distinctly biased.

There are some obvious features that you would want to imitate if asked to write one. One of the most striking things is that, for all their sense of immediacy and spontaneity, blogs do not contain any of the typical characteristics of spoken language. Although the reader is often asked to engage in **dialogue** and leave a track, the blog itself is not interactive: the reader is not in a conversation with the writer, so there is no element of **turn-taking**, a crucial element of chat.

Typical characteristics of blogs seem to be:

- the topics appear chronologically, with the most recent posting first
- they are usually written in response to something that the blogger has read or seen, often on the internet
- they are simply laid out, with clear titles
- most blogs are brief
- millions of them are never read by anyone other than their creator and, perhaps, close friends or family
- many are not edited but are published directly by their creators
- there is a button that allows you to subscribe and be sent updates
- you can often access an archive of previous posts
- if the blogger is selling something, this has to be kept in the background
- there may be links to social media sites like Facebook or Twitter so that you can follow the writer in a number of different ways
- many blogs do not last very long – authors get bored with them when they realise that other people don't find their opinions fascinating.

Exam tip

The consequence of all this is that unstable forms are difficult to engage with in terms of your own writing. If you had to write a blog entry in your exam, you would need to demonstrate understanding of the text type, and not just write what you were going to write anyway and hope that it served the purpose.

Activity 3.8

Type 'blog template' into a search engine. You will quickly discover that much of the formatting work can be pre-determined so that all a blogger has to do is to put in the content. This will help you to establish some of the genre rules.

Typing in the name of your hobby will produce thousands of examples of content. There is even one for people like me who work in garden huts, called Shedworking (www.shedworking.co.uk).

Netspeak

Perhaps the biggest language innovation has been that a hybrid version of English (it may be true of other languages too) called **Netspeak** is starting to emerge. If you go back to the table in Chapter 2 (see page 52) that describes the differences between spoken and written language, it will soon become apparent that many of those distinctions begin to blur once mobile phones and computers are involved.

We have seen some of this at work in our discussion of email. One of the most obvious difficulties is that if we write as if we are speaking, we can't often go back and correct ourselves, or adapt what we say to the audience as we gauge a reaction. This has led to the emergence of emoticons in some sorts of messaging in order to convey tone or mood.

Some messages also use angle brackets or asterisks (*...*) to provide a gloss on what is being said, for example, <smiles, hoping you understand>. Some of these features are trying to do exactly the same thing that happens when a novel writer creates a passage of speech and then characterises it with, for example, 'he said, angrily.' An example of this is the word *facepalm* which indicates ironic despair, as though the writer is dropping their head into their hands and is lost for words. The desire to write stage directions like this fits clearly into occasions where the pragmatics of the situation – almost spontaneous communication without the other person being present – call for signals to ensure that a writer's tone is not being misunderstood.

Moreover, many notionally spontaneous utterances over the internet have elements of pre-planning that could more easily be associated with written texts. The most obvious elements of spontaneous speech (the 'ums', 'ers', 'you-know-what-I-means') are almost entirely absent, so it is clear that Netspeak is a very long way away from natural conversation. Even 'instant' messaging has pauses and a sense of the other person taking a turn that would be slightly different if the conversation was being held face to face.

At the same time, Netspeak is also not nearly as bound up in the rules of writing, as there is a significant difference between a formally laid out webpage and a text message. What we have is a hybrid that is still very much in the process of development. This has implications for your own writing. You may be asked to produce an article for a webpage, and this is deeply problematic because you will have to think about issues of format as well as about the various ways in which issues of interactivity may be relevant to your text.

Text messaging

It's interesting that text messaging (SMS) has gained so much popularity. Although these are early days in terms of research, it seems that many people prefer to communicate by text rather than by speaking on the telephone because they feel that it is less intrusive to others and it means that they can plan what they want to say more carefully. Texting can, of course, be massively abused when one half of a couple dumps the other by text, or, as happened in 2003, over 2,000 workers for a British claims management company were told they were being made redundant by text. Sometimes, face-to-face communication is simply more suitable.

Diaries, autobiographies and biographies

Think back to the work you did on first-person narrative in Chapter 2 (see pages 17–20). Although some diaries are written for publication, the vast majority are a record of events and private thoughts. As such, they will lack formality and may not have the coherence of something that is more fully planned.

↑ **Figure 3.3** How often do you use emojis in the place of words when messaging your friends?

Activity 3.9

■ Find a range of different texts that illustrate your own use of electronic media. Discuss them in terms of genre, language choice and register. Think about your status as producer, audience or joint author of these texts.

■ Now discuss these texts in terms of the characteristics they share with both spoken and written language. Make use of the table in Chapter 2 (page 52) to help you define the differences.

Here's an example by a writer who tried to visit her London home from the country during the bombing of London in 1940.

Text type: diary, UK

Back from half a day in London – perhaps our strangest visit. When we got to Gower St. a barrier with Diversion on it. No sign of damage. But coming to Doughty St. a crowd. Then Miss Perkins at the window Meck S. [Mecklenburgh Square] roped off. Wardens there, not allowed in. The house about 30 yards from ours struck at one this morning by a bomb. Completely ruined. Another bomb in the square still unexploded. We walked round the back. Stood by Jane Harrison's house. The house was still smouldering. That is a great pile of bricks. Underneath all the people who had gone down to their shelter. Scraps of cloth hanging to the bare walls at the side still standing. A looking glass I think swinging. Like a tooth knocked out – a clean cut. Our house undamaged. No windows yet broken – perhaps the bomb has now broken them. We saw Sage Bernal with an arm band jumping on top of the bricks – who lived there? I suppose the casual young men & women I used to see, from my window; the flat dwellers who used to have flower pots & sit on the balcony.

All blown to bits. The garage man at the back – blear eyed & jerky told us he had been blown out of his bed by the explosion; made to take shelter in a church – a hard cold seat he said, & a small boy lying in my arms. "I cheered when the all clear sounded. I'm aching all over." He said that the Jerrys had been over for 3 nights trying to bomb Kings X [a London station]. They had destroyed half Argyll Street, also shops in Grays Inn Road. Then Mr Pritchard ambled up.

10 September 1940,
The Diary of Virginia Woolf by Virginia Woolf

In an early diary entry (20 April 1919), Woolf articulated her aims for her diary.

> 'What sort of diary should I like mine to be? Something loose knit and yet not slovenly, so elastic that it will embrace anything, solemn, slight or beautiful that comes into my mind. I should like it to resemble some deep old desk, or capacious hold-all, in which one flings a mass of odds and ends without looking them through.'

Activity 3.10

(a) In what ways does the entry from 1940 confirm the view that Woolf's diary is:

- loose knit (that is, not formally structured)
- able to 'embrace' a wide variety of experiences
- like 'a deep old desk, or capacious hold-all'?

(b) Write a diary entry – or a series of entries over a number of days – by someone who is confronting problems at school or in a new job.

An autobiography is different from a diary in that it is written to be read by other people.

Look at a piece of autobiographical writing describing a writer's harsh upbringing by a religious mother in the north of England.

Text type: autobiography/memoir, UK

I got myself up for school every day. My mother left me a bowl of cornflakes and the milk in a flask. We had no fridge and most of the year we had no need of one – the house was cold, the North was cold, and when we bought food we ate it.

Mrs Winterson had terrible stories about fridges – they gave off gas and made you dizzy, mice got caught in the motor, rats would be attracted by the dead mice caught in the motor … children got trapped inside and couldn't escape – she knew of a family whose youngest child had climbed into the fridge to play hide-and-seek, and frozen to death. They had to defrost the fridge to prise him out. After that the council took away the other children. I wondered why they didn't just take away the fridge.

Every morning when I came downstairs I blew on the fire to get it going and read my note – there was always a note. The note began with a general reminder about washing – HANDS, FACE, NECK AND EARS – and an exhortation from the Bible, such as Seek Ye the Lord. Or Watch and pray.

The exhortation was different every day. The body parts to be washed stayed the same.

When I was seven we got a dog, and my job before school was to walk the dog around the block and feed her. So then the list was arranged as WASH, WALK, FEED, READ.

At dinner time, as lunchtime was called in the North, I came home from school for the first few years, because junior school was only round the corner. By then my mother was up and about, and we ate pie and peas and had a Bible reading.

Later, when I was at the grammar school further away, I didn't come home at dinner time, and so I didn't have any dinner. My mother refused to be means-tested, and so I didn't qualify for free school meals, but we had no money to buy the meals either. I usually took a couple of slices of white bread and a bit of cheese, just like that, in my bag.

Nobody thought it unusual – and it wasn't. There were plenty of kids who didn't get fed properly.

Why be Happy When You Could be Normal? by Jeanette Winterson

In the next passage, the New Zealand writer Janet Frame recounts an autobiographical childhood episode about her brother (Bruddie/Geordie). The second passage is the re-telling of the same incident by her biographer.

Text type: autobiography, New Zealand

It was not long after Grandad's death that we were awakened one night by a commotion in the house. I heard Mum crying out, 'Bruddie's having a convulsion; Bruddie's having a convulsion.' I ran with the others into the dining room. We sat together on the … sofa, watching and listening while Mum and Dad went back and forth from Bruddie's room to the bathroom. 'A convulsion, a convulsion,' Mum kept saying in her earthquake-and-tidal-wave voice. She fetched the doctor's book from where it was (unsuccessfully) hidden on top of the wardrobe in their bedroom and looked up Convulsions, talking it over with Dad, who was just as afraid.

In the meantime Bruddie had wakened, sobbing. 'A bath,' Mother cried. 'Put him in a bath.' Dad carried the crying Bruddie into the bathroom. We four girls were sent back to our bedrooms, where we cuddled up to one another, talking in frightened whispers and shivering with the cold Oamaru night, and when I woke the next morning, my eyes were stinging with sleep and I felt burdened with the weight of a new awful knowledge that something terrible had happened in the night to Bruddie.

Our lives were changed suddenly. Our brother had epilepsy, the doctor said, prescribing large doses of bromide which, combined with Bruddie's now frequent attacks, or fits, as everyone called them, only increased his confusion and fear until each day at home there were episodes of violent rage when he attacked us or threw whatever was at hand to throw. There had usually been somewhere within the family to find a "place" however cramped; now there seemed to be no place; a cloud of unreality and disbelief filled our home, and some of the resulting penetrating rain had the composition of real tears. Bruddie became stupefied by drugs and fits; he was either half asleep, recovering, crying from the last fit, or in a rage of confusion that no one could understand or help. He still went to school, where some of the bigger boys began to bully him, while we girls, perhaps prompted by the same feeling of fear, tried to avoid him, for although we knew what to do should he fall into a fit at school or outside at home, we could not cope with the horror of it. Mother, resisting fiercely the advice of the doctor to put Bruddie into an institution, nursed him while we girls tried to survive on our own with the occasional help of Dad, who now combed the tangles out of my frizzy hair each morning and supervised the cleaning of our bedroom.

To the Is-Land by Janet Frame

Activity 3.11

Compare the techniques used in this passage with those of Woolf in her diary. Pay particular attention to the voice that each writer constructs and also to the structure of each piece.

Now write a short section of your own autobiography where you try to amuse a reader about a specific episode from your life. You could choose a moment fondly recalled by your family from a holiday, or perhaps an account of your first day at a new school.

How might this have been different if you had been simply writing up the incident in a diary?

↑ **Figure 3.4** Janet Frame, the New Zealand author, and subject of *Wrestling with the Angel*

Text type, biography, New Zealand

Early in 1932 the family discovered a more traumatic and enduring source of tension and grief. One night, not long after Janet had thrown a lump of coal at her brother and hit him on the head, Geordie, now aged nine, suffered an epileptic seizure. Neither parent knew how to cope with this frightening visitation. "A convulsion, a convulsion," Mum kept saying in her earthquake-and-tidal-wave voice. Later, as the fits recurred and the family knew what to do to make it less likely that Geordie would injure himself, the sense of horror and helplessness persisted. And for Janet, who feared that she may have caused this problem, the fits produced additional anxiety and guilt.

There were at this time no effective drugs to mitigate or control the condition. Large doses of bromide, the sole recourse of the family's doctor, only increased Geordie's confusion and fear. '[Each] day at home there were episodes of violent rage when he attacked us or threw whatever was at hand to throw. There had usually been somewhere within the family to find a 'place' however cramped; now there seemed to be [none] … Mother, resisting fiercely the advice to put [Geordie] in an institution, nursed him while we girls tried to survive on our own.' Epileptics were then defined as 'mental defectives' under mental health legislation. And what Lottie actually said as she rejected the doctor's advice was, 'No child of mine is going to Seacliff,' which was the Otago mental hospital. In the case of her son at least this ambition was realized. Geordie, deaf as well as epileptic, left school before he turned twelve and, in the recollection of his siblings, his mother 'devoted all her time to him'.

Wrestling with the Angel: A Life of Janet Frame by Michael King

Conclusion

All the examples in this chapter present us with examples of what linguists call 'communicative competence'. Language is not, as we now know, merely used because it is neutral and grammatically correct; rather, a speaker or writer has to know how, when, and where to use language appropriately, and with whom. A consequence of this is that analysis needs to take into account the social and cultural setting in which the text is produced, looking at the text producers' relationships with potential audiences and at a community's norms, values and expectations for the type of text produced. Linguists therefore see grammatical competence as being only one aspect of a much wider range of pressures that are part of text production and consumption, namely:

- sociolinguistic competence, a knowledge of appropriate language use in specific situations.
- generic competence, an ability to respond to a text by showing awareness of how to construct, interpret and exploit established conventions associated with the use of particular types of texts
- discourse competence, a knowledge of how to connect utterances in a text so that it is cohesive and coherent in its own terms
- strategic competence, an ability to examine breakdowns in communication, or to enhance a communication's effectiveness.

All of these factors joined together are sometimes described as 'textual competence' or 'discursive competence', which is achieved by a text producer or consumer being able to draw on textual, contextual and pragmatic knowledge of what typically occurs in a particular text, how it is typically organised, and how it is usually interpreted, in order to create new texts or respond to texts that are unfamiliar.

In this chapter:

- you have looked at a range of text types and at issues that place textual detail into a wider context
- you have thought more deeply about genre and language use
- you have broadened your understanding of the term 'discourse analysis' to enable you to talk about some of the social, political, practical and ideological issues related to the production and reception of texts.

Activity 3.12

Compare the writers' different presentations of this moment in Janet Frame's life. Pay particular attention to:

- the difference between **subjective** (the writer is involved) and **objective** narration
- ways in which Michael King incorporates some of Frame's own narrative into his writing.

Now go back to the Winterson passage (page 67) and re-write it as though you were her biographer, using the King passage as a model.

Discuss with a partner the narrative choices that you made in order to present an objective view of Winterson's experiences.

Paper 1: Reading

This chapter will:

→ build your skills for answering the questions on Paper 1

→ go through the requirements of each section of the paper

→ consider how to tackle re-purposing a text

→ work through strategies to help analyse your own and other writing

→ show a selection of sample student responses with feedback.

Paper 1 Reading (50 marks) lasts 2 hours and 15 minutes.

The paper is primarily designed to assess your skills and techniques in relation to reading.

The paper has two sections:

■ Section A: Directed response

■ Section B: Text analysis.

You should divide your time equally between the two sections. There will be two questions, Question 1 in Section A and Question 2 in Section B. Both are compulsory.

Section A: Directed response – what's involved?

You have just over an hour for Section A. Question 1 is in two parts: (a) and (b) and is worth **25 marks** in total.

You will be asked to read a text of approximately 550–750 words and then:

1(a) Produce a short piece of your own writing (150–200 words) that uses information from the original, but re-purposes it to fit a specific form, purpose and audience. (10 marks)

1(b) Compare your writing in 1(a) with that of the original, identifying, analysing and comparing characteristic features of the texts and relating these to their purpose, audience and contexts. (15 marks)

Why am I being asked to do this?

The Assessment Objectives (AOs) for this course set out the core skills you need to show.

✓ Writing a 're-purpose' response to a previously unseen text has been found to be a very good way of assessing a student's understanding of that text. AO1 requires that you 'demonstrate understanding of a wide variety of texts'. In order to make the linguistic choices necessary to shift a text from one genre or purpose to another, you need to have a good (implicit) understanding of the construction of the given text and of questions to do with purpose/audience and genre. Your writing will *show* the examiner your understanding.

✓ The second stage – writing a comparative commentary – then follows naturally, and you can make your implicit understanding 'explicit' by making specific comments on choices of form, structure and language (satisfying AO2). Your commentary will *tell* the examiner about your understanding of how writers' choices produce meaning and style.

How am I going to tackle the questions?

Phase 1: Sequencing

You are going to need to get into the habit of **sequencing** what you do. If you stick to the same pattern each time you tackle these questions, it will be a matter of habit by the time you take the examination.

- Read the text, making notes about both style and content.
- Think about the genre requirements of the text you are about to create.
- Write your directed response, selecting material from the original.
- Write brief notes where you outline major points of difference between the two pieces of writing.
- Write your comparative commentary.

> 1 Read a text, annotating points of linguistic interest
>
> 2 Think about re-purposing requirements (genre, etc.)
>
> 3 Write your directed response, selecting material from the original

Let's get started and follow the process through. You will find it useful to refer to the Step 1 and Step 2 tables on pages 83–4 as you write your notes.

Text A is from a medical advice website. The material consists of the expert reactions of four senior health professionals to research into the side-effects of commonly prescribed drugs.

Text A

Expert 1:

The negative effects of anticholinergic drugs on brain and cardiac function have been known for decades and this study reinforces their dangers. The wide use of amitriptyline and related tricyclic antidepressant drugs in primary care for depression, and also unproven indications such as insomnia, is therefore a significant concern. For these reasons most experts have recommended that antidepressants such as amitriptyline should be replaced by the SSRIs which are much safer.

Expert 2:

All drugs have possible side effects, but the results of this study should not lead anyone to stop current medications without discussing this with their doctor first. Before starting any drug, it is important for the doctor and patient to discuss the possible benefits of the treatment, compared with the potential downsides, so that the patient can make an informed decision. As a cardiologist, many of the drugs I use (such as beta-blockers) have been definitely proven to make people with heart disease live longer, so it's important to balance these proven benefits against the risk of side effects.

Expert 3:

This comprehensive study could have some far-reaching effects. The results underline the critical importance of calculated drug prescription. Further investigation needs to establish exactly how and why drugs with an anticholinergic effect are increasing mortality, which might offer clues to influence safer drug design. It's important for people prescribed medicines with an anticholinergic effect not to panic, but to discuss with their doctor the best possible personal treatment plan.

Large cohort research is essential to understanding what might influence the prevalence of dementia in a population. These broad studies can be invaluable in shaping public health policy, yet funding for such research remains shamefully low. With the 820,000 people currently living with dementia set to increase drastically, research is the only answer and we must invest more now.

Expert 4:

Older people are prescribed many drugs, as this study shows. Yet again some of these drugs have been shown to have adverse effects, including an association with cognitive decline. This is an important and very large study and although we cannot assume that the drugs are actually causing the increased decline, there is good reason to think they may be. This study has important clinical lessons for all doctors looking after older people.

As you can see, the target audience for this website is very broad. One of its articles or blogs might be read (at one extreme) by a confident expert in a particular field of medicine or (at the opposite extreme) by an anxious individual with very little medical knowledge.

Phase 2: Creating text

A task for Question 1(a) could be:

Write 150–200 words of an article for a medical website, suitable for the non-expert, explaining some of the possible dangers and side effects of taking medication. Base your writing on the information in Text A.

STEP 1

For the moment, don't worry about the content of your article. Think about the style, tone and register: in other words, how to match the message to the audience.

Let's start by making a basic list of choices about language you might expect to make. Examples are given here but you can add your own ideas too.

Tone/register:	Lexis:
■ friendly	■ simple/colloquial
■ modified formal	■ non-specialist
	■ concrete nouns where possible
	■ avoiding complex nominalisations

Mode of address:

- direct second person, *you*
- inclusive – writer invites reader to join in and agree so first person plural, *we*

Syntax:

- simple (and minor) sentences
- non-standard grammar, with some function words missed out
- active verb constructions
- some abbreviations or contractions ('you'll', 'I've')
- conversational/colloquial

Behind all this there is of course the implicit understanding that you will be thinking about:

- **A**udience
- **P**urpose
- **P**oint of view.

It might be a good idea to remember the acronym APP as a means of ensuring that you cover all these points in an examination.

As you move into this new area, you become the creator of the text. This means that you have to ask yourself the questions about texts from a different point of view.

- Who am I writing this text for? Where will it be read? (do not think about the examiner!)
- What is the text going to be about?
- What sort of a text is it going to be?
- What sort of relationship will I need to establish with an audience?
- What sort of attitudes and values will be conveyed through my text, both explicitly and implicitly?

Think again of the purpose: you are explaining some of the possible dangers and side effects of some medicines.

STEP 2

Go back to the original piece and now choose the examples and information that you need in order to give your article substance. Select a couple of points from each of the paragraphs.

Phase 3: Comparing texts

Question 1(b) will always be the same, and could be phrased in this way:

Your task is to take your own writing and compare it to the original.

You may well find it useful to put your thoughts together in diagrammatic form to start off with. It will be easier to see what is important. After all, you only have a limited amount of time, so you have to get on with essential points straight away. You also need to structure your writing clearly, as you are rewarded for that by the examiner.

Activity 4.1

Now write your piece in answer to the task you considered on the previous page:

Write 150–200 words of an article for a medical website, suitable for the non-expert, explaining some of the possible dangers and side effects of taking medication. Base your writing on the information in the extract in Text A.

Remember the word limit. Make sure that you think about communicating simply and clearly and matching your language to your audience.

Give yourself 10 minutes to re-read the material and make some notes, then 25 minutes to do the writing, and finally 5 minutes to check carefully what you've written. Now go and do something else before tackling Question 1(b). It's worth more marks, so should take longer.

You could use a table like this, or a spider diagram/mind map to help.

Compare and contrast	
Original text	My re-purposed text
How are these alike (what similarities can you spot)?	
1.	
2.	
3.	
4.	
How are these different? (with regard to language; style; layout; techniques; attitude; anything else?)	
Conclusion:	
Technical vocabulary to use in my comparison:	

Activity 4.2

Copy and complete the chart, or a similar diagram, comparing the original text on pages 71–2 and your re-purposed text from Activity 4.1.

You need to use a good variety of 'comparing' words (discourse markers) in your points. They will help you keep the **comparison** of the two texts in mind throughout. For example:

- comparatively
- likewise
- in contrast
- in comparison
- equally
- similarly
- on the other hand
- however
- on the contrary
- but
- whereas
- as with.

Try to deal with the original source text and your own text at the same time, rather than going through one then the other. This will help you really compare the texts, rather than simply talking about them in isolation.

Activity 4.3

Here is the beginning of an answer, with a framework for comparison laid out. Copy and use the structure given to construct part of an answer to the question:

Your task is to take your own writing and compare it to the original.

> All of the opinions in the original text are rather formal (give example) ... On the other hand in the re-purposed text, the lexis is more relaxed and colloquial (give example) ... This shows that the audience for the original text is ... In contrast, in the re-purposed text the writer wants to appeal to a broader, less-expert audience, hence the tone (give example) is more ... This is created by ... Sentences in the original text are often quite long. However, the sentence structure in the re-purposed text is more straightforward with the effect that ...

You get the idea: for each point you make, you should consider how the original/re-purposed text is similar or different. Most importantly, go on to discuss the effect of this.

Once you have finished, you then need to check your answer. The examiner will be looking for very straightforward things such as your ability to:

- identify characteristics of both genres and comment on them
- organise your writing in a clear way
- comment on form, structure and language of the texts
- write in an appropriate, analytical way.

Most important of all, your ability to sustain the comparison will be central to the examiner's assessment of what you have done. Spend a few minutes ensuring your work matches all these requirements.

Moving on

Now you know how to do it, it's time to work through this process independently. On the next few pages are three sets of sample exam questions for Paper 1 Section A. Let's go easy with the first sample question by asking you to write less in Question 1(a) than you would normally do. Spend about 25 minutes on Question 1(a), 35 minutes on Question 1(b) – this reflects the allocation of marks within the hour or so that you are allowed.

Once you have finished, read the discussion that follows.

Sample question 1

1. Text B is the opening from the book *Mirror to Damascus,* which the author Colin Thubron describes as having begun as a 'history and a description' of the ancient city in the Middle East.

   (a) Imagine you work for the tourist board of the area that Colin Thubron describes in the extract. Write a paragraph (70–100 words) for a tourist guide which aims to encourage wildlife enthusiasts to visit.

   (b) Compare the style and language of your tourist guide with the style and language of the original account.

Hint:

Select five negative details from the original which you can 're-position' as positive and encouraging details, slanted to appeal to wildlife enthusiasts.

Text B

We kept climbing up and up. Soon, it seemed, I would be able to stretch out a hand and touch the cloud above the hill. Every now and then the man's foot disturbed a stone, which escaped down the slope in ugly leaps, drawing a dust of pebbles after it. Saffron butterflies fidgeted among the rocks and settled on shrubs whose substance had been blown out by wind and sun. 5

Everywhere up the hill these ghosts attended us: clumps of colourless thistles; filmy-leaved plants whose violet stalks fingered each other obscenely over the stone; bushes which threw up thorns and noxious berries. 10

The sun had drunk up almost all life. The weeds themselves only flowered by miracle. Men had left rubbish behind, familiar objects which assumed a curious importance among the rocks: tendrils of rope, warped shoes, tins, shreds of cloth, corn cobs, broken plates decorated with sad flowers. 15

Reflecting on Sample question 1

This sample exam task required you to carry out an extreme transformation. The original passage describes a hostile landscape and is full of unpleasant images. Even the butterflies seem uncomfortable: first they 'fidgeted', and then when eventually they 'settled', it was on shrubs that were withered. Where natural forms have been given human characteristics, these are even more unpleasant: 'plants whose violet stalks fingered each other obscenely'. Man-made objects have started to develop characteristics of the natural: 'tendrils of rope'.

So what could you possibly have found that you could 'spin' as an advantage?

1. Weeds that only 'flowered by miracle' could be presented as a unique feature: 'Come and see the miraculous flowering weeds!'

2. Saffron butterflies could be 're-positioned' as a marvel of nature: 'Be amazed by the dazzling sunshine-yellow butterflies!'

3. Slant the rubbish as an advantage: 'Man has made his mark on the area. Even the most familiar "objets trouvés" assume a curious importance among these barren rocks.' (A touch of French can work wonders, and not just on restaurant menus!)

Your commentary will probably start by drawing attention to the changes that you have made in order to accentuate the distinctive choices of vocabulary that you have made in your own work in order to adapt its genre. There are, of course, other things that you might have done in order to create a more positive atmosphere, and which you might have also commented upon.

Sample question 2

With the following exam-style question, you need to see if you can do the opposite to Sample question 1, by adopting a negative rather than a positive angle.

---

1. Text C is from a website originating in Bengaluru, India. The writer is describing a National Park. Imagine you recently visited this National Park, but you did not enjoy the experience. Many of the features which are described in such positive terms in the passage were a big disappointment to you and your family.

    (a) You decide to send an email to the director of the tourist board responsible for publicity for the National Park, pointing out how your experience of the attraction fell far short of what it promised. Write the text of this email in 150–200 words.

    (b) Compare the style and language of your email complaint with the style and language of the original website description.

Text C

Tryst with Nature – Bannerghatta National Park

If you keep your eyes and ears open, you will be treated to the delight of exotic species of both flora and fauna. There are gigantic and overwhelmingly beautiful trees that will make you stand and stare in awe. These trees also provide shelter all round the year, helping maintain the temperature and humidity of the park to tolerable   5
levels. The monsoon brings refreshing showers, covering the place in a blanket of lush green so that it is both soothing and pleasing to visit. Bamboos can be seen dotting the park and a small portion of it is dedicated to Eucalyptus plantations.

A diversity of wildlife can be seen in this park. To say so would be   10
something of an understatement indeed. Elephants, cheetal, slow loris, wild boar, fox, squirrels, porcupine, muntjac, bonnet macaque, gaur, leopard, wild pig, sambar, barking deer, langur, bison, white tiger, Bengal tiger, panther and sloth bear can be found in abundance
to name a few. These animals have been preserved in their natural   15
habitat so as to allow them to propagate. If you wish to visit the park

---

A brief language-change detour

Lynda Mugglestone (Professor of the History of English at Oxford University) wrote on 'spin' in an Oxford Dictionary blog from 2011.

'Spin is one of those words which could perhaps now do with a bit of "spin" in its own right. From its beginnings in the idea of honest labour and toil (in terms of etymology, spin descends from the spinning of fabric or thread), it has come to suggest the twisting of words rather than fibres – a verbal untrustworthiness intended to deceive and disguise. Often associated with newspapers and politicians, to use spin is to manipulate meaning, to twist truth for particular ends – usually with the aim of persuading readers or listeners that things are other than they are. As in idioms such as to put a "positive spin on something" – or a "negative spin on something" – one line of meaning is concealed, while another – at least intentionally – takes its place. Spin is language which, for whatever reason, has designs on us.'

to spot wildlife, then doing so between November and June would be a good idea. The collection of wildlife here is sure to spark your interest.

A visit to the Bannerghatta National Park can be aptly described as a Tryst with Nature. The entire area of the park includes 10 reserve forests from the Anekal Range. The forests are lined with hills abounding in ancient temples. The vegetation is mainly scrub land and dense dry and moist deciduous forests. The Suvarnamukhi stream, originating from the Suvarnamukhi Hill, cuts through the park. At a distance of 2km from this hill, the Suvarnamukhi pond is believed to have curative powers. 20

25

The Bannerghatta National Park boasts of a snake park that houses a unique collection of these scaly and slithering beauties. You will encounter innumerable species of snakes here. Other major attractions are a crocodile farm, aquarium and museum.

Source: www.theindianwire.com

Hints:

- Think about your audience. Students doing directed writing tasks that involve letters or emails of complaint or protest often lose sight of who they are writing to: they assume that the recipient is personally responsible, and will be able to put right whatever has been wrong. Here, you are not writing to the author of the website description, but you are writing to someone who you might reasonably expect to take some action.

- Think about the purpose of your email. Do you just want your disappointment to be recognised and acknowledged? Or are you asking for something more specific?

- Think about the context of language use for your text and Text B. Email is often brief and transactional; an article about a place to visit is likely to be more expansive and expressive.

Reflecting on Sample question 2

The simplest level of commentary is to recognise broad patterns and tendencies of language use. For example, the lexical choices in the original passage are likely to be positive, as the writer wants to construct a favourable impression of the National Park. But at AS Level you need to go further and deeper than that: you need to analyse and explore.

In Text C you could have looked for two particular linguistic species:

1. You would expect to find description, and positive evaluative adjectives. These are not difficult to locate in the passage, but you need to think more precisely about how they are used.

    Linguists refer to the process by which one word affects the meaning of another as modification. (You came across the term **modifier** in Chapter 2.) Most often, nouns are modified by adjectives and verbs are modified by adverbs. And, most of the time, the modifying word comes first.

    So we can analyse the following sentence from the end of the first paragraph: 'The monsoon brings refreshing showers, covering the place in a blanket of lush green so that it is both soothing and pleasing to visit.'

    All of the highlighted words are positive evaluative lexical choices. The first two provide adjectival pre-modification: they tell us what kind of showers and what kind of green to expect. The next two provide adjectival post-modification: they tell us what 'it' (the place) is like once it's been bathed by the refreshing showers.

2. The use of active and/or passive verb constructions is always potentially interesting.

    As you'll remember from Chapter 2:

    ■ verbs used in the active voice involve the grammatical subject of the clause or sentence performing some action

    ■ verbs used in the passive voice involve the grammatical subject of the clause or sentence having some action done to them.

    Think about what you would expect to find in a description of a visitor attraction.

    In an article about an activity holiday or a place where you would pursue a particular interest, you might expect lots of active verb constructions, used to draw attention to what you would be doing. You would be the **agent**.

    In an article about a place where you would receive some kind of treatment – beauty therapy, for example – you might expect lots of passive verb constructions, used to draw attention to what you would have done to you! You would be the *recipient*.

    What do we find in this article?

    Right from the start, we find a mixture of active and passive verb constructions:

    'If you keep your eyes and ears open, you will be treated to the delight of exotic species of both flora and fauna.'

    So, the visitor has to do something (active verb: keep your eyes and ears open), but it's something fairly natural and easy, and will lead to a pleasurable experience (passive verb: you will be treated to the delight of exotic species).

Now look back at your directed writing task, your email. It is important that you don't just simply have a 'shopping list' of linguistic features to cover because that may lead you astray. For example, if you do not use verbs in the passive voice, or you don't make significant use of pre-/post modification, then there is no point in raising these as issues.

In other words, as with tools, if the tap is dripping, you will need a spanner and a wrench; if you are painting the house, you need a brush and a ladder. In short, you must make sure that the tool is suitable for the job. If there is nothing particularly interesting to say about, for example, punctuation, you would be unwise to discuss it at length.

Why is that?

Because identification of language features is a basic skill – it's useful, but it's only a start. The real work comes in analysing the workings and effects of what you've found.

You are constantly trying to move forwards in your discussion from observation to analysis. In doing these transformations, you are not particularly interested in the 'what' of a piece of writing (its content), more in the 'how' of a piece of writing in terms of a writer's choices of form, style and language.

> **Exam tip**
>
> Bear in mind, this is quite a literary description: it's not a 'hard sell', full of facts and figures and prices.

> **Exam tip**
>
> Examiners say that the feature of language on which students waste most time is completely unimportant examples of pronoun use. The fact that you can recognise a feature of language doesn't make it significant.

Sample question 3

You are on your own now. Remember that you don't have to use all the information from Text D in your answer to 1(a); and in 1(b), you cannot hope to cover everything, so be selective.

> 1. Text D is from a website, www.coastalcare.org, that concerns itself with environmental matters.
>
>   **(a)** Write the text of a leaflet designed for young people to make them more aware of the environmental issues involved with plastic. Write between 150–200 words.
>
>   **(b)** Compare the language and style of your response with the language and style of the original text.

Text D

When the mermaids cry: The great plastic tide

By Claire Le Guern

Last updated in March 2018.

The world population is living, working, vacationing, increasingly conglomerating along the coasts, and standing on the front row of the greatest, most unprecedented, plastic waste tide ever faced. [...]

For more than 50 years, global production and consumption of plastics have continued to rise. An estimated 299 million tonnes of plastics were produced in 2013, representing a 4 percent increase over 2012, and confirming an upward trend over the past years. In 2008, our global plastic consumption worldwide has been estimated at 260 million tonnes, and, according to a 2012 report by Global Industry Analysts, plastic consumption is to reach 297.5 million tonnes by the end of 2015.

Plastic is versatile, lightweight, flexible, moisture resistant, strong, and relatively inexpensive. Those are the attractive qualities that lead us, around the world, to such a voracious appetite and over-consumption of plastic goods. However, durable and very slow to degrade, plastic materials that are used in the production of so many products all, ultimately, become waste with staying power. Our tremendous attraction to plastic, coupled with an undeniable behavioural propensity of increasingly over-consuming, discarding, littering and thus polluting, has become a combination of lethal nature.

A simple walk on any beach, anywhere, and the plastic waste spectacle is present. All over the world the statistics are ever growing, staggeringly. Tonnes of plastic debris (which by definition are waste that can vary in size from large containers, fishing nets to microscopic plastic pellets or even particles) is discarded every year, everywhere, polluting lands, rivers, coasts, beaches, and oceans.

Published in the journal *Science* in February 2015, a study [...] quantified the input of plastic waste from land into the ocean. The results: every year, 8 million metric tonnes of plastic end up in our oceans. It's equivalent to five grocery bags filled with plastic for every foot of coastline in the world. In 2025, the annual input is estimated to be about twice greater, or 10 bags full of plastic per foot of coastline. So the cumulative input for 2025 would be nearly 20 times the 8 million metric tonnes estimate – 100 bags of plastic per foot of coastline in the world!

Lying halfway between Asia and North America, north of the Hawaiian archipelago, and surrounded by water for thousands of miles on all sides, the Midway Atoll is about as remote as a place can get. However, Midway's isolation has not spared it from the great plastic tide either, receiving massive quantities of plastic debris, shot out from the North Pacific circular motion of currents (gyre). Midway's beaches, covered with large debris and millions of plastic particles in place of the sand, are suffocating, envenomed by the slow plastic poison continuously washing ashore.

Then, on shore, the spectacle becomes even more poignant, as thousands of bird corpses rest on these beaches, piles of colourful plastic remaining where there stomachs had been. In some cases, the skeleton had entirely biodegraded; yet the stomach-size plastic piles are still present, intact. [...]

It is estimated that of the 1.5 million Laysan Albatrosses which inhabit Midway, all of them have plastic in their digestive system; for one third of the chicks, the plastic blockage is deadly, coining Midway Atoll as "albatross graveyards" by five media artists, led by photographer Chris Jordan, who recently filmed and photographed the catastrophic effects of the plastic pollution there. […]

In a 2006 report, *Plastic Debris in the World's Oceans*, Greenpeace stated that at least 267 different animal species are known to have suffered from entanglement and ingestion of plastic debris. According to the National Oceanographic and Atmospheric Administration, plastic debris kills an estimated 100,000 marine mammals annually, as well as millions of birds and fishes. […]

However, most of the littered plastic waste worldwide ultimately ends up at sea. Swirled by currents, plastic litter accumulates over time at the centre of major ocean vortices forming "garbage patches", i.e. larges masses of ever-accumulating floating debris fields across the seas. The most well known of these "garbage patches" is the Great North Pacific Garbage Patch, discovered and brought to media and public attention in 1997 by Captain Charles Moore.

The plastic waste tide we are faced with is not only obvious for us to clearly see washed up on shore or bobbing at sea. Most disconcertingly, the overwhelming amount and mass of marine plastic debris is beyond visual, made of microscopic range fragmented plastic debris that cannot be just scooped out of the ocean.

Reflecting on your work

Once you have finished both parts of the exam-style question, you should try to assess the level of your achievement. Does your work fit the following description below?

For Question 1(a) does it:

- re-work the extract in a way that would be appropriate for the genre requested in the question
- ensure the target audience would read the piece with interest?

For Question 1(b) does it:

- work through a range of points to demonstrate understanding about differences between genres
- back up ideas by close reference to the form and style of both texts
- develop a coherent response?

If not, what could you do to improve your work next time round?

Section B: Text analysis – what's involved?

You have just over an hour for Section B, Question 2. There is only one question to answer.

You will be asked to read a prose text of approximately 550–750 words (it could be in any of the genres listed in the introduction). You will then be asked to produce a stylistic analysis of the piece, commenting on form, structure and language.

Exam tip

With any written assignments done under timed conditions, you need to keep your eye on the clock. The worst mistake you can make is to get towards the end of the time allowed and not have enough time to complete the second assignment. No writing equals no marks.

Why am I being asked to do this?

This will give you an opportunity to show off your ability to:

✓ Comment on what you have read through thoughtful selection, quotation and analysis

✓ Demonstrate an ability to organise material into a coherent, developing argument.

How am I going to tackle the question?

The question asked will be fairly formulaic. There will probably be some background information which will help you identify genre and context, and then you will be asked to: 'analyse the text, focusing on form, structure and language.'

As you read, underline important points: again, remember that it is the style and language of the piece – not the subject matter – that is of prime importance.

Let's just remind ourselves of something we covered earlier. When you deal with a text you need to ask yourself a range of questions.

- Why, when and where am I reading this text? (Remember that readers of the original would not be in an examination situation.)
- What, basically, is this text about?
- What kind of text is it? (genre, type of publication, purpose, register, for example)
  - Is it oral/written?
  - Is it formal/informal?
  - Does it have features of a particular text type that I recognise?
  - What is its function? (to inform, persuade, amuse, irritate, inspire further thought, answer questions, pose problems?)
- Who is talking and who are they talking to through, within and around the text? What relationship are you, the reader/listener, being asked to develop with the text and the writer or speaker?
- What sorts of attitudes and values are being put forward? Are you being persuaded to share them with the text creator? If so, how?

You should also be able to see that there is a logical way to tackle any text you come across, which can be conveyed best in stages as outlined below.

STEP 1: Contextual analysis

Ask the following questions of the text:

genre of text	What sort of text are you dealing with?
	What are the established characteristics of this genre that you already know about? Is this a 'typical' example?
social context	In what context is this kind of text normally produced?
	What constraints/obligations/rules does this impose upon the text?
	Where might this sort of text be found?
	What constraints does its context place upon it (a fashion magazine article may, for example, be surrounded by advertisements)?

purpose	What is the writer aiming to do here?
reader/listener	What role is required of the reader/writer/speaker/audience in this text?
cultural values	What cultural values are shared by both the text producer and the audience of this text? Is this a variation on the normal relationship between producer/recipient in texts of this genre?
formal text features	What shared understanding of this genre of spoken or written English is required to understand this writing or speech fully?

STEP 2: Linguistic analysis

Ask the following questions of the text:

register and tone	What are the significant features of the text in terms of formality/informality? Do they vary within the text?
diction and grammatical features	What features are prominent and worthy of comment? This could also include features of figurative language, alliteration, etc.
text patterns	Can you see any patterns in the text? If so, what is the reason for them?
text structure	How is the text organised into units of meaning? What is the reason for this organisation in terms of text type, audience and intended effect?

Above all, you will recognise that this sort of discussion is firmly based on ideas about language in use, not on feature spotting as you go through the text sentence by sentence.

If you step back from the detail of this for a moment, you will also realise that you now have a strong sense of the main ideas that are central to formal discourse analysis which:

- focuses on language beyond the simple analysis of word, clause, phrase or sentence
- looks at patterns of language in texts and considers the links between the language and the social and cultural contexts in which it is used
- recognises that the use of language presents different views of the world and different understandings and perceptions
- examines the relationship between the participants – speaker/listener or reader/writer
- considers how language creates and influences identities and relationships
- examines how views of the world and identities are constructed through different varieties of discourse and linguistic techniques.

These questions now need to be used along with the tools that you learned about earlier so that you can provide an overall view of the text and show an ability to analyse in detail. You will have to decide which are the most useful tools for the particular challenges that have been presented by a passage. Like a craftsperson, you need to know when to use a hammer and when to use a screwdriver.

Worked example 1

Often you will be given some background information about the author or the genre of the piece. Use it if you can relate it to points that emerge from the written text but don't simply re-write it in other words.

Activity 4.4

The writer of the following extract was part of the British colonial administration in Burma in the 1930s. Using the questions in Step 1 and Step 2, make notes on the passage.

Text type: prose essay, UK

But I did not want to shoot the elephant. I watched him beating his bunch of grass against his knees, with that preoccupied grandmotherly air that elephants have. It seemed to me that it would be murder to shoot him. At that age I was not squeamish about killing animals, but I had never shot an elephant and never wanted to. (Somehow it always seems worse to kill a large animal.) Besides, there was the beast's owner to be considered. Alive, the elephant was worth at least a hundred pounds; dead, he would only be worth the value of his tusks, five pounds, possibly. But I had got to act quickly. I turned to some experienced-looking Burmans who had been there when we arrived, and asked them how the elephant had been behaving. They all said the same thing: he took no notice of you if you left him alone, but he might charge if you went too close to him.

It was perfectly clear to me what I ought to do. I ought to walk up to within, say, twenty-five yards of the elephant and test his behaviour. If he charged, I could shoot; if he took no notice of me, it would be safe to leave him until the **mahout** came back. But also I knew that I was going to do no such thing. I was a poor shot with a rifle and the ground was soft mud into which one would sink at every step. If the elephant charged and I missed him, I should have about as much chance as a toad under a steam-roller. But even then I was not thinking particularly of my own skin, only of the watchful yellow faces behind. For at that moment, with the crowd watching me, I was not afraid in the ordinary sense, as I would have been if I had been alone. A white man mustn't be frightened in front of "natives"; and so, in general, he isn't frightened. The sole thought in my mind was that if anything went wrong those two thousand Burmans would see me pursued, caught, trampled on and reduced to a grinning corpse like that Indian up the hill. And if that happened it was quite probable that some of them would laugh. That would never do.

There was only one alternative. I shoved the cartridges into the magazine and lay down on the road to get a better aim. The crowd grew very still, and a deep, low, happy sigh, as of people who see the theatre curtain go up at last, breathed from innumerable throats. They were going to have their bit of fun after all. The rifle was a beautiful German thing with cross-hair sights. I did not then know that in shooting an elephant one would shoot to cut an imaginary bar running from ear-hole to ear-hole; I ought, therefore, as the elephant was sideways on, to have aimed straight at his ear-hole, actually I aimed several inches in front of this, thinking the brain would be further forward.

When I pulled the trigger I did not hear the bang or feel the kick – one never does when a shot goes home – but I heard the devilish roar of glee that went up

---

from the crowd. In that instant, in too short a time, one would have thought, even for the bullet to get there, a mysterious, terrible change had come over the elephant. He neither stirred nor fell, but every line of his body had altered. He looked suddenly stricken, shrunken, immensely old, as though the frightful impact of the bullet had paralysed him without knocking him down. At last, after what seemed a long time – it might have been five seconds, I dare say – he sagged flabbily to his knees. His mouth slobbered. An enormous senility seemed to have settled upon him. One could have imagined him thousands of years old. I fired again into the same spot. At the second shot he did not collapse but climbed with desperate slowness to his feet and stood weakly upright, with legs sagging and head drooping. I fired a third time. That was the shot that did for him. You could see the agony of it jolt his whole body and knock the last remnant of strength from his legs. But in falling he seemed for a moment to rise, for as his hind legs collapsed beneath him he seemed to tower upward like a huge rock toppling, his trunk reaching skyward like a tree. He trumpeted, for the first and only time. And then down he came, his belly towards me, with a crash that seemed to shake the ground even where I lay.

I got up. The Burmans were already racing past me across the mud. It was obvious that the elephant would never rise again, but he was not dead. He was breathing very rhythmically with long rattling gasps, his great mound of a side painfully rising and falling. His mouth was wide open – I could see far down into caverns of pale pink throat. I waited a long time for him to die, but his breathing did not weaken. Finally I fired my two remaining shots into the spot where I thought his heart must be. The thick blood welled out of him like red velvet, but still he did not die. His body did not even jerk when the shots hit him, the tortured breathing continued without a pause. He was dying, very slowly and in great agony, but in some world remote from me where not even a bullet could damage him further. I felt that I had got to put an end to that dreadful noise. It seemed dreadful to see the great beast lying there, powerless to move and yet powerless to die, and not even to be able to finish him. I sent back for my small rifle and poured shot after shot into his heart and down his throat. They seemed to make no impression. The tortured gasps continued as steadily as the ticking of a clock.

In the end I could not stand it any longer and went away.

*__mahout:__ *person who works with and rides the elephant*

Shooting an Elephant by George Orwell

One way to begin to look at the style and language used is to pick out one aspect and see how far you can get simply using that one idea. You might, for example, focus on figurative language in the Orwell passage. There's lots of it:

- 'grandmotherly air'
- 'a toad under a steamroller'
- 'as of people who see the theatre curtain go up at last'
- 'an enormous senility seemed to have settled upon him'
- 'like a huge rock toppling'
- 'caverns of pale pink throat'.

But simply picking out examples won't do. They have to be shaped into some sort of an order to demonstrate their function in the writing. For example, you could write the following:

> The image of the elephant as 'grandmotherly' makes it seem unthreatening, as does the idea of 'senility' later on; we are invited to feel sympathy for the helplessness of the elephant. This is contrasted with the images of size later on with the 'huge rock toppling' and the 'caverns of pale pink throat'. The images demonstrate the narrator's uncertain attitude towards the creature. Similarly, he himself feels under threat but tries to deal with this by making a joke of what might happen: if squashed, he will be like a 'toad under a steamroller'. His feeling of being watched and judged by the Burmese is made explicit by him talking about them as 'people who see the theatre curtain go up at last'. The elephant itself could be seen as metaphor for the British Empire which, by the time Orwell was writing, was lumbering out of control. Orwell clearly has in view an audience for his writing that would be sympathetic to the ambiguous emotions expressed about colonialism in the passage.

Activity 4.5

Using your understanding of discourse markers and sentence structure, discuss Orwell's presentation of the narrator's uncertain state of mind in this passage.

Start by collecting your examples ('but', 'besides', for example) and then see if you can shape them into a paragraph. You could perhaps also talk about his choice of verbs ('shoved', for example) to make your points about him being unwilling and disconcerted by what happens.

What you will become aware of is that all of these different features work together to create an overall impression. So it doesn't really matter which ones you choose, as long as you are prepared to argue the case.

In other words, you are taking elements of the passage and starting to construct an argument. The features discussed are all contributing to your understanding of how the writer is conveying attitudes and values. An approach like this encourages you to take an overall view of the passage, not simply to go through it line by line. In short, you are moving through a clear process, one that you need to practise until it is a matter of habit:

- locate
- describe
- analyse
- synthesise.

Reflecting on Activity 4.5

You could take other elements of the passage and develop them in similar ways into separate paragraphs. This is how you start to build up a discussion in an argumentative/discursive piece of writing. There will be lots more on this in the next chapter.

You will see that you are building up a series of paragraphs, each with a very specific, language-based focus. During the course of an examination you will probably have time to create four or five paragraphs like this. You will want to ensure, too, that you have linked them, possibly using discourse markers, so that a reader can see that you are making logical progress through your points. Notice that you have not gone through the passage line by line. Nor have you been particularly concerned with the content of the passage. The focus has been on language and its effects throughout.

Under test conditions, you probably won't have time to do the very formal things that might normally be expected of essays such as an opening paragraph or a summarising conclusion. Don't worry about this. It is vital that you get on with the task. Think of it as like making a sandwich: you want it to be stuffed with tasty ingredients, with the bread (the opening and the conclusion) merely holding it all together.

One crafty trick is to leave a space at the beginning and then write your opening once you have written the essay. This means that you know precisely what you are going to say, so you can introduce it briefly. It also means that you won't promise more than you can deliver. Never fall into the trap of an over-elaborate announcement of what you intend ('In this essay, there are fourteen important issues that will be considered.'). because if you only get to number three in the time allowed, your reader will feel disappointed.

It is important to recognise that your response does not have to be comprehensive. You should not sacrifice detail for coverage. The examiner is only asking you to write interestingly about points that *you* find significant for the author's creation of meaning and significance.

Worked example 2, with student responses and examiner commentary

You might find it helpful to see some work from candidates who were given a speech to work on. The speech on the following page was given by Nelson Mandela at his inauguration as the first President of the Democratic Republic of South Africa on 10 May 1994. Before this, during the time of apartheid (white rule with different laws for the black population), Mandela spent many years as a political prisoner. The start of the speech has not been reproduced here, indicated by the [...].

The question – as you might imagine – asked the students to comment on the structure, tone and language of the passage.

↑ **Figure 4.1** Nelson Mandela was the first President of South Africa following the dismantling of apartheid

---

Text type: scripted speech, South Africa

[...] We, the people of South Africa, feel fulfilled that humanity has taken us back into its bosom, that we, who were outlaws not so long ago, have today been given the rare privilege to be host to the nations of the world on our own soil.

We thank all our distinguished international guests for having come to take possession with the people of our country of what is, after all, a common victory for justice, for peace, for human dignity.

We trust that you will continue to stand by us as we tackle the challenges of building peace, prosperity, non-sexism, non-racialism and democracy.

We deeply appreciate the role that the masses of our people and their political mass democratic, religious, women, youth, business, traditional and other leaders have played to bring about this conclusion. Not least among them is my Second Deputy President, the Honourable F.W. de Klerk.

We would also like to pay tribute to our security forces, in all their ranks, for the distinguished role they have played in securing our first democratic elections and the transition to democracy, from blood-thirsty forces which still refuse to see the light.

The time for the healing of the wounds has come.

The moment to bridge the chasms that divide us has come.

The time to build is upon us.

We have, at last, achieved our political emancipation. We pledge ourselves to liberate all our people from the continuing bondage of poverty, deprivation, suffering, gender and other discrimination.

We succeeded to take our last steps to freedom in conditions of relative peace. We commit ourselves to the construction of a complete, just and lasting peace.

We have triumphed in the effort to implant hope in the breasts of the millions of our people. We enter into a covenant that we shall build the society in which all South Africans, both black and white, will be able to walk tall, without any fear in their hearts, assured of their inalienable right to human dignity - a rainbow nation at peace with itself and the world.

As a token of its commitment to the renewal of our country, the new Interim Government of National Unity will, as a matter of urgency, address the issue of amnesty for various categories of our people who are currently serving terms of imprisonment.

We dedicate this day to all the heroes and heroines in this country and the rest of the world who sacrificed in many ways and surrendered their lives so that we could be free.

Their dreams have become reality. Freedom is their reward.

We are both humbled and elevated by the honour and privilege that you, the people of South Africa, have bestowed on us, as the first President of a united, democratic, non-racial and non-sexist South Africa, to lead our country out of the valley of darkness.

We understand it still that there is no easy road to freedom.

We know it well that none of us acting alone can achieve success.

We must therefore act together as a united people, for national reconciliation, for nation building, for the birth of a new world.

Let there be justice for all.

Let there be peace for all.

Let there be work, bread, water and salt for all.

Let each know that for each the body, the mind and the soul have been freed to fulfil themselves.

Never, never and never again shall it be that this beautiful land will again experience the oppression of one by another and suffer the indignity of being the skunk of the world.

Let freedom reign.

The sun shall never set on so glorious a human achievement!

God bless Africa!

Thank you.

Nelson Mandela's inaugural speech

Student response 1

Mandela's lexis is primarily positive, wholly reflecting on the mood and atmosphere of not only himself, but the nation of South Africa.

Firstly, Mandela's use of a tripartite structure, "Let there be justice for all. Let there be peace for all. Let there be work, bread, water and salt for all," illustrates how Mandela is attempting to raise spirits of South African people, through his use of emphatic linguistic features. The use of the abstract nouns shows how Mandela will attempt to bring such things as 'justice' and 'peace' a true sense of meaning during his time in power, whereas previously these things may have seemed abstract and unreachable. For him to then mention basic necessities and simple human wants such as 'bread', 'water' and 'salt' shows how Mandela believes that the abstract nouns spoken of above, should be and will be as simple to obtain or see as bread and water. Finally, Mandela assures this to his people through the imperative 'let'. The imperatives makes it seem as if this plan of his is certain to be achieved but through the use of the dynamic verb "let", it has a sense that he is asking the inhabitants of South Africa to not stop these changes and allow him to change their country for the better.

Secondly, throughout his speech, Mandela uses the personal pronoun 'we' on a number of occasions. In using this Mandela makes the speech personal to every person listening, giving them a sense of accomplishment in helping towards his release. Also, by making the speech so personal, it makes the listeners feel more involved in what he's saying, therefore listening closer to every word.

Finally, Mandela tries to reflect himself in a manner of high intellect, trustworthiness and reliability all through his use of polysyllabic, high register, low frequency lexis. This is illustrated though lexis such as 'emancipation', 'reconciliation' and 'discrimination' with the effect being that he appears to the audience as a man who they feel comfortable in giving the power of their country to.

Consequentially, as Mandela refers to the "distinguished international guests" present at his inauguration, this sophisticated lexis reflects well on South Africa, with countries leaders possibly thinking of starting a trade partnership with Mandela's South Africa as a result of how Mandela has presented himself and his country.

In conclusion, Mandela's style is sophisticated and flamboyant and his language reflects this as well. He is aiming on making a good impression on his voters and it is clear that he achieves it.

Commentary

The response deals carefully with a range of linguistic points that are linked to matters of content. Points are usually clearly made, although there is a slight lack of fluency in the paragraph about inclusive pronouns. There is a logical structure. However, there is not much overview, and this leads to the points appearing to be slightly randomly presented. The discussion about lexis makes clear, interesting points about Mandela's emerging status as a world leader and how he tries to engineer this. More could be made of the speech as an example of scripted spoken language. The final paragraph adds little to the discussion. The writer has avoided the temptation to go through the passage line by line. This is competent work that demonstrates ability, though its lack of depth would prevent it from receiving a top-level mark.

Student response 2

The prepared speech by Nelson Mandela has many linguistic features. There is a huge repetition of 'we' and 'us' which presents the idea that Mandela has wanted to make sure the people of South Africa know that they are united and the use of the pronouns 'we' and 'us' creates a sense that the country is whole, as well as engages all of the audience together, which is reinforced when he says "we must therefore act together as a united people," the use of the word 'must', emphasising the force of his words which also highlights the idea that he is sure of what he is saying, so the audience has no doubt to his words and may also have been used to persuade the audience that they must act in this way or the country will fall again, and there will be different laws for the black population again. Therefore 'must' could have been used as a scare tactic, as it is a command which is reinforced by use of another strong modal verb 'will' which is also repeated throughout the text. By using the modal 'will', Mandela has again managed to create a sense of certainty to his words, whilst reinforcing the idea to himself and persuading the audience that everything he is saying – "will be able to walk tall", "you will continue to stand by us" is true, and it will happen, managing to gain the trust of the audience.

The text also contains imagery. The use of the imagery "humanity has taken us back into its bosom," "implant hope into the breasts of the millions of our people", "out of the valley of darkness", helps the audience to visualise the consequences, and emphasises the severity of the situation. In the first piece of imagery, the use of the phrase "taken us back into its bosom", gives the imagery of being cared for and safe, which is reinforced by when he says "implant hope into the breasts". This imagery of breasts, highlights back to when people were cared for when they were babies by their mothers, which creates a sense of purity and innocence, whilst being cared for and looked after in this new South Africa. This contrasts when he says "out of the valley of darkness", which presents the imagery that pre Nelson Mandela being freed was a very dark, sinister place, with the use of the common noun 'valley' emphasising the idea that it was a deep area, giving the imagery that it was a hard place to come out of, and that the depth of the darkness was hard to be freed from and perhaps they were trapped. This contrast reminds the audience of how horrible the old South Africa was, which gives a greater sense of freedom and happiness to Mandela's speech. This is also reinforced by his use of the phrase "rainbow nation", creating a sense of being a happy, bright future, as the black population and white population can live together peacefully. In this speech separate lines start with "let": "let there be work, bread, water and salt for all." This highlights the gravity and forcefulness of his words again, as each line holds more importance than the next. In this, Mandela is building up the tension, which would help to encourage the crowd to believe in his words and pull together and highlight what he is stating to achieve while being president and what he considers is best for the country and its people. By using tripartite structure and lists, Mandela has created the sense that the country and its people can achieve more than what he has just stated "for justice, for peace, for human dignity".

He has also left 'human dignity' until the end of the line, and thus he is emphasising human dignity, possibly implying that without it, justice and peace can't and will not follow. By leaving this till last, he is stating that it is the most important quality people can have.

Finally, Mandela uses polysyllabic lexis 'humbled and elevated', 'honour and privilege', 'bestowed', because as it is a prepared speech and he is educated, he will need to sound sophisticated. It also helps to persuade the audience of the certainty of his words, especially with the juxtaposition of 'humbled' and 'elevated' implying his overall mood is elevated, and he considers this to be most important and possibly what he wants the people of the country to feel also.

Activity 4.6

Compare the two student responses in terms of their strengths and weaknesses. Thinking about the strengths of the second response, in what ways might you improve student response 1?

Commentary

This is sophisticated and perceptive work, worthy of a high mark even though there are some moments where the writing is not completely fluent. The writer has a clear list of linguistically based points to discuss, and they are reviewed one by one in paragraphs that analyse in order to develop an overall view of the methods, strategies and context of the original. Points about the language of the passage are discussed first, and then the writer moves on to matters of syntax. This gives the response a clear line of argument because the writer has dealt with things serially, rather than with the slightly random approach taken in response 1. Quotation from the speech is used selectively and with discrimination to substantiate the points made.

Reflecting on your work

You need to judge your response through the Assessment Objective for this task. You will need to show that you have understood the passage given and that you are aware of matters of structure, form, audience and purpose. Discussions of genre and style will be central. Without trying to comprehensively cover every aspect of the passage, you will need to demonstrate how language creates effects. To do this, you will need to move easily between matters of detail and of general significance. Your work should be presented in a logical form, with your points supported by direct reference to the text.

We can simplify all of this out into a series of prompts that you could use each time you undertake an analysis. Ask yourself if, in terms of the passage, you have:

- communicated a secure knowledge of the text and its context (if given)
- given relevant responses to key themes and ideas in the text
- used suitable terminology
- analysed and shown an understanding of the form (shape) of the text
- looked at the structure of the text
- analysed aspects of the text's language.

And in terms of your own writing, you need to be confident that you have:

- supported your ideas with relevant, brief quotations
- checked for errors in expression and punctuation.
- produced coherent, accurate and well-structured writing.

As far as your own writing is concerned, the Roman orator Cicero summed it up neatly. To write well, you need to:

- ✔ find good arguments *(inventio)*
- ✔ put them in a logical order *(dispositio)*
- ✔ choose suitable words and expressions *(elocutio)*
- ✔ explain in an interesting way *(actio)*.

We will be coming back to the idea of logical order in the next chapter when we deal with discursive and argumentative writing. If it was good enough for Cicero, it's good enough for AS Level!

Conclusion

In this chapter you have:

- analysed how to re-purpose a text for a given form, purpose and audience
- worked on strategies for writing a commentary on your own and other writing
- seen sample work by other students and considered the effectiveness of their responses.

Paper 2: Writing

In this chapter you will:

→ build your skills for answering the questions on Paper 2

→ go through the requirements of each section of the paper

→ consider how to respond to a given prompt in the exam

→ work through strategies to help analyse your own and other writing

→ analyse examples of different types of writing and practise creating your own.

Paper 2 Writing (50 marks) lasts 2 hours.

This paper is primarily designed to assess your skills and techniques in relation to writing.

The paper has two sections, Section A: Shorter writing and reflective commentary, and Section B: Extended writing. You should divide your time equally between the two sections.

You will answer one compulsory question in Section A, but have a choice of three questions in Section B from which you will choose one.

Section A: Shorter writing and reflective commentary – what's involved?

You have an hour for Section A. Question 1 is in two parts: (a) and (b) and is worth **25 marks** in total:

- Question 1(a) asks you to write a short piece (up to 400 words) in a particular genre/form. (10 marks)
- Question 1(b) asks you to write a commentary on your writing in 1(a) which explains the choices that you made and how they fulfilled the task. (15 marks)

Why am I being asked to do this?

As with Paper 1, Question 1(a), this assignment is designed to demonstrate your ability to write in a given form, for a particular purpose and audience, choosing a suitable structure and using appropriate language (AO2).

Your commentary in Paper 2, Question 1(b) allows you to explain your thinking in 1(a), showing the examiner that you made conscious and appropriate decisions in order to craft your writing (AO3).

How am I going to tackle the questions?

As always, you need to break the questions down into bits and have a strategy, even before you go into the examination.

Here is an example of the sort of question that you might be asked to tackle.

> Write an article for a teenage magazine directed at young adults who are about to live away from home for the first time. You should aim to give both practical advice and reassurance.

From your experience of Paper 1, you know that you need to think strategically.

The first thing to do is to take the question apart. Four pointers will help you do this.

Register   **A**udience   **P**urpose   **P**oint of view

You might note the following things:

> Write an article for a **teenage magazine** directed at **young adults** who are about to live away from home for the first time. **You should aim to give both practical advice and reassurance**.

The **audience** is teenagers but it will appear in a magazine. That has implications from the genre of magazine articles (headlines, etc).

As the purpose is to advise and reassure, the article needs to be written from the **point of view** of someone who can convince a reader that they have the authority to give advice.

As the reader needs advice and reassurance, the **register** – the sort of lexis chosen – needs to be friendly and not off-putting. So you might need a slightly casual tone, with your sentences reasonably short and snappy if your **purpose** is to be fulfilled.

If you think about it, your preparation and note taking at this stage (have a sneaky look at part (b) of the question on page 97) will be directly relevant for the shaping of the second part of your answer.

Sample student responses

Here are two sample student responses to the exam-style task you have just completed. Read them through carefully.

Student response 1

> Problems You May Not Have Considered Before Leaving Home
>
> Congratulations: you're successfully leaving the nest! Whether it's to university or your own house or flat, there are some things you probably won't be prepared for. Even if you're totally confident about leaving home, it's best you give this a read. Y'know, just to check. So, in reverse order of importance:
>
> 3 BILLS
>
> This is the big one that everyone harps on about, but just before you roll your eyes and abandon this article, just think: are you absolutely certain you know how much utilities in your area cost? Or how about balancing your bank account? Or even how to budget properly? If you feel even a hint of doubt about any one of those subjects, you need to learn fast.
>
> Luckily there's a readily available source of information from people who have to do that sort of thing every day. Yes! We are talking about your parents. Your parents would much prefer to spend half an hour teaching you how to budget your student loan/wages than have to bail you out in a couple of months when you don't have enough money to eat. Really – just ask them.
>
> 2 CLEANING
>
> While this may sound like a strange one, all homes get dirty fast, and at some point you will have to start cleaning.
>
> This is a problem relatively easily solved: just clean constantly. Cleaning constantly doesn't mean being obsessive or even particularly neat. It just means washing up every other day instead of once a week, and vacuuming every other week, instead of once every three months. After a while, cleaning will just become routine, and you'll never be faced with a two-foot pile of plates in your sink, or having literally nothing to wear!

Activity 5.1

Using the exam-style question and the annotations above, write the text for this part of the question. Spend about 40 minutes on this.

1 FOOD

For the first time in your life you'll be completely in control of your eating habits, but don't break out the ice cream and chips just yet, and remember that the same rules still apply – bread still makes you fat, you have to eat your greens and living on noodles and crisps will kill you. We're not saying stop eating what you like. Just rein it in a bit so you don't end up with scurvy.

So there you have it: 3 Problems You May Not Have Considered Before Leaving Home. Remember these and you won't mess up completely. Good luck!

Student response 2

Taking the big step: Moving Out

Moving out from home can seem daunting to many teenagers, but once you've settled in it really is the best time of your life. Here are just a few simple steps to take that allow you to get the most out of your time at university and become a fully independent young adult.

Firstly, once you have chosen the universities that you are going to apply to, you should go on Open Days and make the most out of the opportunity to look around the accommodation on offer, to get a feel for how the students function and live. Having done this, you will feel much more comfortable when you actually move in.

So, secondly, have a look online at the accommodation and decide what suits you personally. Think – 'Do I want catered or non-catered, en-suite or shared facilities?' Really look into each choice of accommodation to decide which suits you personally. Making sure you've picked the right choice for you will make getting into the regime much easier.

When you are happy with your choice of accommodation and you have applied through the university website you can relax; all the hard work is done.

On the big day, when you arrive at the university and settle into your room, make it as personal as you can to make it seem like your own space. Then head out to the main university building or wherever you have been told, to start making friends. Remember that everyone here is in exactly the same situation as you. So however nervous you feel, they are no different. This is a fresh new start and an exciting time, so start chatting to people and introducing yourself. After this there really is nothing to worry about! Try to find people in the same accommodation as you as you'll be seeing a lot more of them over the next few years. The university knows that the first few days can be tough, but induction week is designed for you to get to know people you live near, as well as those who share your interests or are studying the same subjects. Although it is your first time living away from home, it is also a chance to meet new people who think like you, share the same interests as you, and are jumping into this new experience alongside you. Don't panic. Don't fear it. Just go and have fun.

Making a judgement

Having read both of these answers, which do you think is better? Remember that in this section of the paper, the responses should be judged through the Assessment Objective for this task (AO2) by asking if the student has been able to write 'effectively, creatively, accurately and appropriately for a range of audiences and purposes'.

Writing your reflective commentary

If you made notes before you started on the exam-style Question 1(a) task in Activity 5.1, this should be very straightforward.

Question 1(b) will be generic – you will always be asked to do the same thing, phrased along these lines:

> Write a reflective commentary on your text, explaining how your linguistic choices contribute to fulfilling the task.

You need to know that in this instance, 'linguistic choices' covers all aspects of the subject, not just lexis and syntax. Nonetheless, the steer suggests that you should start from the detail.

Here are two examples of commentaries written by the same two students whose shorter writing texts you read on pages 95 and 96.

Exam tip

Treat your Question 1(b) commentary in this exam as though you are writing a text analysis for Paper 1, Section B. Go through the same process as you do there before starting to write (see pages 82–4 in Chapter 4).

Reflective commentary: Student 1

I wanted to lay out the piece very clearly and give it a strong structure and a clear, summative conclusion. I did this using numbers to make it easy to follow. There is awareness of the form and genre characteristics of a piece of journalism, through the title and the subheadings. Paragraphs are kept short and to the point. Lexical choices are carefully made and colloquial expressions used to maintain an informal, friendly tone throughout ('Y'know, just to check', 'harps on about'). Different grammatical structures, including fragments such as 'Yes!', give variety and create a voice that is trying to be helpful rather than giving a list of do's and don'ts. The aim was to make the reader pay attention by adopting a light tone ('scurvy') and showing some humour.

Reflective commentary: Student 2

The article I have written demonstrates one of the genre conventions of magazine journalism by providing a headline. A friendly tone is maintained throughout, and the question requirement for reassurance is well met through the last paragraph. The piece has a clear structure, but there is quite a lot of repetition over the issue of accommodation. The structure of the piece suggests a time line, which would be useful for the reader as it underlines the process of moving away from home for the first time. Addressing the reader directly is an effective way of engaging interest. I felt that I had not quite got the tone and structure right as the long paragraphs suggest that a reader has to absorb a narrative. The strongest element of my writing was probably the end where I fulfilled the instruction to offer reassurance. My choice of language is perhaps more formal than would be suitable for a magazine for teenagers.

Making a judgement

Exam tip

If you find it easier, it is certainly acceptable to write the reflective commentary in the third person. It may help you to be more detached about what you have written.

Activity 5.2

The first commentary is obviously much better than the second. Try to explain why. You need to judge your response through the Assessment Objective for this task (AO3) by asking if the student has been able to 'analyse the ways in which writer's choices of form, structure and language produce meaning and style.' It will be clear that the more specific you can be, the better. You could produce a table of strengths and weaknesses for each piece of writing.

Moving on

Now you know how to do it, it's time to work through this process independently. Don't feel that time spent on writing notes is wasted; it will help you clear your mind and you will have something to refer to when you come to Question 1(b).

Below is a sample exam question for Paper 2 Section A. Spend about 40 minutes on Question 1(a), 20 minutes on Question 1(b) – this reflects the allocation of marks within the hour that you are allowed.

Activity 5.3

1. Answer the following exam-style Question 1. Allow yourself a maximum of 1 hour to complete **both** tasks.

   (a) Write a letter to your eleven-year-old self in which you explain what you would have done differently if you had known then what you know now.

   (b) Write a reflective commentary on your text, explaining how your linguistic choices contribute to fulfilling the task.

2. Once you have completed your work, reflect on how far you have succeeded in fulfilling the requirements of AO2 and AO3 for the different parts.

Section B: Extended writing – what's involved?

You have an hour for Section B. Question 2 asks you to write between 600 and 900 words in a particular form. You will have a choice of three questions. Each of these forms is always on the paper:

- imaginative/descriptive writing
- discursive/argumentative writing
- review/critical writing.

The question you choose is worth **25 marks** in total. Depending on the category, examples of the text types you may be required to produce include advertisements, brochures, leaflets, editorials, news stories, articles, reviews, blogs, investigative journalism, letters, podcasts, biographies, autobiographies, travel writing, diaries, essays, scripted speech, narrative writing and descriptive writing.

Why am I being asked to do this?

This is your opportunity to show off your ability to fulfil AO2 and write at length in a particular genre and with a particular audience in mind. It will test your ability to write fluently, creatively and – no matter what genre you choose – with a strong sense of organisation.

From here on, there are different paths. You might have time to walk them all; you might choose to focus on one. The important thing to remember is that different people have different strengths and weaknesses. If, for example, you really like persuading people and arguing a case, then discursive/argumentative writing is for you.

How am I going to tackle the question?

The most important thing that you have to do is to work out what sort of writing you are good at. All three types of writing are marked in the same way, but fairly obviously there are some people who enjoy writing stories and others for whom it is a complete nightmare. There is a simple rule here: you need to decide what sort of writing you like doing *before you go into the exam*. Like a sports coach, you need to have worked out your tactics before the match.

You would be wise to work on a couple of the potential routes, just in case one of the questions doesn't appeal on the day.

Route 1: Imaginative writing/descriptive writing

The task for this route will either be an imaginative writing task OR a descriptive writing task. If you want to consider it as an option you need to prepare for both these types of creative writing.

Imaginative writing

Ideally, you will take an original, imaginative approach to the task. This means not worrying about what anyone else might write but concentrating on your own ideas and how to make these fresh and avoiding cliché. Your originality might be expressed through an unusual point of view, the creation of an interesting voice or through structural devices, if not also through originality of subject matter. You will be aiming to create a tight structure and to craft effects through your use of language. Your writing will be fluent and relevant, with few mechanical errors. Above all, you will want to create a piece of writing that sustains a reader's interest throughout.

As you write, therefore, you need to ensure that you are paying attention to the following:

- voice and point of view
- originality, either of content or technique
- imaginative and controlled use of language and syntax
- clear expression.

Before moving on to thinking about specific examples of this sort of writing, you need to reflect on what is possible in 900 words or less.

In a piece like this, you are often asked to write a story or the beginning of a novel. It will be very tempting to get involved in telling too much of a story, so here is some advice.

- Keep it simple – often only a couple of characters will be enough.
- Remember that lots of events (plot) is not the purpose of a short story.
- Try to get inside the characters and make them believable.
- Write about places you know well – that will give your writing individuality.
- If there is to be dialogue in your story, use characters whose speech patterns you know and can imitate.
- Think hard about whether you want to tell the story using a first-person narrator.
- Think about whether you need to play around with a timeline in order to create surprise or suspense.
- Start with an engaging opening.
- Aim to create a scene rather than giving unrelated background detail.

Let's think about the following examples from published novels.

Text type: prose narrative, fiction, UK (162 words)

Whether I shall turn out to be the hero of my own life, or whether that station will be held by anybody else, these pages must show. To begin my life with the beginning of my life, I record that I was born (as I have been informed and believe) on a Friday, at twelve o'clock at night. It was remarked that the clock began to strike, and I began to cry, simultaneously.

In consideration of the day and hour of my birth, it was declared by the nurse, and by some sage women in the neighbourhood who had taken a lively interest in me several months before there was any possibility of our becoming personally acquainted, first, that I was destined to be unlucky in life; and secondly, that I was privileged to see ghosts and spirits; both these gifts inevitably attaching, as they believed, to all unlucky infants of either gender, born towards the small hours on a Friday night.

David Copperfield by Charles Dickens

Text type: prose narrative, fiction, UK (265 words)

One evening of late summer, before the nineteenth century had reached one-third of its span, a young man and woman, the latter carrying a child, were approaching the large village of Weydon-Priors, in Upper Wessex, on foot. They were plainly but not ill clad, though the thick hoar of dust which had accumulated on their shoes and garments from an obviously long journey lent a disadvantageous shabbiness to their appearance just now.

The man was of fine figure, swarthy, and stern in aspect; and he showed in profile a facial angle so slightly inclined as to be almost perpendicular. He wore a short jacket of brown corduroy, newer than the remainder of his suit, which was a fustian waistcoat with white horn buttons, breeches of the same, tanned leggings, and a straw hat overlaid with black glazed canvas. At his back he carried by a looped strap a rush basket, from which protruded at one end the crutch of a hay-knife, a wimble for hay-bonds being also visible in the aperture. His measured, springless walk was the walk of the skilled countryman as distinct from the desultory shamble of the general labourer; while in the turn and plant of each foot there was, further, a dogged and cynical indifference personal to himself, showing its presence even in the regularly interchanging fustian folds, now in the left leg, now in the right, as he paced along.

What was really peculiar, however, in this couple's progress, and would have attracted the attention of any casual observer otherwise disposed to overlook them, was the perfect silence they preserved.

The Mayor of Casterbridge by Thomas Hardy

In both pieces, the writers are in no great rush to give you a lot of action or to move the plot along. Instead, Dickens is gently introducing you to a character; Hardy is setting up an atmosphere. If you are asked to write the opening of a novel, you have to bear in mind that the allowed number of words (600–900 words) is only the beginning of something that could be 100,000 words long. The implication here is that you must not be too impatient to move on to matters of plot and storytelling. Usually the question will give you a hint about the sort of story you are going to write and instruct you to create a strong sense of mood, sense of place or suspense, perhaps.

Therefore you need to focus on:

- building a character or a relationship that is going to be important later on
- creating atmosphere
- creating a relationship with the reader through voice and point of view.

It's important, too, that you think hard about a good opening paragraph and that even this early you draw a reader into the world of the novel.

Here are some more examples.

Cannery Row in Monterey in California is a poem, a stink, a grating noise, a quality of light, a tone, a habit, a nostalgia, a dream. Cannery Row is the gathered and scattered, tin and iron and rust and splintered wood, chipped pavement and weedy lots and junk heaps, sardine canneries of corrugated iron, honky-tonks, restaurants, [...] and little crowded groceries, and laboratories and flop-houses.

Cannery Row by John Steinbeck

There was a lark singing somewhere high above. Light fell dazzling against my closed eyelids, and with it the song, like a distant dance of water. I opened my eyes. Above me arched the sky, with its invisible singer lost somewhere in the light and floating blue of a spring day. Everywhere was a sweet, nutty smell which made me think of gold, and candle flames, and young lovers. Something, smelling not so sweet, stirred beside me, and a rough young voice said: "Sir?"

The Hollow Hills by Mary Stewart

If you want to find Cherry Tree Lane all you have to do is ask the Policeman at the crossroads. He will push his helmet slightly to one side, scratch his head thoughtfully, and then he will point his huge white-gloved finger and say: "First to your right, second to your left, sharp right again, and you're there. Good morning."

Mary Poppins by P. L. Travers

Call me Ishmael. Some years ago – never mind how long precisely – having little or no money in my purse, and nothing particular to interest me on shore, I thought I would sail about a little and see the watery part of the world. It is a way I have of driving off the spleen, and regulating the circulation. Whenever I find myself growing grim about the mouth; whenever it is a damp, drizzly November in my soul; whenever I find myself involuntarily pausing before coffin warehouses, and bringing up the rear of every funeral I meet; and especially whenever my hypos get such an upper hand of me, that it requires a strong moral principle to prevent me knocking people's hats off – then I account it high time to get to sea as soon as I can. This is my substitute for pistol and ball. With a philosophical flourish Cato throws himself upon his sword; I quietly take to the ship. There is nothing surprising in this. If they but knew it, almost all men in their degree, some time or other, cherish very nearly the same feelings toward the ocean with me.

Moby Dick by Herman Melville

It was very still in the house. The sweet and solemn dusk was falling after one of the loveliest of September days, and high above the smoke of town and city the harvest moon was making for herself a silvered pathway through the stars.

The Better Part by Annie S. Swan

Call me Jonah. My parents did, or nearly did. They called me John.

Cat's Cradle by Kurt Vonnegut

The storm-force wind was blasting squalls of incredibly wet and heavy rain across the loch, blotting out the hills and the sky and flaying the rusty grass of the crofts until it cringed back into the ground from which it had sprung so ebulliently only a few short months earlier. All day there had been semi-dusk and when I had returned soaked and shivering from the moors that morning after a long hunt to give Bonny her morning hay, I had promised myself I would do nothing but change into dry clothes, put some food on a tray and then sit by the fire with a book. Nothing, that is, until it was time for me to don my sticky oilskins and my coldly damp sou'wester, strain on wet gumboots and go seeking Bonny again with her evening feed.

The Loud Halo by Lillian Beckwith

Ours is essentially a tragic age, so we refuse to take it tragically. The cataclysm has happened, we are among the ruins, we start to build up new little habitats, to have new little hopes. It is rather hard work: there is now no smooth road into the future: but we go round, or scramble over the obstacles. We've got to live, no matter how many skies have fallen.

Lady Chatterley's Lover by D. H. Lawrence

"Yes, of course, if it's fine tomorrow," said Mrs. Ramsay. "But you'll have to be up with the lark," she added. To her son these words conveyed an extraordinary joy, as if it were settled, the expedition were bound to take place, and the wonder to which he had looked forward, for years and years it seemed, was, after a night's darkness and a day's sail, within touch.

To the Lighthouse by Virginia Woolf

Our coal-bunker is old, and it stands beneath an ivy hedge, so that when I go to it in wet weather, I catch the combined smells of damp earth and decaying vegetation. And I can close my eyes and be thousands of miles away, up to my middle in a monsoon ditch in India, with my face pressed against the tall slats of a bamboo fence, and Martin-Duggan standing on my shoulders, swearing at me while the rain pelts down and soaks us. And all around there is mud, and mud, and more mud, until I quit dreaming and come back to the mundane business of getting a shovelful of coal for the sitting-room fire.

The General Danced at Dawn by George MacDonald Fraser

Through the fence, between the curling flower spaces, I could see them hitting. They were coming toward where the flag was and I went along the fence. Luster was hunting in the grass by the flower tree. They put the flag back and they went to the table, and he hit and the other hit. Then they went on, and I went along the fence. Luster came away from the flower tree and we went along the fence and they stopped and we stopped and I looked through the fence while Luster was hunting in the grass.

The Sound and the Fury by William Faulkner

Once upon a time, many years ago – when our grandfathers were little children – there was a doctor; and his name was Dolittle – John Dolittle, M.D. "M.D." means that he was a proper doctor and knew a whole lot.

The Story of Doctor Dolittle by Hugh Lofting

Activity 5.4

Use the extracts from the novels on pages 100–4 to work through the following tasks.

STEP 1

Put yourself in the position of someone setting examination questions for your class. What focus could you give a question that might, as a result, produce the opening of each novel? For example, with the first extract, this might have come from the prompt: 'Write the opening to a story for children. You should create a strong sense of the central character from the beginning.'

STEP 2

Having established a question for each of the passages, now see if you can write your own opening paragraph or two for each of the tasks you have devised. You do not need to imitate the original. Remember here that the focus is on drawing your reader into your piece of writing.

STEP 3

Choose one or two of the openings given here and write a continuation, picking up characters, point of view, themes or atmosphere.

We slept in what had once been the gymnasium. The floor was of varnished wood, with stripes and circles painted on it, for the games that were formerly played there; the hoops for the basketball nets were still in place, though the nets were gone. A balcony ran around the room, for the spectators, and I thought I could smell, faintly like an afterimage, the pungent scent of sweat, shot through with the sweet taint of chewing gum and perfume from the watching girls, felt-skirted as I knew from pictures, later in miniskirts, then pants, then in one earring, spiky green-streaked hair. Dances would have been held there; the music lingered, a palimpsest of unheard sound, style upon style, an undercurrent of drums, a forlorn wail, garlands made of tissue-paper flowers, cardboard devils, a revolving ball of mirrors, powdering the dancers with a snow of light.

The Handmaid's Tale by Margaret Atwood

When asked to write a story, there's often a temptation to fill in all the details instead of letting a reader's imagination go to work on a situation. Many writers prefer to let their narratives work by implication, rather than explicit statement. In the following complete short story, Raymond Carver tells you a lot about the family and their relationships without having to describe each character in detail or fill in much background to the tale.

Text type: fiction, short story, USA

The baby lay in a basket beside the bed, dressed in a white bonnet and sleeper. The basket had been newly painted and tied with ice blue ribbons and padded with blue quilts. The three little sisters and the mother, who had just gotten out of bed and was still not herself, and the grandmother all stood around the baby, watching it stare and sometimes raise its fist to its mouth. He did not smile or laugh, but now and then he blinked his eyes and flicked his tongue back and forth through his lips when one of the girls rubbed his chin.

The father was in the kitchen and could hear them playing with the baby.

"Who do you love, baby?" Phyllis said and tickled his chin.

"He loves us all," Phyllis said, "but really he loves Daddy because Daddy's a boy too!"

The grandmother sat down on the edge of the bed and said, "Look at its little arm! So fat. And those little fingers! Just like its mother."

"Isn't he sweet?" the mother said. "So healthy, my little baby." And bending over, she kissed the baby on its forehead and touched the cover over its arm. "We love him too."

"But who does he look like, who does he look like?" Alice cried, and they all moved up closer around the basket to see who the baby looked like.

"He has pretty eyes," Carol said.

"*All* babies have pretty eyes," Phyllis said.

"He has his grandfather's lips," the grandmother said. "Look at those lips."

"I don't know …" the mother said. "I wouldn't say."

"The nose! The nose!" Alice cried.

"What about his nose?" the mother asked.

"It looks like somebody's nose," the girl answered.

"No, I don't know," the mother said. "I don't think so."

"Those lips …" the grandmother murmured. "Those little fingers …" she said, uncovering the baby's hand and spreading out its fingers.

"Who does the baby look like?"

"He doesn't look like anybody," Phyllis said. And they moved even closer.

"*I* know! *I* know!" Carol said. "He looks like *Daddy*!" Then they looked closer at the baby.

"But who does Daddy *look* like?" Phyllis asked.

"Who does Daddy *look* like?" Alice repeated, and they all at once looked through to the kitchen where the father was sitting at the table with his back to them.

"Why, nobody!" Phyllis said and began to cry a little.

"Hush," the grandmother said and looked away and then back at the baby.

"Daddy doesn't look like *anybody*!" Alice said.

"But he has to look like *somebody*," Phyllis said, wiping her eyes with one of the ribbons. And all of them except the grandmother looked at the father, sitting at the table.

He had turned around in his chair and his face was white and without expression.

The Father by Raymond Carver

Activity 5.5

Discuss some of the ways in which Carver creates atmosphere and a sense of unease in this story.

Sample student writing

Here are two sample student responses to the same exam-style task. Read them through carefully.

Write the opening to a novel called *The Visitor*. In your writing, create a mood of anxiety and uncertainty.

Student response 1 (733 words)

I woke. Sounds filled the space around me, but I heard them distorted, indirectly, as one might hear a voice when submerged in a pool of water. I decided best to keep my eyes closed for the time being, for as long as it took me to regain my hearing properly, allowing each sense to return individually lest I should be overwhelmed by my new surroundings. How I had come to be here was not entirely absent from my memory, but rather came through in short flashes of the mind: an image here, a half-remembered sentence there. Contrary to my plan to allow each sense its own time to adjust and return to me, my sense of tough acted of its own accord altogether, bringing with it the sensation of metal – yes, some form of cold metal against which my hands and feet were pressed. Touching about the place, I found my location to be cylindrical, scarcely more than three feet in diameter and extending a mere inch or two above my head in its height. It was I that moment too that my olfactory senses jumped the gun: smoke, seeming almost viscous as it poured into my lungs with my next breath, causing a hacking cough. I knew I had to escape from it before I choked on the heavy fumes. Upon opening, it was of course unsurprising that my eyes were stung by the self-same smog I sought to free myself from; though they watered, I could make out a thin, luminous outline in the dark. I reached out my hands, pushed against it with all I could muster in my recently-returned conscious state, and it gave way. This panel of metal toppled outwards, and I with it.

Face-down atop the fallen panel, I felt the area round the metal, touching out at my surroundings in order to establish some sense of location. My left hand tapped along the panel slowly and steadily, much as a robin redbreast might hop along the ground tentatively in its search for worms. It met with the feeling of something smooth, cold, porous and unyielding to the touch. I reasoned that I must have stones around me. My right hand moved then with a greater ease, more secure in the knowledge that there was some solid ground beneath me. Its journey took it along much the same sensation to the other side of me, of rock, before finally reaching something different: coarse strands, dry and somewhat prickly, reaching some five-and-a-half inches or so in height. Some sort of plant life, a long grass or thistle, perhaps? Beyond the immediate sensations of my active hands, my body as a whole felt warm, as though bathed subtly in heat – not uncomfortably so, but perhaps a little more than I was used to. The air here was a faintly sweet smell, that of plants in bloom on a warm day, although tainted somewhat by the smoke from within the cylinder spilling out, polluting the breeze.

I decided to properly open my eyes now so as to better inspect the strange land I now found myself resident in. My first mistake, in hindsight, came from looking upwards as my eyelids lifted, straight into the blistering orb of a sun which burned through my skull. The bright light laid waste to my vision in an instant, rendering me effectively sightless. The difference between one's eyes being voluntarily closed and one's vision being made useless lies in the distinction of consent: whereas before my hands and nose had been explorers, forward parties to assist in my discovery of this landscape, they were now fallen back on as a last line of defence in desperation; I was no longer a man seeking knowledge, now little more than a blind, groping child grasping aimlessly into a white void to try and find help. This lasted for perhaps two minutes, but to me it seemed an eternity, being robbed of my window into the world; after that, my vision slowly returned, although very much blurred. I saw naught but desert, endless expanses of rock punctuated only by the occasional sparse thistle or desert bush, as though placed as a token gesture to Mother Nature. Alone, a foreigner in some alien land with little recollection of what brought me here, and with severely hampered eyesight for the time being, I would have to survive.

Commentary

Narrative voice is clearly established here. From the rather arresting beginning onwards, a reader shares the speaker's puzzlement about what is going on.

The use of the senses acts effectively to help build the atmosphere of anxiety and uncertainty as the narrator starts to explore a strange world. The relationship between the title given and the writing is not entirely clear, though it is implied throughout. Some of the **imagery** and metaphorical language ('like a blind groping child') is effective; the image of the robin perhaps less appropriate. At times the language register is slightly mixed, with words like 'naught' used; there may, however, be an attempt to characterise a narrator here because he or she often uses complex words ('viscous', 'punctuated') or makes unusual lexical choices. The writing does not feel fully controlled; this would need to be improved if this student wanted to access the higher marking bands.

Student response 2 (591 words)

I don't quite know what happened or what went wrong ... Was it a mistake on my behalf? Or was it all just destined to turn out how it did? If only I had known the consequences of answering the door that fateful day, I would never have ... I suppose I should start at the beginning.

It had been another typical day for me. I got up, brushed my teeth, ate breakfast and went to work. I felt no relief when I returned that afternoon, no comfort. You see, living in a dying city never seems to have a bright side. I'd appreciate any weather these days rather than the dull, cloudy skies that hang over our heads. Whenever I cross the threshold into my 'humble abode', I am welcomed by that damp, stale air that is always happy to see me apparently.

I turned on the TV and collapsed on the couch, and by the looks of it, I wouldn't be surprised if the couch collapses too one of these days. I looked round the living room. Peeling wallpaper, almost antique furniture and a distinct lack of heat. The heater works just fine but the living room seemed as though no living actually occurred there.

Why am I telling you all this? It's simple. What I'm trying to get at is that I lived a solitary life. I don't want to talk about my parents – too painful. My only friends are the sights and sounds of my home. I have plenty of partners in crime but that's just business. Even three cockroaches seem to be walking out on me. So you can only imagine how I felt when the doorbell rang. What am I saying? It wasn't the sound of cheerful bells as you'd expect – no. Just a short electronic inhuman buzz. It sounded so foreign. The sky was beginning to form an ugly mauve colour as I glared towards the window. I hesitated. Who could it be? I wasn't expecting anyone, nor was there any doubt that there is definitely something strange about a visitor at this time of day. What should I do? If it's the men in blue then I may have to use force but that won't do me any good. No it can't be. They promised to keep me safe if I did as they said. Would they go back on their word?

I sluggishly rose from my chair and approached the door. My mind was racing but my body was in the lead. All sorts of questions flooded my mind but I had to keep calm. It seemed so quiet. The TV was on showing a programme about renovations but all that seemed to slowly fade away; another world, distant from mine. I was sweating. Globs of perspiration formed on my forehead. Darn it! Why couldn't I get a hold of myself? All I had to do was see who it is! Who was it?

I forced the key into the lock and twisted it with much force. I yanked open the door and prepared for the worst.

A boy.

A boy and a young woman.

He was dressed in a plain white hoodie with faded jeans and yet she was wearing an expensive high quality suit that you would wear only to the most formal of occasions. So this was the visitor? Should I have been scared? Certainly I should have, as now the events had been set in motion. Right now, I was intrigued.

"Greetings," the boy whispered. "May we come in?"

Commentary

This is imaginative and original work. The reader is plunged straight into the situation and is immediately engaged with the first-person narrator's voice and wonders what sort of a person is talking. There is a clear sense of the narrator wanting to engage the reader's sympathy, particularly when remarks are explicitly addressed to the notional listener ('Why am I telling you all this?'). The narrator's feelings of gloom are vividly caught, with even the sofa, the personified damp air, and the unyielding key in the lock seeming to contribute to his or her negative feelings. There is a strong feeling of events unfolding in a rather uncomfortable way. There is complexity of narrative method because we have a present time introduction which then takes us back in time. The reference to 'the men in blue' suggests he or she might be expecting a visit from the police, and this helps build up the reader's enthusiasm to find out what happens next. Much is implied without being explicitly stated, and this means that a reader has to try to decode the smallest of signs – a clear indication that he or she will be fully engaged. The last line builds suspense and makes us want to read on.

Descriptive writing

When the focus of the imaginative/descriptive question is specifically on description, or creating a particular atmosphere, then you must ensure your writing moves from writing an imaginative story to writing a descriptive piece of text. You may need to evoke a narrator and have a time line in what you write, but don't get yourself distracted into telling a story; you are building description.

You may be given an instruction about a particular atmosphere that you should aim to create. Here is an example of this type of writing.

> **Text type: prose narrative, fiction, descriptive, USA**
>
> We went out at the French doors and along a smooth red-flagged path that skirted the far side of the lawn from the garage. The boyish-looking chauffeur had a big black and chromium sedan out now and was dusting that. The path took us along to the side of the greenhouse and the butler opened a door for me and stood aside. It opened into a sort of vestibule that was about as warm as a slow oven. He came in after me, shut the outer door, opened an inner door and we went through that. Then it was really hot. The air was thick, wet, steamy and larded with the cloying smell of tropical orchids in bloom. The glass walls and roof were heavily misted and big drops of moisture splashed down on the plants. The light

Exam tip

Imaginative writing does of course include description! And descriptive writing requires imagination. In the exam, what you need to work out is the primary focus of the question: is it crafting a story? Or is it building a description? You can then use description in your imaginative writing and vice versa, as it helps you to achieve that primary focus.

Activity 5.6

Read the extract from *The Big Sleep* and comment on Chandler's methods for creating a scene.

had an unreal greenish color, like light filtered through an aquarium tank. The plants filled the place, a forest of them, with nasty meaty leaves and stalks like the newly washed fingers of dead men. They smelled as overpowering as boiling alcohol under a blanket.

The Big Sleep by Raymond Chandler

Reflecting on Activity 5.6

You will notice that Chandler has made strong use of descriptive words (adjectives and adverbs) and that he aims to give you a very visual picture to establish the **setting** (time and place) of his story. The orderly set-up of the garden is strongly contrasted with the murk of the greenhouse. Note too that he plays particular tricks with imagery.

Many of the words – 'larded' and 'cloying' – give a strong sense of excess and discomfort and suggest that the speaker has a negative view of the situation he finds himself in. These words are associated with decaying food. There is also the distasteful image of the stalks, 'like the newly washed fingers of dead men', combined with something slightly sinister too – 'the light had an unreal, greenish colour.' The writing is setting up a strong sense of anticipation. You will also have started to have some view of the sort of man telling the tale. He has told you nothing explicitly about himself, but you have a strong view of his world view, which seems rather obsessed with death and corruption. It will be no surprise to learn that we are at the beginning of a murder mystery.

What you will also have noticed is that the writing here is setting up a series of possibilities but is in no great rush to get on with telling you a story. For the time being, plot and character are less important than the setting up of the scene.

In your own writing

You are allowed a narrative voice, as here, but you must remember that, in this sort of question, your prime objective is to create atmosphere, not to tell a story.

Text type: prose narrative, description, travel writing, UK

Lahore, 1997

It is barely dawn, and the sky is as pink as Turkish delight. Yet already, at 5.45 a.m., Lahore Central Station is buzzing like a kicked hive.

Bleary-eyed, you look around in bewilderment. At home the milkmen are abroad at this time, but no one else. Here the shops are already open, the fruit and vegetables on display, and the shopkeepers on the prowl for attention.

'Hello my dear,' says a man holding up a cauliflower.

'Sahib – what is your good name?'

'Subzi! Subzi! Subzi!'

'Your mother country?'

↑ **Figure 5.1** Lahore Station in Pakistan

A Punjabi runs up behind the rickshaw, waving something horrible: a wig perhaps, or some monstrous vegetable. 'Sahib, come looking! Special shop OK! Buying no problem!'

Lahore station rears out of the surrounding anarchy like a liner out of the ocean. It is a strange, hybrid building: The Victorian red-brick is imitation St Pancras[1], the loopholes, battlements and machicolations are stolen from some Renaissance palazzo – Milan, perhaps, or Pavia – while the towers are vaguely German, and resemble a particularly Wagnerian stage set. Only the chaos is authentically Pakistani.

As a tape of the Carpenters' greatest hits plays incessantly on the tannoy, you fight your way through the surge of jammed rickshaws and tottering red-jacketed coolies, through the sleeping villagers splayed out on the concrete, past the tap with the men doing their ablutions, over the bridge, down the stairs and onto the platform. In the early-morning glimmer, Platform 7 seethes with life like a hundred Piccadilly Circuses[2] at rush hour. Porters stagger towards the first-class carriages under a mountain of smart packing cases and trunks. Further down the platform, near third class, solitary peasant women sit stranded amid seas of more ungainly luggage cases and boxes, ambiguous parcels done up with rope, sacks with lumpy projections – bits of porcelain, the arm of a chair, the leg of a chicken. Vendors trawl the platform selling trays of brightly coloured sweetmeats, hot tea in red clay cups, or the latest film magazine. Soldiers wander past, handlebar moustaches wobbling in the slipstream.

1. *St Pancras – an elaborate Victorian station in central London*

2. *Piccadilly Circus – a major traffic interchange in central London*

The Age of Kali by William Dalrymple

Activity 5.7

Write a short piece describing a busy place that you know well. Try to see it as an outsider, from the point of view of someone for whom it is a new experience.

In thinking about this piece you could focus on the use of the following:

- the second-person pronoun 'you'
- European references
- metaphorical language
- the present tense
- senses of sight, sound, taste, smell, touch
- attitudes and values, both implied and explicit.

In the next extract, a character in a novel contributes contrasting blogs to a website as a response to government demolition of illegal roadside food shops in Lagos, Nigeria.

Text type: blog within prose fiction, Nigeria

It is morning. A truck, a government truck, stops near the tall office building, beside the hawkers' shacks, and men spill out, men hitting and destroying and levelling and trampling. They destroy the shacks, reduce them to flat pieces of wood. They are doing their job, wearing "demolish" like crisp business suits. They themselves eat in shacks like these, and if all the shacks like these disappeared in Lagos, they will go lunchless, unable to afford anything else. But they are smashing, trampling, hitting. One of them slaps a woman, because she does not grab her pot and her wares and run.

She stands there and tries to talk to them. Later, her face is burning from the slap as she watches her biscuits buried in dust. Her eyes trace a line towards the bleak sky. She does not know yet what she will do but she will do something, she will regroup and recoup and go somewhere else and sell her beans and rice and spaghetti cooked to a near mush, her Coke and sweets and biscuits.

It is evening. Outside the tall office building, daylight is fading and the staff buses are waiting. Women walk up to them, wearing flat slippers and telling slow stories of no consequence. Their high-heeled shoes are in their bags. From one woman's unzipped bag, a heel sticks out like a dull dagger. The men walk more quickly to the buses. They walk under a cluster of trees which, only hours ago, housed the livelihoods of food hawkers. There, drivers and messengers bought their lunch. But now the shacks are gone. They are erased, and nothing is left, not a stray biscuit wrapper, not a bottle that once held water, nothing to suggest that they were once there.

Americanah by Chimamanda Ngozi Adichie

↑ **Figure 5.2** The writer of *Americanah*, Chimamanda Ngozi Adichie

In analysing these two contrasting paragraphs from *Americanah*, we can see the following:

- Continuity is created by the use of the simple present tense in both paragraphs. This creates a sense of immediacy, as does the use of the present continuous tense, which is used for rather different purposes in each paragraph, with verbs like 'smashing, trampling, hitting' making the violence of the first paragraph more aggressive, whereas in the second the tense is used to create tranquillity because it is the daylight that is fading, the buses that are waiting.

- References to the time of day and the fact that both the demolition crew and the office workers might use these hawkers' stalls create parallels. The plight of the female hawker ('a woman') with her business reduced to nothing and the female office workers ('the women') with their 'high-heeled shoes' demonstrates disparities of wealth and opportunity, and the connection is made absolutely clear as the demolition workers wear their overalls 'like crisp business suits'.

- Links are also provided through the use of the word 'they' to open sentences in both paragraphs. Even the reference to biscuits in paragraph one, followed by the littered biscuit wrapper in paragraph two, creates a connection.

- In both paragraphs the voice is objective and distant, but a clear sense of the narrator's attitude to these events can be inferred through the writer's decisions about tone and register.

- A story is not being directly told, but an audience is being invited to piece one together from the contrasts and comparisons.

Activity 5.9

Choose one of the sample prompts below and write a two-paragraph response.

- Describe your school or college as it might be in the middle of the night.
- Describe your school or college as it might be seen by the youngest pupil or the oldest pupil.
- Describe your school or college as being like a prison.
- Describe your school or college as being like a holiday camp.

Activity 5.8

Look again at the writing that you did for Activity 5.7. Write a contrasting piece, describing the same place from the point of view of someone who has lived there since childhood.

Exam tip

In descriptive writing you will need to plan out what you want to say. Remember that you will be seeking to create atmosphere. You want your readers to feel that they are with you and sharing the experience. This will certainly have implications for the writing in terms of point of view and voice.

When creating an atmosphere in your writing, it's always good to try to appeal to a reader's sense of touch, smell, hearing, vision and taste.

Sample student responses

Students were asked to write a short piece about a place both **before** and **after** a natural disaster.

The aim of the writing was to create a sense of the impact that the place has on the narrator. Read the student's work carefully.

Student response

Before

A pair of bright red Converses stroll along the busy pavement, jumping from paving stone to paving stone to playfully avoid the cracks. Anywhere else, the bold shoes would have made a statement, but here in the buzz of city life, they fit perfectly. They seem to dance down the street to the sound of car horns beeping in frustration and the hum of human voices as they pass by, all completely oblivious of one another. There is something uniting every person in that city – the fact that each is focused on living their own life in this shiny playground. Looking up, there is something wonderful about the skyscrapers that tower over the people reaching into the heavens. These giants are perhaps the only solid thing about this city. They observe the chaos of change below, witnessing each individual moment of joy or disaster which go unnoticed by passers by. The colour and the noise and the continuous motion of the city gives it a life of its own. Its energy is overpowering.

After

Then the Converses descend to the Underground, perhaps seeking refuge from the intense experience above. But here is not the place. They weave between the lawyers, the bankers, the teachers and the artists whose faces are never registered. They wander past the beggar as the song of his guitar fills the space but ignore him. They jump into the carriage just as the doors begin to close, and they are, for a little while, trapped inside the intense atmosphere of the train. The people inside are thrown about like children's toys in a fast-paced game. Not soon enough the train stops, the doors open, and the Converses burst out onto the platform. Fighting upwards though the swarms of people, being pulled in every direction as though caught in an undercurrent, they reach the street once more. And in a strange and surprising way, the exhilarating experience only makes the city sweeter.

A pair of ripped shoes pick their way through the rubble, carefully treading where pavements used to be. The city is eerily silent. The noise of cabs' horns would be a welcome surprise – anything to bring back to life the city so many love.

Men, women and children struggle through the streets they used to strut down, any sense of purpose destroyed by the earthquake. Dust and dirt mar their faces, the faces that used to go unacknowledged. Not any more. Strangers comfort one another in an uncharacteristically friendly way. Who knew that one day could change a city so completely? The big shot bankers who used to unapologetically barge their way to work now sit, head in hands, in front of what used to be home. The shining towers that once dominated the skyline now lie on the floor, crumbled in shame. The initial confusion of sirens and shouting has given way to a numbness that fills every corner of the city. There is no escape from it. Like a burst balloon, the shape of the city has been destroyed in an instant and the idea of getting back to that exciting place that was once here seems impossible. The confident swagger of the city has been replaced by a lame limp as its people wander around in a dazed state of shock. All its power has been crushed, falling along with its buildings. The entrance to the Underground still stands, inviting the red shoes in once more. But it no longer promises the excitement it did as the trains that charged through the tunnels have been brought to a standstill.

Commentary

There is an oddly disembodied but engaging feeling about the writing in both these pieces because the focus is on two pairs of shoes (Converses are a type of trainer), an original way to tackle the topic. Images used in the first part are re-used (the personification of the towers, for example) to different effect in the second. The use of the present tense gives the writing immediacy. The idea of the shoes is picked up as a vivid personification as the city's forward striding of the first part is reduced to a 'lame limp' in the second. The writing is complex, fluid and highly controlled in order to create specific effects. Throughout, the reader wants to know how this writing will resolve, and this level of engagement with the writing suggests that the writer will do very well in this assignment.

Route 2: Review/critical writing

There is no one way of writing in this genre. There are, after all, lots of different sorts of reviews (films, restaurants, art shows, plays, books, hotels, computer games, mobile phones, to name a few), let alone the fact that different reviews are directed at different audiences, depending on whether they find the review in a newspaper, magazine or on the internet.

On pages 114–6, you will find two reviews, one of an American TV show from a website for parents with young children; the other from a website of film reviews. Both are dealing with children's shows.

Dancing with the Stars: Juniors TV Review ✕

www.commonsensemedia.org/tv-reviews/dancing-with-the-stars-juniors

HOME   STUFF   CONTACT   ABOUT   SEARCH

Dancing with the Stars: Juniors

TV review by Emily Ashby, Common Sense Media

Common Sense says age 8+

Pint-size dance contestants impress in fun reality spin-off.

Parents say: No reviews yet   Add your rating

Kids say: No reviews yet   Add your rating

Common Sense is a nonprofit organization. Your purchase helps us remain independent and ad-free.

We think this TV show stands out for:

- Character Strengths

WHAT PARENTS NEED TO KNOW

Parents need to know that *Dancing with the Stars: Juniors* is very similar to *Dancing with the Stars* in structure but features teams of child and young teen stars and professional dancers. Contestants come from a range of backgrounds […] As such, their dance abilities and ease in the spotlight varies greatly, but all seem to genuinely enjoy the experience of learning to dance and competing on this big stage. Contestants must learn to work with their partners and their adult mentors/choreographers and to step outside of their comfort zones to take chances on the floor. Judges encourage but offer honest criticism when it's warranted, and all of the cast members show sportsmanship in victory and defeat.

WHAT'S THE STORY?

Like its parent series, *Dancing with the Stars: Juniors* is a reality competition that pairs accomplished ballroom dancers with celebrities for a series of performances and the chance to take home the coveted mirror ball trophy. Here the competitors are kids and young teens who have made names for themselves in entertainment, sports, reality TV, and even in one case a spelling phenom. Each week the couples will perform a dance in a different ballroom discipline, including foxtrot, salsa, and jive. At the end of each round of competition, a combination of judges' scores and studio audience voting determines which team is eliminated.

IS IT ANY GOOD?

This exuberant spin-off of a long-running reality competition favorite is a genuinely enjoyable watch, thanks to the enthusiastic young cast of stars and pros. There's a decided absence of hesitation among the contestants who, regardless of their dance skills (or lack thereof) coming into the competition, throw themselves into training and performing with gusto. Even when their stage work gets a little off beat, they obviously have fun doing it and seem to revel in the opportunity to learn something new. The whole package makes for great family entertainment.

The only thing missing in *Dancing with the Stars: Juniors* is audience involvement that helps drive the drama of the contest. Because eliminations are determined onsite by the judges and the live audience, viewers at home are left without any say in the results, which is a big miss for a show that has such broad appeal for families. Even so, there's a lot to like about the contestants' enthusiasm for the challenge, the diversity among the cast members that defies stereotypes about dancing, and the lessons in teamwork and perseverance that the endeavor holds for them. Oh, and the dancing itself is pretty spectacular considering many of the juniors are grade-school age.

TALK TO YOUR KIDS ABOUT …

- Families can talk about this show's messages about stereotypes in dance and the performing arts. Did any of the pros surprise you in how they looked or performed? Before watching, did you think of ballroom dance as something that young girls and boys would enjoy? Does this show change your assumptions about that?

- To what degree does a positive attitude influence the stars' performance success? Were there dances that lacked finesse but won you over because of the partners' personalities? How does this competition reward ability over attitude, or is there balance between the two factors? Did you agree with the elimination decision?

- Besides teamwork, what other strong character strengths are evident in some or all of the competitors' efforts? How did the mentors and judges act as role models for the contestants? Were there times when the stars had to rely on their own strength to overcome a challenge? Were they successful in doing so?

www.nerdist.com/paddington-2-review/

HOME　　STUFF　　CONTACT　　ABOUT　　SEARCH

PADDINGTON 2 MAY HAVE ACTUALLY CHANGED MY LIFE (REVIEW)

POSTED BY M. ARBEITER ON JANUARY 11, 2018

Of the hundreds of movies I see every year, I love plenty. I'm awe-stricken by several. I'm totally and permanently bowled over by one or two. But it's only the occasional miracle that'll rip me straight from my body and the trials of whatever late afternoon with which it is contemporaneously plagued and drop me face first into, say – just for example – a barbershop in London, where one might find a well-meaning bear using a handful of marmalade to reattach the scattered follicles of a customer he's just accidentally embaldened.

At seven or eight, I was launched into a lifetime of devotion to the cinematic majesty I'd just discovered in a diluted VHS copy of *Close Encounters of the Third Kind* viewed in the living room of my family's Queens[1] duplex. Twenty-odd years down the line, I've mined from that devotion a dogmatic regard for the big screen experience and the spiritual efficacy of a 35mm film print; I've pursued it through dozens more screenings every year; I've embedded myself ever deeper to evade the jowls of a reality with thinning patience for the kind of wonder committed to screen in the final 20 minutes of Steven Spielberg's 1977 masterpiece.

But everything I've become makes true spectacle on movie night all the more elusive. It's perhaps impossible to reconvene the magic I felt when Richard Dreyfuss boarded the mothership. But if Paddington Brown would have me walk away with anything from his latest adventure, it'd be that the good, the fine, and the whole are all still in there, tucked away, and worth digging up. And dug up they were. All it took was a dobbet of orange preserves slathered on a grouchy man's dome.

In 2014, I had the pleasure of meeting an unexpected gem in *Paddington*, a delightfully chipper and righteously witty film adaptation of Michael Bond's *Paddington Bear* children's books and television series. Owing to the sheer stupefaction of how much fun I – not to mention the herd of giggling critics in my company – was having, I maintained footing in my own head all the while, noting how stunned I was to be enjoying the film so much. This time around, I was prepared to avoid the surprise. But even with expectations as high as they were, *Paddington 2* still managed to supply something I didn't foresee: a trip out of this world.

I was right there with our fuzzy hero, emancipated from my anxious frame and the daily news that created it, as he coated his dozing customer's scalp in citrus jam. I remained by his side as he played matchmaker around his London cul-de-sac, rode a scraggly stray dog across town in hot pursuit of a stolen pop-up book, and turned a state penitentiary filled with grizzled criminals into a carnival of goodwill and better meals. For a swift 103 minutes, I was along for the ride with Paddington, and with Paddington, I was free.

What's especially impressive about this feat is how timely *Paddington 2* is. Timeless all the while – comedic influences range from Charlie Chaplin to Abbott and Costello to *Rocky and Bullwinkle* to Monty Python to plenty from today's treasure trove of British hilarity – but unmistakably reactive to the cultural mores infesting England and America here and now. Paddington's overarching messages of kindness and compassion may ring like bipartisan truths, but the film pulls no punches in asserting that certain ideological movements, represented here by a bigoted Peter Capaldi, aren't living up to the code.

In the hilarious company of Hugh Grant's cartoon supervillain – a master of disguise on a demented treasure hunt – elements like a Brexit-banner-wielding Capaldi are what make *Paddington 2* reverberate well beyond the form of an hour-and-40-minute vacation. *Paddington 2* gives us a world decidedly better than our own, that's for sure, but not one so unrecognizable as to suggest that our own might not make it there with a little work, hope, and love.

After all, the most transportive cinematic experiences aren't simply ones that take you someplace new. It wasn't only the curiosity of a planet unlike our own that made the ending of *Close Encounters of the Third Kind* such a dazzling conceit. It was what I saw of myself, my life, my world in those final moments, and what new possibilities now seemed open to me, that allowed this movie to change my life so many years back.

I don't know exactly what I saw in *Paddington 2*, or why it struck me with such wonder when the little bear slapped a glob of vermilion jam on the glistening noggin of an ill-tempered patron. All I know is that it took me somewhere. It was somewhere a bit like our world, and all the same, a bit unlike any. Somewhere I really needed to go.

RATING: 5 MARMALADE-FILLED BURRITOS

[1] **Queens**: a suburb of New York City

Activity 5.10

Go back to your work on genre and register in Chapter 2. Try to establish the rules that apply to the writing of reviews. Look too at differences and variations that are obviously acceptable within the genre. You will recognise the following table from Chapter 2. Copy and complete it for both these reviews.

	Dancing with the Stars: Juniors	Paddington 2
author		
audience		
purpose		
situation		
physical form		
constraints/rules		
content		
level of formality/register		
style		
written language		
structure		

Activity 5.11

Thinking about the genre table in Activity 5.10, and paying particular attention to register, write a review of a film or a TV show that you have seen recently. Not all reviews have to use the cheery, informal register of the pieces that we have seen thus far, so think carefully about whether your review will be negative or positive and the effect this would have on your writing.

No matter what types of reviews you have read, you will probably have noted that they have some of the following in common:

- they report what happens without providing 'spoilers' that might ruin the experience for someone who goes to the movie or watches the TV show
- they evaluate the event in terms of its qualities and deficiencies

- they provide a personal response
- they engage with a particular, specific audience.

Route 3: Discursive/argumentative writing

This is the sort of writing that you did for Paper 1, Question 2, though we didn't call it that. It means that you are putting forwards a case, making an argument.

Structure

Your writing will benefit from a strong sense of organisation. This means that it is worthwhile creating a plan. Some people like to do this as a mind map, with the central idea in the middle and then a series of links to minor ideas.

For example, you could be asked if home schooling is a good or bad thing for children and come up with a diagram such as Figure 5.3:

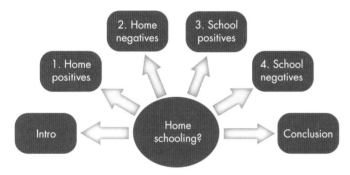

↑ **Figure 5.3**

The trouble here is that you haven't really thought about the different relationships between the points that you want to make or ranked them by importance.

It might be better to see your planning as being like a tree. You have a big idea, and then each of the paragraphs is a branch as in Figure 5.4:

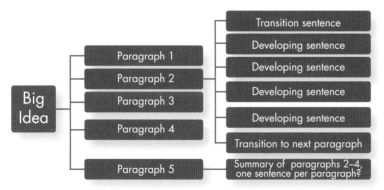

↑ **Figure 5.4**

Exam tip

If you are writing under timed conditions, keep an eye on the time to ensure that you are moving through your plan and won't get left with half of what you wanted to say unwritten because you went into too much detail early on.

Exam tip

In writing where you are trying to develop an argument, it may be useful to leave a space and only write the opening paragraph at the end, so that you will not promise more than you can deliver in the time allocated.

Everything grows out of the big idea, and the sentences all feed back through the paragraphs to the 'trunk' of the tree. This model encourages you to see which ideas are central and to treat them equally. It also gives you the possibility of shaping a case by contrast ('on the one hand', 'on the other hand') within a paragraph; a sophisticated approach to dealing with a topic. Notice, too, that your plan is limited to a few words – just enough to keep you on track as you write.

In an essay of only 600–900 words you have limited space to develop ideas, so five or six paragraphs is probably about right: it gives you space to go into some detail on each of the points that you want to make. If you are writing a speech you may want to write more and shorter paragraphs because you will want more pauses for an audience to reflect on what you have said.

In commentaries and argumentative essays you will probably want to make use of words that help to move your discussion forwards. These are called discourse markers. You saw some of them at work in Lincoln's Gettysburg Address in Chapter 2 (page 24): *now*, *but*. They are vital if you are to give a sense of logical forward movement to your writing, and can often get you over the rather difficult issue of how to move from one paragraph to the next.

Furthermore (see exactly such a transition there!), you can use them to demonstrate that you have a variety of strategies for developing a discussion, something that will improve your writing (see table below).

Discourse markers					
Ordering	**Consequence**	**Continuation**	**Simultaneity**	**Concession**	**Conclusion**
Firstly	Because of this	Furthermore	Meanwhile	However	Finally
Secondly	Therefore	Moreover	At the same time	On the one hand … On the other hand	In conclusion
Thirdly		Another aspect to consider	While	Admittedly	To sum up
Next		In addition	In the meantime	Yet	Overall
Ultimately		Another		Notwithstanding	
Lastly		Then		Nevertheless, nonetheless	
		Similarly		In spite of this	

You need to anchor some of these words into your everyday writing and get used to them as the 'oil' that allows you to move from one thing to another. This can be useful when you are writing commentaries too.

Activity 5.13

Tell a story (it will need to be nonsense), in which the first word of each sentence moves the tale on in one of the ways described in the headings of the discourse markers table above.

For example:

> The other day I went to the zoo with my brother and his pet crocodile. Meanwhile my mother went shopping. Because of this …

Review the table of discourse markers and see if you can add some other words or short phrases that serve the same purpose.

Activity 5.14

For the time being, leave aside matters of audience. Here are three essay topics. Write a plan for each one. Get someone else to evaluate their effectiveness.

- Is it better to support local shops rather than large supermarkets?
- 'There is too much money in sport.' How far do you agree?
- 'A woman's place is in the boardroom.' Discuss this statement.

The important thing is that the structure should be solid – think of it as being like building a table that doesn't wobble. It may not be the best table ever built but it should do the job it was designed to do and be serviceable.

Style

Now that we have established how to build a structure, it's time to work on matters of audience, form and style. You must bear in mind that you are writing *for* someone, so you need to put yourself in their position and ask yourself if you would want to read or listen to the material that you are preparing. This takes us back to earlier discussions about genre in Chapter 2. Look again at the table on page 14 and use it in your planning from now until the end of this section.

Questions may also ask you to include strong elements of persuasion or argument. Fundamentally, there are three possible lines of attack:

- you can argue strongly *for* a given discussion topic
- you can argue strongly *against* a given discussion topic
- you can argue about a given discussion topic in a *balanced* way, as you might do in any essay if asked the question 'To what extent …?'

You are perfectly entitled to put in examples from your own reading and personal experience, and this will often make your work stand out as original or highly individual, something that will be well regarded.

Getting started

It can be difficult to get going, so you may want to adopt one of the following methods. Let's imagine that we have been given the statement 'Team sports should be compulsory in schools.' The topic is usually quite generally framed, so the skill of this assignment is to make something interesting of the prompt you are given. You will not be required to have any specific knowledge about the topic. You will be rewarded for your ability to shape a case and hold an audience's attention, not for gathering lots of evidence.

You need to draw the audience in from the start. You can choose from a wide variety of strategies for this. You can be:

- provocative – 'No one in their right mind would subject themselves to the ritual humiliation at school that disguises itself as "team sports".'
- balanced – 'Although many children dislike being forced to participate in school sports, there are strong reasons why they should be considered a compulsory part of the school day.'
- illustrative – 'There is nothing better than the sight of a game of school cricket, with all it implies about the values of sportsmanship and good health.'
- anecdotal, telling a story – 'The thought of soccer practice makes me sick. It's not that I'm really sick. It's just that I have to spend time faking illnesses in order to avoid it.'

You could also try using a quotation, or a misquotation: '"If at first you don't succeed, try and try again." Or in my case, on the school sports field, "If at first you don't succeed, give up."'

One of the best things that you can do to grab hold of a reader's attention is to present your points in relation to personal experience, as the anecdotal approach demonstrates. You are trying to hook your audience into your writing, to make them carry on reading. Don't be afraid of using your own stories and history to make your points. The best pieces of writing are praised for their originality, in terms of either voice or content, and this is most easily achieved by making some of what you say personal.

Writing headlines

If you are writing a newspaper or magazine article, comment column or blog, remember that you should also write a headline to get a reader interested in what you have to say. There are many ways of doing this, but you might like to consider some of the following tried and tested methods.

- Include a number:

> **10 ways to gain promotion at work** 📈

- Provide an offer:

> **The secrets of promotion at work revealed**

- Make someone want to find out more:

> **How I gained four promotions in three months**

- Be useful and make a promise:

> **How you can win the promotion race at work**

- Be controversial and cheeky:

> **They all hate me, but now I'm the boss.**

- Ask a question:

> **Are you stuck in a rut at work?**

Activity 5.15

Write five different openings for an article on compulsory team sports by using each of the strategies outlined here.

It could even be seen as a formula (use with care!):
trigger word or number + adjective + keyword + promise.

For example:

Six surefire tricks to achieve promotion in a week

Above all be brief.

Activity 5.16

Collect a range of newspaper or magazine articles and discuss the methods they use to make a reader want to read on, such as layout, sub-headings, different print fonts, illustrations, and so on.

Again, you may want to leave a space at the top of your writing and then come back to the headline at the end once you are clear about the shape and general direction of your writing.

Writing a letter

Another task you might be asked to do is to write a letter, most often to a newspaper. The task is usually to outline an issue of concern. You need to remember that this is a formal communication and that it will therefore need to be written using a formal register and tone. This is a specific genre, with very particular conventions.

You are writing as a member of the public in order to argue a point, and you will be addressing both the editor of the newspaper and the wider public.

Make sure that you do the following:

- open the letter formally
- use the first person, either singular (I) or plural (we)
- state clearly the problem or issue that concerns you
- expand on your point by explaining how this problem affects you or others, and give some examples
- try to suggest some possible resolutions to the problem
- review any positive steps that have already been taken to deal with the issue
- be clear about what needs to be done, when and by whom
- sign off formally.

An example is given on the following page.

Activity 5.17

Discuss the structure and effectiveness of this letter.

Text type: letter to newspaper, USA

June 3, 2018

Springfield Herald
Main Street
Springfield

Re: Graduation report, Springfield High (May 31)

To the Editor,

On behalf of the 65 young women who make up over 60% of this year's graduating class, we are writing to express our disappointment with the sexist nature of your May 31 coverage of our graduation.

Of course, the female members of the class are pleased to be able to dress up and make a night of it, but it was a shame that you did not make more in your reporting of the achievements of the girls rather than simply naming them and describing what they were wearing. Tom O'Connor was singled out, for example, for his ambition to study Math at Yale, but his twin sister Martha (who has a scholarship to Harvard to study History) was simply described as wearing a chiffon teal ball gown and carrying matching accessories.

Whilst we appreciate that there is not much that can be said about tuxedos, it seems astonishing to us that the men seem to be written about in terms of their achievements and aspirations (Captain of Football) etc., whereas the women are discussed in terms of their looks and clothes. This year's class president was a woman, as was the editor of the yearbook, but none of this was mentioned in your write up.

We are drawing this to your attention because we feel that the media's unfair portrayal of women plays a serious role in the undermining of female aspiration and confidence about the world. We do not wish to undermine or belittle the achievements of our fellow (male) students, but we feel that you should be aware that your reporting gives a false impression of the female graduates who have worked so hard and contributed so much.

In future years, when we aim to hold positions of power and influence in society, we very much hope that people will be chosen for jobs on the basis of their resumes, not their wardrobes.

Sincerely,

Giovanna Benetti/Dora Siegel
2018 Graduates, Springfield High School

Activity 5.18

(a) Find an article in a paper or magazine where you disagree with the writer's point of view and then write a letter to the editor.

(b) Find some further examples of letters to newspapers or magazines that conform to this genre of letter writing. You could contrast them, perhaps, with the sort of letters that appear on the 'problems page' of a magazine.

You could also be asked to write an informal letter where, for example, you are writing to a younger relative about how to cope with the transition to a new school. In this case, colloquial language and register would be perfect, but you still need to plan carefully so that you are making logical progress through a range of points. The key here is to keep the audience for your writing clearly in view throughout. If you are writing for an 11-year-old, for example, you need to ensure that you use words that are not likely to puzzle them and sentence structures that are easy to follow. Remember, too, that an 11-year-old's preoccupations and concerns might be different from yours, with questions about lunch and making friends looming far larger than those about how the school admissions programme is organised.

Another possibility is that you might be asked to write the text of a speech that is intended for spontaneous delivery to an audience.

Read the following speech from a student in India who was asked to address a conference of teachers about the power and influence of the media.

Activity 5.19

Write a letter to a friend in which you explain your ambitions in life.

Text type: planned speech, India

The model on the glossy magazine cover page captivates its readers, as she wears a gorgeous Versace outfit revealing her paper-thin, fragile body. Her soft-cushioned flawless white skin attracts and mesmerises the reader's eyes, but there is something disturbing about that model's lean, sleek, malnourished body structure, almost mocking the reader for an unattainable body just like hers.

The readers fantasise about this 'size 0' cult and develop an obsession about this 'utopia' world of fashion.

The media, thus, definitely has a major impact on the masses, overshadowing the 'realistic' world. The growth of the impact is so rapid that without media's influence, businesses slack out and brand ambassadors may not survive and influence the people. Admittedly, the 'visual media' brings about this obsessive state of mind and changes the patterns of brain chemistry in most young teenage women.

Children also are desensitised at a very early age as they believe that the 'violent' animated shows are not so different from reality.

The first global impact of the media is to imitate the super glamorised images of paper-thin models. Women who view such models further feel worse about themselves and that leads to extremely low self-esteem and, ultimately, depression.

According to statistics, 80% of the teenage girls mimic their favourite celebrities on screen and feel insecure about their own self-image.

Has the media any right to destroy an individual's identity?

The media has immense power to drive the society in a stereotypical way. Consequently, media betrays its own purpose of projecting 'the truth' to the society, as it is controlled by influential people. Instead of making people aware of various scams and scandals of the political or social world, it successfully hides and reverses the picture. It promotes the wrongful acts of the political leaders and allows hooliganism and vandalism.

Furthermore, media has developed the power to mislead the masses while portraying deceitful images of famous people. Market gimmicks are practised in the name of charity and noble causes. These could be utilised in better developmental areas of health and education.

In conclusion, though media has immense power to influence its readers, it also uses its power to contradict its own purpose. Nevertheless, it can utilise its power in a more positive way and build a bond of trust with its readers.

Thank you.

Student, India

Activity 5.20

How effective do you find this speech? You should think about:

- structure
- audience
- content
- creation of voice
- fluency in terms of a text that is to be spoken, not read.

If there are any parts that you find difficult to follow, re-write them.

Using the original, see if you can expand some of the ideas so that the speaker could give a rather more detailed talk. You should stay with the original structure but aim to develop the ideas already presented.

Orwell's checklist of good practice

This is a checklist of good practice that can be used no matter what sort of text you are trying to produce. It was written by the author George Orwell in his book *Politics and the English Language*.

- Never use a metaphor, simile or other figure of speech that you are used to seeing in print.
- Never use a long word where a short one will do.
- If it is possible to cut a word out, always cut it out.
- Never use the passive when you can use the active.
- Never use a foreign phrase, a scientific word or a **jargon** word if you can think of an everyday English equivalent.
- Break any of these rules sooner than say anything outright barbarous.

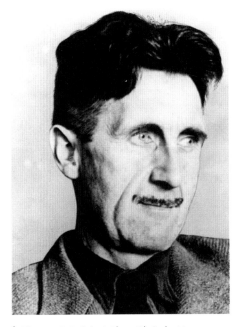

↑ **Figure 5.5** Eric Arthur Blair, better known by his pen name, George Orwell

Activity 5.21

- Discuss Orwell's rules for effective writing in the box above. Do you agree that these are sound principles? Are the any further rules that you would like to add? Cicero might help (see page 93).

Conclusion

In this chapter you have:

- thought about how to produce shorter writing in response to a given prompt
- worked on strategies for writing a commentary on your shorter writing
- thought in detail about your own writing strategies for producing a wide variety of extended texts by analysing examples of others' writing.

6 Conclusion to AS Level

We've come a long way, so let's summarise what you have achieved in the previous five chapters.

- You have worked on suitable vocabulary and strategies for the analysis of texts, both written and, to an extent, spoken.
- You have responded to a wide variety of extracts in order to demonstrate your understanding of how texts create meaning.
- You have developed your own writing skills in terms of writing in a variety of genres and for a number of different purposes.
- You have looked at other students' work in order to establish how you might be assessed and to analyse your own strengths and weaknesses.

At the same time, you have gained an understanding of some of the central debates that confront linguists when they try to study a language in use.

- In any language, change is natural and unstoppable.
- Both spoken and written texts are legitimate territory for analysis, though the methods of analysis are slightly different.
- There will be variations of English within cultural and social groups, even though the broad outlines of the language are shared.
- Standard English enables diverse groups to communicate both within a country and internationally.
- The varieties of English and points of contrast with standard English are worthy of study and analysis.
- Non-standard varieties of English are not inferior – they allow people to express their regional, cultural and national identities.
- Standard and non-standard English are both subject to change, and there is natural variation between the written and spoken forms.
- Standard and non-standard English are differentiated by variations in both grammar and lexis.
- Non-standard versions of the language may influence and change the standard form over time (the incorporation of 'loanwords' into the standard form is an example of this).

If you go on to A Level, these discussions will form the basis of much of what you study there.

For now, good luck with the AS exams!

Introduction to A Level English Language

This chapter will:

→ remind you of what you did in the first year of your course, and give you an idea of what the A-level year will involve

→ invite you to consider what language is for, and to reflect on terminology used to describe kinds of language use

→ introduce terminology for the analysis of meaning

→ outline what this part of the course involves

→ describe the skills you need

→ explain how you will be assessed.

Thinking about language

Throughout Part 1 of this book, you have been developing your knowledge and understanding of English Language by practising and using skills and techniques of reading and writing. In other words, you've been *learning* by *doing* – which is a simple but very successful method of learning almost anything.

Now, in Part 2, as you progress through the A-level year of the course, you will need to spend more time *thinking* about the English language. And as you absorb more knowledge of linguistic concepts and theories, you will be able to practise *thinking like a linguist*.

We'll start by considering a question about language in general, a simple-looking question which might produce some complicated answers:

What do we use language for?

Activity 7.1

Using a table like the partially-completed one on page 128, make a list of ten different situations in which you've used language in the last week.

Include:

■ spoken language as well as written language

■ electronic communication as well as face-to-face communication

■ situations where you were the receiver/consumer of language

■ situations where you were the transmitter/producer of language.

Link

→ You have considered the way language is used already, in activities 1.4 and 1.5 on page 12.

Situation: Sender/ Recipient	Reason/purpose	What kind of language?	Ideas/concepts/ theories
sending a text message to a family member	e.g. letting them know what time you'll be home → hoping someone will have food waiting for you	– informal – **elliptical** – non-Standard	
receiving an email from a company	e.g. advertising a special offer → hoping to persuade you to buy	direct address: – personal pronouns – your name	
posting on a special-interest website		– technical lexis (vocabulary)	reinforcing a shared or group identity or interest → using language to **include** or **exclude**
a *No Smoking* sign			**politeness strategies**

Reflecting on Activity 7.1

Did you manage to come up with ten different situations? Did you complete all columns of the table?

You may have wondered about the four columns. The first two are quite straightforward: you became accustomed at AS Level to thinking about **audience** and **purpose**, and how together these aspects contribute to the **context** in which language is produced and received.

You should have had to spend a longer time *thinking* about the third and fourth columns.

From your studies at AS-level, you have learned some *linguistic terminology* to help you explain in a more precise way *what kind of language* is being used in a particular situation and *what linguistic concepts/theories* might be involved:

- you might use **vague** or **deictic language** when communicating with someone you know well, because they know what you mean even when you're not **explicit**; for example, you could say/write '*that shop at the end of the road*' without naming the road because you and the person you're communicating with have shared general/contextual knowledge (which shop and which road)

- you might use **technical** or **field-specific language** when communicating in a situation where you share specialist knowledge with anyone likely to hear or read what you say/write

- you might (deliberately or otherwise) use **exclusive** or **inclusive** language to construct or reinforce your relationship with another person; and, similarly, you might use (or avoid using) **politeness strategies**.

Exploring meaning

People use the word *meaning* in a general, everyday way. But you need to think like a linguist, which means using such terms in a precise, exact way.

Linguists use the term **semantics** to refer to the study of meaning. We will look at different kinds of **semantic change** in the next chapter (on language change).

But for now we will consider just one distinction, based on the difference between **explicit** (= clearly-stated and obvious) meaning and **implicit** (= suggested) meaning.

This will not be a new concept for you, but the terminology may be new.

- **Denotation** refers to the literal meaning of a word, the 'dictionary definition'. For example, if you look up the word *apple* in a dictionary, you will discover that its primary **denotative** meaning is 'the round fruit of a tree of the rose family, which typically has thin green or red skin and crisp flesh'.

- **Connotation** refers to the associations that are connected to a certain word or the emotions suggested by that word. The **connotative** meanings of a word exist at the same time as the denotative meanings. The connotations for the word *apple* could include innocence, wholesomeness or purity.

Activity 7.2

1. Let's see how this works with one apparently simple **concrete noun** and one apparently simple **adjective**. Read the examples in the following table, and make sure you understand how the literal denotative meaning leads to connotative meaning and **idiomatic** usage.

idiom ← literal denotative meaning → *connotative meaning*

Simple word	Usage – e.g. idiomatic	Denotative meaning	Connotative meaning
apple		(noun) 1. edible fruit of the apple tree	Symbol of temptation: Adam and Eve in the Garden of Eden
	'an apple for the teacher'		a gift offered in the hope of being in favour
	'a rotten apple'		an immoral person who may corrupt others
	'the apple of his father's eye'		a child favoured above her/his siblings
Apple		2. an internationally-known brand of computers and other consumer electronics	
green		(adjective) 1. colour between blue and yellow in the spectrum	a green light suggests it's safe to proceed
		2. covered with grass or other vegetation	concerned with protection of the environment
		3. (of a plant or fruit) young or unripe	innocent and naïve
	'the green-eyed monster'		[from Shakespeare's *Othello* (Act 3, Scene 3, 166)] = jealousy personified.
	'green with envy'		

2. Now give yourself 40 minutes to copy and complete the table with eight more examples of your own.

Hint: Think about examples of this process from your own experience. The dominant 'variety' of English in your own culture might not be British-English: it might be American English or Asian English or Caribbean English. If so, you may be able to think of a number of more 'local' idiomatic uses that would fit in the second column.

? Hmm...

You should have noticed that connotation is a two-way (and 'iterative') linguistic process. We know that the word *apple* occurs in various idioms such as 'the apple of his eye' (meaning something or someone valued and cherished above all others) with a connotative meaning of 'perfection'. The more often such idioms are used, the more likely it becomes that the word will in future *connote* such ideas.

What's involved?

I hope you feel encouraged when you think about the skills you've acquired through your AS-level course, and how far you've come in a year. Even if the ideas and terminology in Activities 7.1 and 7.2 gave you some difficulty, you should remember that you are now working at a higher conceptual level than you were a year ago. You now read and think and write with *knowledge* and *skills* which you didn't have at the start of the course. I hope you find yourself naturally applying linguistic knowledge and skills to your everyday life, not just when you're in an English language class or doing English language homework.

It's good to be aware of your linguistic environment, to be aware of and be able to assess your own progress. However, you also need to be aware of the new concepts your A Level course will bring which you didn't encounter last year – new *knowledge*.

You will learn about:

- how the English language has changed over time, from c.1500 to the present day
- how language is acquired by children and how it develops in the years 0–8
- the status of English as a world/global language
- how language can be used to construct aspects of personal identity.

In Chapters 8–11 we will focus on each one of these subject areas in turn.

What skills do I need?

You will write the answers to your A-level examination questions in the form of academic essays, and you will need to begin practising the planning of such essays very soon – new *skills*.

You will be expected to learn how to:

- read and understand transcripts of spoken language
- read and understand linguistic data – graphs and tables of information about changes and trends in the use of the English language
- integrate your understanding of material in the question papers with the knowledge you have gained from your wider (term-time) study of the English language.

How will I be assessed?

At AS Level, the assessment took the form of two written examinations. To gain the full A level qualification, you will need to take **two** more papers.

Paper 3 Language Analysis (50 marks) lasts 2 hours 15 minutes.

The paper has two sections, Section A: Language change, and Section B: Child language acquisition. There will be two questions, one in each section. Both are compulsory.

Section A: Language change, Question 1 (25 marks in total) provides you with three texts to read and to make use of in an essay answer.

- Text A (approximately 300–400 words) will be a passage of **prose** written at some time between 1500 and the present day, chosen to illustrate some ways in which the English language has changed over time.
- Texts B and C will be an *n*-gram graph and a table of corpus (language) data, linked to the language features in Text A.

You will analyse how Text A exemplifies ways in which the English language has changed over time, supporting your response with reference to Text B and Text C, and also to your wider study of language change.

Text A could be any of the following text types: advertisements, brochures, leaflets, editorials, news stories, articles, reviews, blogs, investigative journalism, letters, podcasts, biographies, autobiographies, travel writing, diaries, essays, scripted speech, narrative writing and descriptive writing.

Section B: Child language acquisition, Question 2 (25 marks in total) provides you with a transcript of spoken language featuring language spoken by a child or children in the early stages of language development (0–8 years), possibly alongside older speakers.

You will analyse ways in which the speakers in the transcript use language, referring to specific details from the transcription, and linking your observations to ideas and examples from your wider study of child language acquisition.

Paper 4 Language Topics (50 marks) lasts 2 hours 15 minutes.

The paper has two sections, Section A: English in the world, and Section B: Language and the self. There will be two questions, one in each section. Both are compulsory.

Section A: English in the world, Question 1 (25 marks in total) provides you with a text of about 400–500 words on the topic of 'English in the world'. You will write an essay discussing the most important issues the text raises in relation to a specified aspect of the role and status of the English language in the world.

You must refer to specific details from the text, relating points in your discussion to ideas and examples from your wider study of the topic of English in the world.

Section B: Language and the self, Question 2 (25 marks in total) provides you with a text of about 400–500 words on the topic of 'Language and the self'. You will write an essay discussing the most important issues the text raises in relation to a specified aspect of the relationship between language and the self.

You must refer to specific details from the text, relating points in your discussion to ideas and examples from your wider study of the topic of language and the self.

Conclusion

We have established a number of things in this introductory chapter for A Level.

- You have revised ideas about what language is for and begun to think about what kind of language is being used in a particular situation and what linguistic concepts/theories might be involved.
- You have considered what linguistic concepts and theories might be involved in analysing communication.
- You have explored terminology relating to semantics that you will develop in later chapters.
- You know what is involved in the course.
- You know how you will be assessed in the examinations.

What can you do to help yourself?

Here are some suggestions about easy good habits – ways in which you can make yourself more aware of your linguistic environment without having to make a huge amount of effort.

1. Start (and maintain) your own Personal Collection of Linguistic Artefacts – a PCLA – examples of language use that you find interesting or amusing. This collection can 'live' in your laptop or your phone, or in an old-fashioned notebook. You can easily take a quick photograph of a sign or an advertisement that uses language in an interesting (or irritating!) way; you can easily record a snatch of a broadcast interview.

2. Pay more linguistic attention to news media: print journalism, radio and television and online news outlets. Hardly a day passes by without some news story with a basis in the usage of the English language, and often it will be connected to one of your four specialised subject areas. Pay extra attention to any online comments sections. Even when the original subject has nothing to do with the use of the English language, people who disagree with each other's views will often direct their criticism to the other person's English rather than her/his ideas and arguments. Add these to your PCLA!

3. Share with your fellow-students. Some of them may be members of groups (for example, online gamers) who belong to a **linguistic community** because of their specialised interest and who therefore use **inclusive language** with each other – language which you might find **excludes** you.

Language change

This chapter will:

→ look at some attitudes to language change

→ develop your understanding of how to deal with historical language data

→ explore some of the ways in which the English language has changed between 1500 and the present day

→ consider how changes in language reflect changes in society and culture, politics and technology

→ explore some of the consequences of language change in English.

Language change and general knowledge

Most people have ideas about various ways in which they believe language might have changed or might still be changing.

Here is a series of typical statements and questions about language change from people with general knowledge of language.

1 It's bad English to use slang.

2 The language of business and finance is everywhere these days. Corporate-speak is changing the way we think.

5 Allowing American spellings and vocabulary is wrecking the English language.

4 I don't like the way television broadcasters and politicians are using the word 'disinterested' to mean the opposite of 'interested'. It's wrong to do that: look in a dictionary and you can see that the opposite of 'interested' is 'uninterested'. 'Disinterested' means something quite different.

8 Do I need to use 'her/she' as well as 'his/he' when I write this sentence: 'The Prime Minister shouldn't just pick his closest friends when he chooses who is to be Home Secretary or Foreign Secretary'?

7 Official letters – like the ones you get from the tax inspectors – are friendlier in tone these days. And nurses and doctors use fewer technical words than they used to: they explain things in more patient-friendly language.

3 Does texting damage people's use of English?

6 Young people are less accurate in the way they use grammar than older people.

Activity 8.1

You're now going to approach each one of these statements and questions with the benefit of your linguistic knowledge.

Make a four-column list in which you:

■ identify the underlying linguistic issue or concept – e.g. **'correctness'** or levels of **formality** – which may not occur to someone not studying A Level English Language

- consider whether there's any evidence to support the statement, or to explain why someone might ask the question

- explore whether there's any misunderstanding going on because general knowledge isn't precise enough to deal with a linguistic issue

- consider what other factors (societal, political, cultural) might be influencing language choice and thus language change.

You can copy and complete the columns provided below; or you might prefer to devise your own columns, based on the chapter objectives.

Number(s) and issue(s)	Evidence?	Evidence? View limited by lack of linguistic knowledge?	Changes in culture and society?
7: **formality** and **tone** in 'official' or expert communication			Society becoming more open and egalitarian?
1, 3 and 6: differences according to age and generation	Are there any research studies on how texting affects other aspects of language use?	6: Comment is about 'grammar' – but the general public often use the term 'grammar' when what they really mean to criticise is the accuracy of spelling or punctuation in written communication	
8: **'gendered' language**			**'Political correctness'** → concern not to offend or exclude groups

Exam tip

Think back to the tip about terminology after Activity 7.1 in the last chapter (page 128). It's always helpful if you can use more precise terms to describe language use – e.g. you can make a distinction between more **formal** or more **informal** language rather than using everyday terms like 'friendly'.

But don't make the mistake of thinking that just using a more technical-linguistic term is all you have to do. You need to go on and use that more precise term to help you develop a more detailed analysis.

Reflecting on Activity 8.1

Did you manage to complete the table?

You should now make a list of any *linguistic issues and/or concepts* which emerged from your thinking there.

You will have noticed a number of situations in which the general/everyday view of language is limited or mistaken when compared to the view of someone with precise linguistic knowledge.

These are situations in which you can now offer a more informed view – being able to refer, for example, to the debate between **prescriptivists** and **descriptivists** in discussing notions of Bad English and Good English.

If you've never come across these distinctions and this terminology before, now is a good time to start your independent research.

Language change and linguistic knowledge

What we are studying under the heading of 'language change' is the second of two main branches of language variation:

- **synchronic variation** = differences in language use at <u>one time</u>, according to the place or the context – e.g. the difference in how people pronounce the **noun** *bath* according to whether they live in north-west England, south-east England or North America

- **diachronic variation** = differences in language use over <u>different times</u> – e.g. the semantic broadening of the noun *mouse* to mean a peripheral device for a computer as well as a small rodent.

So, what the A Level English Language syllabus calls 'language change' involves looking at the history of the language. Some of the statements and questions in Activity 8.1 were more to do with synchronic variation, but from here on in this chapter we will be concentrating on diachronic variation.

The most obvious examples of diachronic variation are those we can observe at the level of single words.

Link

→ This links back to **semantics** (the study of meaning) – Activity 7.2 in the previous chapter.

Semantic change

You can see in the example of *mouse* above how the meaning of a word can change over time. Some meanings are lost altogether: no-one nowadays uses the adjective *artificial* to denote (or connote) something that's been created with great skill, although this was what it originally meant (from the noun *artificer* = a skilled craftsman or inventor). Over time, social attitudes to man-made things have changed, and it's now fashionable to prefer (for example) *natural* fabrics over man-made fabrics. So the adjective *artificial* has developed negative connotations while the adjective *natural* has developed positive connotations.

This process is called **semantic change**. You'll learn more about it below, together with terminology for particular kinds of semantic change: **narrowing**, **broadening**, **amelioration**, **pejoration** or indeed a combination of these.

Narrowing and broadening involve shifts in *denotative* meaning, while amelioration and pejoration also involve shifts in *connotative* meaning.

Semantic narrowing

This is the process by which a word's meaning becomes less general over time. For example, the word *accident* nowadays means an event that is at least unfortunate and possibly disastrous, and which was not foreseen. In previous times, it could mean any event that was not foreseen, so a 19th-century writer could innocently refer to a chance meeting with a long-lost friend as a 'happy accident', whereas now this meaning would only be employed in a joking or ironic way.

Semantic broadening

Not surprisingly, this is the opposite process, where a word gains broader or additional meanings over time. Some people would argue that this is happening at a faster rate now than at other times in history because of information technology: not only do words spread around the globe, changing meaning as they go, but additional words are needed for new technology and new processes. The obvious example is *mouse*, which no longer denotes only a small furry rodent.

Some words shift **word class** as well, for example from noun to **verb**. The word *friend* was for a long time only a noun; now people use it as a verb and talk of being *friended* (or *unfriended*) on social media.

Semantic amelioration

This is the process by which meaning undergoes an improvement over time, coming to represent something more favourable than it originally referred to. A simple example is the word *nice*, which nowadays is a vague or empty adjective meaning 'pleasant' or 'agreeable', but which originally (when it entered the English language from French) meant 'stupid', then later on 'precise'. Occasionally you might find *nice* being used to mean *precise* in the expression 'a nice distinction', but this usage is mostly thought of as **archaic**.

Semantic pejoration

Pejoration involves a word acquiring negative connotations that it didn't have previously. For example, the word *attitude* has begun to have the connotation of 'disagreement' or even 'aggression'. Formerly, it had a more **neutral** meaning of a person's mental state or way of thinking, without any suggestion that this was a positive or a negative state in a particular situation. Now – especially in American English – to say that someone 'has attitude' is to suggest that he/she is uncooperative. The word *issue* has undergone a similar **shift**, moving from a relatively neutral meaning of a topic to be discussed to a more negative sense of 'problem' or 'complaint'.

Reflecting on semantic change

All of the examples of semantic change which we've considered have involved looking at just one word at a time: we've been considering language use at *word-level*.

The developing linguist – that's you! – will have been wondering if there's any way of exploring hard **objective** evidence of language change at single-word level without having to depend on the **subjective** memories of people who speak and read and write the English language, but whose prejudices about language use might distort any data they can offer. For example, as we saw in Activity 8.1, people might believe that more American English expressions and spellings are being used in British English – but is that actually true? And can we possibly find hard evidence of it?

As a developing linguistic researcher, you will be delighted to learn that the answer is Yes! We can indeed find hard evidence about trends and changes in language use, thanks to the existence of collections of language data, both spoken and written. Such a collection is called a **corpus** (from the Latin word for a *body*), and this branch of study is called **corpus linguistics.** (The plural form is **corpora**.)

Later in this chapter we will move on to examples of language change at clause level, sentence level or whole-text level. But first you're going to learn the basics of how to use **linguistic corpora** for independent research.

How to deal with language data

As far as the A Level English Language syllabus is concerned, you will need to be prepared to deal with *sources of* **quantitative language data** in the exam. The term **quantitative** refers to data which can be counted – for example, the number of times a particular word or combination of words (a **collocation**) occurs in a text or a corpus of texts.

These sources will appear as Texts B and C on the question paper, and they will be of two particular types:

- **n-gram graphs** representing changes in language use over time – such as comparisons of related words, **parts of speech**, inflections, collocations
- **word tables** derived from corpus data – such as collocate lists and synonym lists.

It's likely that you will never have come across either *n*-gram graphs or word tables derived from corpus data before. They will make sense when we look at some examples and try out the approaches needed.

We're going to look at a scaled-down version of a Paper 3 exam-style question on language change, and practise some approaches to dealing with the data.

Reflecting on language data

You may have been wondering how word tables of corpus data and *n*-gram graphs are generated, and how they might be used.

They both depend on developments in computational linguistics. Search engines make it possible to search a database of language – a linguistic corpus – for particular words or combinations of words across a particular time-period.

So, for example, *n*-gram graphs are generated by searching the texts of published books whose texts are available on the internet. You can search for the occurrence of individual words or phrases, or you can compare the frequency of alternative words and phrases.

How to approach an exam-style question on language change

STEP 1

Read the question and make sure you know what you're being asked to do. Identify the key words in the question.

Text A will contain various features of language which are typical of the time in which it was written. It will be up to you to identify some of those features and then to decide which ones you can write about in relation to what you already know from your wider study.

> **Read Texts A, B and C.**
>
> Analyse how **Text A** exemplifies the various ways in which the English language has changed over time. In your answer, you should refer to specific details from **Texts A, B** and **C**, as well as to ideas and examples from your wider study of language change. (25 marks)

→

Exam tip

This task prepares you for what you will be doing in your final examination. By the time you reach the end of the course, you will be able to combine examples from your own wider study with examples from the texts on the question paper.

And here's a reminder of what these texts will be:

- Text A: a passage of English Prose (300–400 words) written at any time from 1500 to the present.
- Texts B and C: graphs and tables containing language data linked to language use in Text A.

Exam tip

You should treat the texts which you are given in the Paper 3 exam as a free gift. They offer you a choice of possible material that will allow you to display your knowledge and skills. They're not the sort of gift you can refuse to accept altogether, but their purpose is to help you, not to give you problems.

Texts B and C will be linked to a small number of those features in Text A, and will provide you with more specific detail. So, some of the work of identifying significant features has been done for you. That might be a reason for looking quickly at Texts B and C before you read Text A.

STEP 2

Read the texts and annotate them on the question paper itself.

- You can read and make notes on Text A first
- Or you can look at Texts B and C first, then note down what there is in Text A which relates to the language data in the graph and table texts.
- Give yourself 15 minutes to do Step 2.

Text A

Excerpt from *Rural Rides* (1821) by William Cobbett, in which the writer describes his journeys by horseback through the countryside of England.

Saturday night, 10 November 1821

Went to Hereford this morning. It was market-day. My arrival became known, and, I am sure, I cannot tell how. A sort of buz got about. I could perceive here, as I always have elsewhere, very ardent friends and very bitter enemies; but all full of curiosity. One thing could not fail to please me exceedingly: my friends were gay and my enemies gloomy: the former smiled, and the latter, in endeavouring to screw their features into a sneer, could get them no further than the half sour and half sad: the former seemed in their looks to say, "Here he is," and the latter to respond, 'Yes, G - - d - - - him!'

I went into the market-place, amongst the farmers, with whom, in general, I was very much pleased. If I were to live in the county two months, I should be acquainted with every man of them. The country is very fine all the way from Ross to Hereford. The soil is always a red loam upon a bed of stone. The trees are very fine, and certainly winter comes later here than in Middlesex. Some of the oak trees are still perfectly green, and many of the ashes as green as in September.

Rural Rides by William Cobbett

Text B

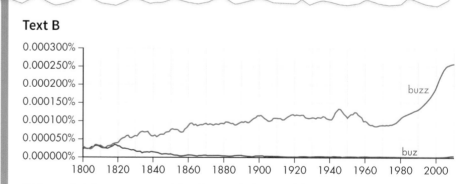

↑ **Figure 8.1** An *n*-gram graph for the words *buzz* and *buz* (1800–2008)

Text C

'bitter'	'ardent'
disappointment	supporter(s)
taste	feminist
pill	desire
blow	suitor
dispute	Royalist

↑ **Figure 8.2** Top five collocates (nouns only) for *bitter* and *ardent* from the British National Corpus (1980–1993).

STEP 3

Look at your notes from Step 2. They should show what you thought were significant features of language in Text A, and connections with the data in Texts B and C – in other words, your observations about language change.

In an exam, you would need quickly to organise these observations into groups of ideas which would lead to a paragraph structure for an essay.

When you look at these annotations, can you see connections between them?

- If the answer is 'Yes', take a fresh sheet of paper and try to organise your observations about language change into groups which could be developed into paragraphs of sensible discussion. (Columns or rows might help.) Then go on to 'Language change at word-level and beyond' and Activity 8.4.

- If the answer is No, continue reading below before you go on to 'Language change at word-level and beyond' and Activity 8.4.

Making simple observations and more complex inferences from language data

One of the reading skills you practised and mastered at AS-Level was making **inferences.**

Looking at the graph and table in Texts B and C, and using our linguistic knowledge, what can we observe?

- (From Text B) *Buz* and *buzz* were found almost equally from 1800–1820.

- (From Text B) After 1820, the use of *buz* declines sharply, and by 1960 it has almost disappeared.

- (From Text B) The use of *buzz* rises sharply after the early 1980s.

- (From Text C) Neither of the Text A combinations/**collocations** with 'bitter' and 'ardent' (*ardent friends* and *bitter enemies*) occurs in the top five collocates for 1980–1993.

- (From Text C) *Bitter* collocates with **abstract nouns** (*disappointment* and *dispute*) and a concrete noun (*pill*) to create **metaphorical** or **figurative** meanings – e.g. *a bitter pill (to swallow)* is a common **idiom** meaning something unpleasant that you have to force yourself to accept.

Now, from what we know about semantic change, what can we <u>infer</u>?

- Perhaps *buz* and *buzz* were interchangeable between 1800–1820, and possibly before that too.

- Perhaps the two variants went through a **divergence** in meaning from 1820 onwards: Cobbett seems to be using *buz* to mean 'rumour'.

- The variant *buzz* became dominant after 1820 – it's an **onomatopoeic** word for the sound made by insects, so perhaps we should be applying the concept of **phonology** (= sound) rather than semantics.

Inference ↔ speculation

There are two dangers at this point:

1. Anyone who is less than fascinated by language change is likely to have fallen asleep.

2. Sensible and informed inference can turn into half-informed speculation if we push it too far.

However, you could build a sensible argument about how the **phonology** of the word *buz/buzz* mimics the sound of a whispered rumour as well as the sound of an insect. You could then move on to how *buzz* has acquired new meanings throughout the 20th century because of developments in technology: a low-flying aircraft can be described as having buzzed people on the ground; you can ask someone to buzz you in when you want to get into a block of flats (British English expression for American-English apartment block!)

And in terms of **slang** – a not-very-technical term for **non-standard English** – a buzz can mean a feeling of euphoria, with positive **connotations** of an exciting and/or dangerous physical activity (like skiing or rock-climbing).

Language change at word-level and beyond

So far, we've been concentrating on changes in language use at the level of individual words. There are still many aspects of change at word-level that we could consider – three of which (**antonyms, archaisms** and **orthography**) we will look at below, based on examples from Text A and Text C.

After that, in Activity 8.4, you will have the chance to do some independent research.

Antonyms

Looking at the collocate list (Text C), *bitter* and *ardent* don't seem to be antonyms at the end of the 20th century in the way that they might have been in 1821. They don't now collocate with *friends* or *enemies* in the way they might have done in 1821.

Of course, we don't know from personal experience of language how often they collocated in 1821 – they might be unusual choices, peculiar to Cobbett – but we could generate some new quantitative data of our own. And you will soon be doing just that.

We can say from personal experience of language which pairs of adjectives and nouns do commonly collocate in contemporary English in the **lexical field** of personal relationships, in terms of friendship and hostility.

Archaisms

If *gay* and *gloomy* don't function as antonyms in contemporary English, it may be that either or both adjectives have undergone semantic change, so that the meaning intended by Cobbett would now be archaic.

Similarly, his use of *perceive* to mean 'see' might now be thought a bit over-formal or old-fashioned. And nowadays we would say *please me very much* rather than *please me exceedingly*.

Orthography

We looked at Cobbett's use of *gay* and *gloomy* as a contrast in Text A. He makes the contrast more obvious by using *italics* for these adjectives.

He also uses dashes to represent missing letters when he imagines the reaction of his enemies to hearing that he was in Hereford: *"G - - d - - - him!"* He does this to avoid causing the offence to some readers which they would feel if he wrote words of swearing and blasphemy in full.

Reflecting on making observations and inferences about language change

Having looked exhaustively (and exhaustingly!) at language change at word-level, where could we go next? We might look yet again at Cobbett's writing in Text A and think about ways in which it is different from contemporary English at phrase-level, sentence-level or whole-text **(discourse)** level. And we will certainly adopt that approach with some further texts later in this chapter.

But now it's time for you to do some research. You will be looking into your own memory and knowledge of the English language, and also into some resources available on the internet.

Activity 8.4

Use your own resources to explore language change.

Look at the collocations in the table overleaf, involving elements from Texts A, B and C on pages 138–9.

For each pairing of noun and adjective, make notes on:

- how likely you think it would be to find that collocation
- what connotations each might have (including current usage)
- anything interesting about the etymology/derivation of either of the words as used in that collocation.

Some parts have been completed for you.

Activity 8.2

Try to think of a situation in which someone would deliberately use archaic forms.

Activity 8.3

What other **orthographic methods** do we have in contemporary written English to avoid writing every letter of a potentially-offensive word?

Collocation	How common/ likely? Where?	Connotations? Current usage?	Etymology?
close friend(s)			
old friend(s)		- (possibly) connotes a sense that they share past secrets and would protect each other's privacy	
best friend(s)	- everyday conversation - more popular with younger speakers	- - BFF	
sworn enemies		- serious hostility - rather archaic	
ardent feminist			ardent derived from Latin for 'burning'
bitter blow			

Searching the internet for language change data

You can use the internet for independent linguistic research in many ways.

- Using a general search engine, you can research the <u>usage</u> of individual words or phrases. You can limit these searches to usage within defined time-periods and/or individual countries.

- You can search for <u>information</u> (e.g. for meaning or etymology) about individual words in online dictionaries or on the huge number of websites devoted to the study of English Language and Linguistics. By using quotation marks and the + sign, you can search for words and phrases (collocations or clusters or 'strings') occurring together.

- The English Language and Linguistics faculties of many universities have websites which 'host' ways into linguistic corpora. You may have to sign up or register for some of these; others are open-access.

- You can generate *n*-gram graphs and word tables similar to those which you will have to deal with in the exam.

Look back to what you wrote in response to Activity 8.1 – where you were taking a more precisely linguistic approach to issues of language change, though at the time you had no quantitative linguistic data to support your argument.

We are now going to search for quantitative linguistic data to support or to criticise some of the ideas about language use in Activity 8.1. That will mean choosing one of the statements from Activity 8.1 and then exploring some

Link

→ Look again at the questions and statements in Activity 8.1.
Remember, your answers were based on personal feelings and general knowledge.

specific examples. And for the purpose of this exercise, we will accept the terminology of statement 2:

The language of business and finance is everywhere these days. Corporate-speak is changing the way we think.

↑ **Figure 8.3** 'Buzzword' *Dilbert* cartoon strip, 22 February 1994

Figure 8.3 shows another contemporary meaning for *buzz*, and in an interesting **compounding** with *-word*. So, before we even start to look for other examples of corporate-speak, we have one to start us off. Like many examples of compound words, *buzzword* probably occurred first in hyphenated form. A search of online dictionaries might tell you when and where it was first used.

Reflecting on corporate-speak: a language-change 'fashion'?

Another quick internet search reveals many articles about corporate-speak. **Synonyms** for this fashion in language include *management/business jargon* and *office-speak*. Searching for examples generates a number of terms from other lexical fields which have been imported into the business field.

Alongside *buzzword* we're going to explore two other examples of expressions which are often used in the discourse of business, finance and politics in contemporary English: *heads-up* and *wake-up call*. Both of these expressions are hyphenated in the text here to make it more obvious that they have undergone the process of compounding.

Once again, it's up to you to look up the etymology (and thus the meaning) of these two expressions. You may discover alternative explanations. And the developing linguistic researcher will be thinking about why business leaders and politicians would be keen to use lexical items from the fields of sport or science.

The explanation lies in how language constructs images, and how it can be used to represent aspects of social and personal identity.

This is a very complex area, and we'll come back to it in Chapter 11. But you'll also have noticed that our general-knowledge statement about language change included the assertion that *corporate-speak is changing the way we think*. This touches on advanced linguistic theory: **linguistic relativity**, **linguistic determinism** and the **Sapir-Whorf Hypothesis**. This **hypothesis** (theory) puts forward the idea that we only think about concepts which we have words for. Is it true?

Link

→ Chapter 2 (a toolbox for textual analysis) discusses metaphorical language (pages 49–50) and Chapter 11 (language and the self) discusses language in relation to themes of personal identity

Activity 8.5

Research the following key terms:

- linguistic relativity
- linguistic determinism
- Sapir-Whorf hypothesis.

Hyphenation – an example of orthography

Deciding whether or not to hyphenate *buzzword*, *heads-up* and *wake-up call* is partly a matter of taste and fashion. When a new word is first **coined** through the process of compounding, it's likely that it will be hyphenated to show its origins. As the word becomes accepted into mainstream usage, the hyphenation tends to be lost – sometimes gradually, sometimes suddenly.

One example of hyphenation disappearing quite quickly is *e-mail/email*. Most people are happy to type or write *email* without the hyphenation which showed the word was an **abbreviation** of *electronic mail*. Most 'style guides' recommend *email*.

In contemporary English, there are many compounds which were once hyphenated but now are not. There are also many compounds which retain hyphenation.

Activity 8.6

Copy and complete the table below – ten examples for each column.

Compounds that are no longer hyphenated, and why not	Compounds that are still hyphenated, and why	Questions/contradictions/inconsistencies
mainstream – no risk of misunderstanding or *mis-reading* as another word	*t-shirt* – the initial letter is pronounced as a separate **phoneme**	A Level? A-Level? ALevel? A-level?

Exploring *n*-gram graphs and corpus data

STEP 1 Deciding on *n*-gram search terms

The Google *n*-gram viewer will allow you to search the texts of books printed between 1500 and 2008. Typing 'ngram viewer' into its search page brings up the default display position, which shows a frequency graph resulting from a search for the three terms *Albert Einstein, Sherlock Holmes, Frankenstein* from the corpus of books in English for the years 1800-2000.

You can adjust which corpus you want to search – for example, to one for British English or American English only. You can change the span of years. And you can type in whatever search terms you want up to a maximum of five words at a time. So, for example, you could complicate the default search to *Einstein's theory of relativity, Sherlock Holmes and Dr Watson, Bride of Frankenstein.*

If you feed *buzz-word, heads-up* and *wake-up call* into the *n*-gram viewer both with and without hyphenation, you will discover that the decision to hyphenate (or not) is crucial to how we choose our search terms in any exploration of *n*-gram graphs and corpus data.

Running a comparison between hyphenated *buzz-word* and un-hyphenated *buzzword* for the years 1960–2008 produces the *n*-gram in Figure 8.4.

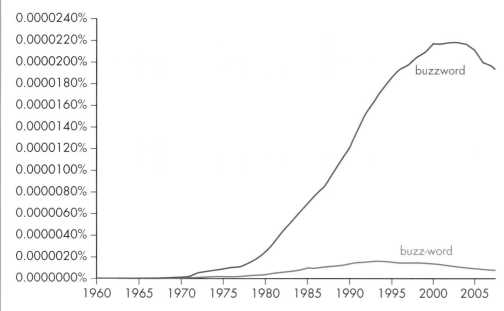

↑ **Figure 8.4** A comparison between hyphenated *buzz-word* and un-hyphenated *buzzword* for the years 1960-2008

And running *buzzword*, *buzz-word*, *heads-up* and *wake-up call* for the same years gives us this:

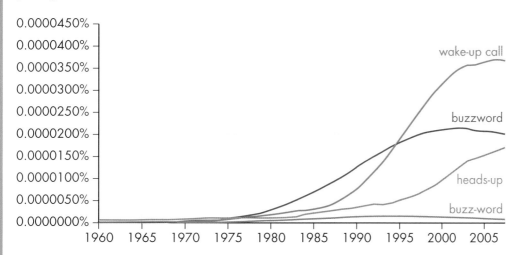

↑ **Figure 8.5** A comparison between *buzzword*, *buzz-word*, *heads-up,* and *wake-up call* for the years 1960-2008

The developing researcher of quantitative linguistic data will have realised that removing the hyphenation from *heads-up* and *wake-up* creates new complications.

You could try running *headsup* and *wakeup* as un-hyphenated compound words. If you run them as separate words – *heads up* and *wake up* – then the search will take in all uses of these terms as phrasal verbs (e.g. *He heads up the European branch of the company/It's time to wake up and smell the coffee*) and thus blur the attempt to find out how frequently they appear in their more modern sense as abstract nouns in the discourse of business.

STEP 2 Trying out *n*-gram searches

The most useful thing you can do now is to experiment with running a variety of *n*-gram searches.

- You might try some searches for words and phrases which you think are examples of fairly recent language change – e.g. expressions which you would use with friends and contemporaries, but not with older family members. By searching different spans of years you might be able to determine roughly when a particular word or phrase passed into general usage.

- You could also try searching for much earlier examples of language use. Perhaps you can think of words which would now be seen as archaic. Try earlier spans of years.

- Try two different approaches. (a) Start with a text from a particular period – many old texts have been digitised – and look for examples of features of language which you think have changed. (b) Start with words (or spellings) which you feel are archaic, and see if you can work out when changes occurred, and why.

- Record your findings. The developing researcher of quantitative linguistic data – that's you! – is perfectly capable of devising a way of doing that, but use a table like the one below if you like:

Link

→ End of Chapter 7 Introduction to A Level English: What can you do to help yourself?

If you're particularly surprised by any of your *n*-gram search findings, you should add them to your Personal Collection of Linguistic Artefacts.

Word/phrase; search-years	Reason for search	Results → inferences
troll – as verb or noun 1800–2008	Is it a modern usage arising from the internet?	Increase in incidence around 1865 – was there an edition of fairy tales then? Fairly consistent 1880–1980, then significant increase late 1990s onwards → internet trolling
bungalow 1700–2008	I know it's a **loanword** (a **borrowing**) from India. When did it start to be used in English?	Hardly any use before 1830. Most commonly used in the mid-1920s → but probably for a social reason (more building) and not a linguistic reason
wrought 1600–2008	I know it's an **archaic past-tense verb-form** (past tense of *work*). When did it start to fall out of use in English?	Most common 1650–1700; steady decline in use from 1750; *worked* became more common than *wrought* in 1850s → fashion to have more **regular past-tenses** ending in *-ed*?

STEP 3 Locating and navigating a corpus of written texts

So many digitised e-texts are available online through websites, such as Project Gutenberg, that the range is completely bewildering. You could narrow your field of research to https://www.gutenberg.org/browse/scores/top which shows the current top 100 searches.

But starting like that won't allow you to choose a particular subject or period, so you could begin by looking for lists of books/authors related to one subject (e.g. travel: https://en.wikipedia.org/wiki/List_of_travel_books) or books from one period (https://en.wikipedia.org/wiki/List_of_travel_books#17th_century).

At this point, things can become more difficult still. The most useful approach for you is one that will lead you quickly to an interesting-looking text with examples of language change which are worth exploring – in other words, a prose text like the text you will be given in the exam as Text A.

The *Oxford Text Archive (OTA)* is more manageable and more accessible than most historical corpora of written texts. Here are some possible ways of using it.

(i) Find the Oxford Text Archive at http://ota.ox.ac.uk/catalogue/index.html

This will offer you three alternatives from the 'browse' function, any of which you could follow:

- TEI texts – texts created following the guidelines of the **Text Encoding Initiative**, available in a variety of formats to read, download or link to.

- Corpora – 84 different collections of language data, comprising a number of texts from different sources (including the British National Corpus), usually compiled for the purposes of linguistic research.

- 'Legacy formats' – a mixed assembly of more than 1600 online text resources which have been collected since the OTA came into existence in 1976. For example, the first 309 are from the Jonathan Swift Archive and consist of multiple versions of Swift's works, including ten versions of his most famous book, *Gulliver's Travels*. Other resources are a bit more surprising, including *The World Factbook 1991*, produced by the Central Intelligence Agency of the United States!

Some of these resources have restricted access, which means that you have to ask for permission to use them – though, even more surprisingly, not *The World Factbook 1991*. Some are in formats which some users may find difficult to use, although most are plain text.

(ii) Alternatively, you could explore the separate catalogue for the **Text Creation Partnership** (**TCP**) texts at http://ota.ox.ac.uk/tcp/. There are over 60,000 texts in this collection, dating from 1473 to 1820, more than half of which can be accessed free, without restriction.

Searches can be filtered by date, so that you could look for texts from a single year. For example, typing in '1628' produces 98 'hits'. This is a manageable number: you could then quickly browse the 'Terms' column to see each text's subject and/or **genre**.

Some of these texts will be of more interest to researchers of highly specialised subjects than to students of language change. If you choose a text whose subject seems to be of more general interest then you can concentrate on what it reveals about the development of the English language at the time it was published.

One random choice from this random year is http://downloads.it.ox.ac.uk/ota-public/tcp/Texts-HTML/free/A14/A14325.html. The (lengthy!) title of this text is *THE BATHS OF BATHE: OR, A NECESSARY COMPENDIOVS TREATISE CONCERNING THE Nature, vse and efficacie of those famous hot waters: PVBLISHED FOR THE BENEFIT OF all such, as yeerely for their health, resort to those Baths: With an Aduertisement of the great vtilitie that commeth to mans body, by the taking of Physick in the Spring, inferred vpon a question mooued, concerning the frequencie of sicknesse, and death of people more in that season, then in any other.*

Exam tip

You can follow these steps in any search of your own, making different choices in order to generate your own data.

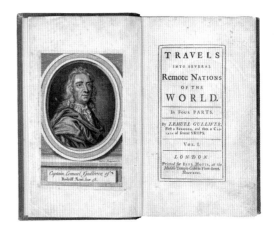

↑ **Figure 8.6** The first edition title page of *Gulliver's Travels*, of which ten versions appear on the OTA

Link

→ Implied meaning is referred to in Chapter 5 (Paper 2: Writing) on pages 107, 108 and 110.

The author is Tobias Venner (1577–1660), described as *Doctor of Physick in Bathe*. It's helpful to know a little historical and social context here. You might not know that health treatments involving sea-bathing and spa waters became increasingly popular throughout the 17th, 18th and 19th centuries in Britain. But if you apply your AS-level skills of reading for implied meaning just to the title of this text, you can work out that the writer is trying to persuade readers that it will be good for their health to come to the city of Bath.

Activity 8.7

Read the extract below. It consists of the first 250 words of *The Baths of Bathe*. Make a note of any feature of language use which is different from contemporary English – or indeed of any feature of language use which is interesting. Give yourself 15 minutes to do this. You could use a table like the one below or devise your own.

Bathe, so called from the Baths in it, is a little well-compacted Cittie, and beautified with very faire and goodly buildings for receit of strangers. Although the site thereof, by reason of the vicinity of Hills, seeme not pleasant, being almost inuironed with them; yet for goodnesse of ayre, neerenes of a sweet and delectable Riuer, and fertilitie of soyle, it is pleasant and happy enough; but for the hot waters that boyle vp euen in the middest thereof, it is more delectable and happier, then any other of the Kingdome.

There are in it foure publike Baths, so fairely built, and fitted with such conueniencie for bathing, as the like (I suppose) is not else-where to be found; besides a little Bath for Lepers, called The Lepers Bath.

They all haue the originall of their heate from one matter, namely, Sulphur, burning in the cauities of the earth, thorow which the waters flowing receiue their heate. They partake of no other minerall that I can finde: what may lye hid *in visceribus terrae,* I know not: of this I am sure, that such diseases as cannot receiue cure else-where, here doe.

These Baths as they differ in their heate, so in their operations and effects. The *Kings Bath* is the hottest, and it is for beautie, largenesse, and efficacy of heate, a Kingly Bath indeed, being so hot as can be well suffered. This Bath is of strong-heating, opening, resoluing, attracting, and exiccating facultie, and therefore onely conuenient for cold and moist bodies, and for cold and moist diseases.

Features of language use which are different from contemporary English			
Spelling	Orthography	Lexis/semantics	Grammar/syntax

Reflecting on Activity 8.7

However you recorded your notes, I hope you found some significant linguistic differences between Tobias Venner's use of language and contemporary English.

I hope also that it occurred to you to organise your ideas into groups, since that would be the next step in planning an essay answer to an exam question.

The other element in an essay answer to a language change exam question is the pairing of Texts B and C, which will offer you *n*-gram graphs and tables of corpus data. We looked earlier at how to generate n-graph data. Now we'll look at ways of exploring corpus data and generating tables of information; and we'll link our exploration to *The Baths at Bathe*.

STEP 4 Trying out corpus data searches

You saw previously how to explore the online Oxford Text Archive and locate whole texts, from which we could study extracts for examples of language change. The OTA has a search function at https://ota.ox.ac.uk/about/search.xml but this is limited. You can try it out for yourself: as time goes on and more texts are digitised and added, more functions may become available.

You can also find out about the **Oxford English Corpus** (OEC) and access a great deal of other interesting information at https://en.oxforddictionaries.com/explore/oxford-english-corpus/

The **British National Corpus** (BNC), spoken and written English 1980s–early 1990s, is accessible in a number of ways. One of the easier ways is via the website of Brigham Young University, Utah at https://corpus.byu.edu/bnc/old/

The **Corpus of Contemporary American English** (COCA) is taken from the years 1990–2017 and is also available through Brigham Young University: https://corpus.byu.edu/coca/old/

A simple search for a word in either the BNC or the COCA will generate a table of the instances in which that word appears in the corpus – a simple **concordance**.

We're going to take another word from *The Baths at Bathe* for a simple concordance search – a word which is **low-frequency** in contemporary English, but whose spelling has not changed over time. The word *efficacy* is an **abstract noun** which occurs in the **noun-phrase** *efficacy of heate*. In modern English we would be more likely to use the word *efficiency* or the compound *heat-efficiency*.

But can we regard *efficacy* as an **archaic** term? My feeling is that it is now archaic. But I might be quite wrong – and a simple concordance search will give us some quantitative data to support my feeling or to show me that my sense of language use in this instance was mistaken.

A simple search for *efficacy* in the BNC returns 509 uses; a similar search in COCA returns 6091.

Reflecting on corpus data searches

It's clear that I was mistaken in my hunch/feeling/suspicion that *efficacy* was archaic. If you look beyond the simple number of 'hits' to the full results from the BNC and COCA searches, you'll see that *efficacy* is used in a variety of **contexts** to mean *effectiveness* or *efficiency*.

The thinking linguistic researcher will have realised that it might be interesting to run an ***n*-gram search** plotting *efficacy*, *effectiveness* and *efficiency*. Go on, then, do it!

Link

→ If you want to see an example of how you can organise your ideas into groups, an answer to Activity 8.7 is available at **www.oxfordsecondary.com/9780198445760**

Exam tip

In the exam, be careful not to jump to conclusions from your first look at the data. 6091 is 12 times as many 'hits' as 509, but much of that difference might be explained by the sizes of the two corpora: COCA is 560 million words of American English, 1990–present; and the BNC is 100 million words of British English, 1980s–1993.

Context and collocate searches

We have been concentrating on language change over time. The results of a simple concordance search of COCA are organised according to years, so you may already have been able to detect some changes in the use of a word over time.

But the **context** of use of a word is not just to do with time. It is also to do with text-type. The full COCA and BNC searches both show what type of text (e.g. scientific, medical, spoken, magazine) each example comes from. And this aspect of context will affect how the word we have searched collocates with other words.

So in our COCA and BNC searches for *efficacy*, there are examples of words from the lexical fields of medicine (*cholera vaccine/rapid absorption*) and government (*inner-urban policy/deregulation*).

We can go further.

- A **KWIC** search (**Key Word in Context**) can show you each occurrence of a word (or pattern) in a text or corpus, presented with the words surrounding it highlighted according to what **part of speech** (**PoS**)/**word class** they belong to.
- A **collocates** search can be limited to a particular **PoS**, or to a certain number of terms to the left or to the right of the search term.

All of the linguistic corpora which you can access online will have their own sets of instructions as to how you can perform different types of search.

Collocations and lexical fields

Here's one more search activity based on *efficacy/efficiency/effectiveness*, using the BNC hosted by the University of Lancaster at http://bncweb.lancs.ac.uk/bncwebSignup/user/login.php

---

Activity 8.8

1. Register for an account at http://bncweb.lancs.ac.uk/bncwebSignup/user/login.php

2. Keep your account details safely!

3. Log in, and you will go to the Standard Query screen at http://bncweb.lancs.ac.uk/cgi-binbncXML/BNCquery.pl?theQuery=search&urlTest=yes

4. Type in *efficacy OR efficiency OR effectiveness* and click Start Query.

5. When you reach the results screen you can choose Sentence View or KWIC View, both of which offer exactly what they say! Have a look at both – you can shift between them.

6. From the New Query drop-down box on the far right, choose <u>Collocations</u>.

7. On the next screen you will be offered three sets of BNC Collocation <u>Settings</u>. Leave these in their default positions – you might want to 'play' with them when you become more familiar with the process – and <u>Submit</u>.

8. On the next screen of collocation results you will have the opportunity to set further limits to your search.

   – <u>Collocation window span</u> allows you to reduce or increase the number of words to the left or right of your search term.

– In the <u>Filter results by</u> row, you can choose any particular part of speech, or leave the collocate search open as <u>no restrictions</u>.

So, for example, if you wanted to search for <u>any adjective</u> which collocates within one place to the right or left, you can set these new parameters, and then you can click 'Go!' in the Submit Changed Parameters box (far right).

9. Record the results of your search in some way. Some corpora will store your searches under a 'history' tab and some will not. But you can easily record your findings in a simple table. As you record the data you have generated, think about straightforward collocates and wider lexical fields. For example, a search starting with *effectiveness* and then limited to <u>any noun</u> and two places to the right and left in the collocate search will generate many terms from the lexis of modern business practice: *efficiency/cost/quality/safety/audit/participation/evaluation/training*.

10. Repeat the process for all three of our original terms: *efficacy/efficiency/effectiveness*.

11. Record all your results and consider possible inferences about language use and language change.

Conclusion

You have coped with a great deal of new knowledge and practised many new skills in this chapter. Some of the concepts involved in corpus linguistics would challenge the understanding of students following an English Language and Linguistics course at university. So you should be pleased with yourself … though you can't afford to relax!

Sometimes it's more interesting to look at a map after you've been somewhere than before. So, to remind you …

In this chapter you have:

- looked at some attitudes to language change
- developed your understanding of how to deal with historical language data
- explored some of the ways in which the English language has changed between c.1500 and the present day
- considered how changes in language reflect changes in society and culture, politics and technology
- explored some of the consequences of language change in English.

Where do you go next?

As with the *n*-gram graphs, the most useful thing you can do now is to experiment with the search functions of different on-line corpora until you feel comfortable with the ways in which information is generated.

For example, you could explore how two words with apparently similar denotative meanings – i.e. two synonyms – have actually been used at certain times. This would allow you to reach inferences about their connotative meanings over a certain time period, and then to explore whether either word has undergone semantic change.

This chapter will:

→ look at ways of representing spoken language in a written form

→ consider the main stages of children's early development in language

→ explore some of the functions of children's language

→ analyse transcripts of children's spoken language

→ develop your understanding of concepts, theories and research studies in child language acquisition (CLA)

→ end by providing some revision and reinforcement exercises.

Transcripts of children's spoken language

Link

→ Chapter 7 Introduction to A Level English Language: How will I be assessed?

As you know, in the examination question for Paper 3, Section B (Child language acquisition) you will be required to analyse a transcript featuring language spoken by a child or children. These children will be in the early stages of language development (0–8 years), possibly accompanied by older speakers.

You will have to *analyse ways in which speakers in the transcript use language, referring to specific details from the transcription, while linking your observations to ideas and examples from your wider study of child language acquisition.*

Nothing you will have done at AS Level has prepared you directly for dealing with written transcriptions of spoken language. So before you look at transcripts of children's speech, you will need to learn about ways in which spoken language can be presented in a written form.

Spoken language in a written form

Before we look at how children acquire language, you need some more terms and tools for language analysis:

✓ **conventions** = accepted ways of doing something – e.g. the 'rule' that in a game of cards you deal clockwise, or the rule that in Britain, India, Australia, New Zealand and South Africa you drive on the left-hand side of the road, while in France, Germany and the USA you drive on the right

✓ **interaction** = communication or direct involvement with someone or something; in linguistics, it is a two-way process using language

✓ **transcription** = a written or printed version of a process which uses language, e.g. the formal proceedings of a law court or a parliament; an informal conversation involving two or more people

✓ **utterance** = a continuous stretch of speech produced by one participant in a conversation.

Link

→ Look back at the transcript you wrote for the TV series/soap opera in Chapter 2, Activity 2.26.

You are going to try out those tools on a transcription of conversation between two adults later in Activity 9.2. But even before you do that, you're going to try some transcription of your own in Activity 9.1.

Activity 9.1

Ask a friend or classmate or family member for permission to record a short extract of their conversation. It might be conversation with you or with someone else – but make sure you have everyone's agreement.

- Make your recording. A minute is plenty!

- Then play it back, listening carefully to the **dynamics** of the interaction – the ways in which different speakers break off their utterance and other speakers take over the conversational **turn**.

- Play it back a second time, this time trying to write some of the interaction down on paper. Use lots of space – leave plenty of room to add changes and corrections later. You may find you have to keep stopping and re-winding in order to capture everything that was said.

- Involve the other participant(s) in the conversation in listening to the recording. They can help in your attempt to transcribe the interaction as accurately as possible.

- When you think you've captured all the words actually spoken, and who is speaking at any one time, you have a draft transcription and you're ready for the last step.

    Listen to the recording one more time, with your draft transcription in front of you. Try to add details of the pace and tone of the interaction. Include ways of showing where more than one speaker was talking at the same time, and some method of indicating that a speaker paused in her/his utterance.

    If your transcription now looks hopelessly chaotic, you've done a good job! Don't try to 'tidy up' the interaction. Normal everyday spontaneous conversation <u>is</u> chaotic, and one of the most amazing things about the human brain is the way we cope with all these signals and all this information.

    When you feel you've got your written transcription as close as possible to the audio recording, store it safely for a day or two.

    After a day or two, have another look at your transcription, and make a list of the methods you've used to represent features of spoken language in a written form.

Reflecting on Activity 9.1

What methods did you use to show who was speaking, what they said, how others reacted?

You might have used some of the **conventions** which playwrights use in writing scripts, such as colons after each speaker's name, or brackets to show non-verbal (**paralinguistic**) **cues** or **signals** – the kinds of signals we all automatically give and receive when we're interacting with other people.

Analysing spoken language

Whenever we listen to a conversation or join in a conversation, we are automatically analysing language without even thinking about it. We listen to the **topic** of conversation, and if we're interested we join in at what seems to be a suitable point – what linguists call a **transition relevant place.**

We might **overlap** with what someone else is saying, to agree or disagree or support; and we might do any of these things with **verbal** or non-verbal (paralinguistic) cues or signals. Sometimes we might **initiate** (begin) the topic; sometimes we might **shift** the topic to something closely related or to something different.

All of the time our brains are processing the **utterances** of other speakers in their **interactions** during everyday conversation. We are analysing the la nguage that we hear – the **speech acts** of other people – and working out what to say and when to say it. Most of the time we will try to be **co-operative**: we will consider the needs of other people, and we will **accommodate** what we say and how we say it to help them understand what we are trying to communicate. If we think we haven't made our meaning clear, we might re-phrase or **re-formulate** what we're saying.

The terms in **bold** above have a specialised meaning for a student of language, but they are all things we do all the time, naturally and quickly and without much time for thinking.

And the student of English language has the advantage of being able to study spoken language in the written form which we refer to as **transcription**. For more advanced linguistic study (at university level or for linguistic researchers) these transcriptions can be very complex, representing much more information about the spoken language than simply recording the words (the **lexical** and **grammatical** items) used by the speakers.

The transcriptions you will have to deal with will not be so complex, but they will still look strange to you at first.

Analysing a transcription

Activity 9.2

Look at the transcription key below. It sets out some of the **conventions** which can be used to represent a spoken interaction in a written form. This is the level of detail you will have to deal with in your exam.

Transcription key

(1)	= pause in seconds	underlined	= stressed sound/syllable(s)
(.)	= micropause	[*italics*]	= paralinguistic features
//	= speech overlap	UPPER CASE	= words spoken with increased volume

1. Now read through the following transcription of a conversation between two young women who are studying English Literature at university.

Hollie:	you havent read the great gatsby yet (.) have you
	//
Liz:	no (1) whats it about
Hollie:	er its er its basically about this this really <u>real</u>ly rich american guy in the nineteen twenties who er throws these ma <u>mass</u>ive parties (.) and er people dont really know how he got rich (.) and things like that (.) and then in the end it go it kind of turns

out that the <u>whole</u> reason why he throws the parties and why he moved to this part of new york is just that he (.) he was looking for his old love (.) like his old girl (1) but shes <u>mar</u>ried now and so you know theres a whole (.) unhappily married (.) so theres a whole <u>tragedy</u>

//

Liz:　　　　　　　　hap (.) <u>happily</u> married

Hollie:　　　　　UNhappily married (1) yeah

//

Liz:　　　　　　　　　　　　UNhappily

Hollie:　　　　[*laughs*] yeah

Liz:　　　　　oh (.) right

Hollie:　　yeah (.) and so theres a whole (.) be (.) because her husband <u>cheats</u> on her (.) and then gatsby come (.) you know kind of comes <u>back</u> into her life (.) and (.) but its

//

Liz:　　　　　　　　　　　　　　　to the <u>rescue</u>

//

Hollie:　　　　　　　　　　　　yeah (.) basically (.) but its a <u>tragic</u> ending (.) and its just (.) yeah (.) but i didnt

//

Liz:　　　　　　　　　　　　mm hmm

2. Did you understand the <u>content</u> of that interaction? It wouldn't be surprising if you didn't fully understand everything that Hollie and Liz said to each other. What reasons can you think of for that? (Tip: think about the nature of spoken language.)

3. Now read the transcription again, not worrying too much about whether you can understand all of the content. Instead, as you read, make a note of:

   ■ any features of language which seem to you more typical of <u>spoken</u> language than <u>written</u> language

   ■ features of conversational interaction which show the two speakers communicating with each other in ways beyond just the meanings of the words they speak.

On page 156 is what one student wrote as an answer to the following exam-style question:

Analyse ways in which Hollie and Liz are using language in this conversation. You should refer to specific details from the transcription, as well as to ideas and examples from your wider knowledge of spoken language.

*Note: Key terms used are in **bold***

The two **interlocutors**, Hollie and Liz, seem comfortable speaking to each other. Several times Liz **overlaps** Hollie's **utterances** without waiting for her friend to finish, but it's usually to **clarify** her own understanding – *hap (.) happily married* – rather than to disagree.

Hollie's second **turn** is a long uninterrupted explanation of the plot of this book – *The Great Gatsby* – which Liz has not read. Even though both young women are studying English Literature at university, Hollie is not giving Liz a complicated **formal** literary analysis of the book. This is a **casual** conversation, and Hollie uses **vague language** (*and things like that .... it kind of turns out ... and so you know theres a whole ....*) to avoid having to go into very specific detail.

Several turns are taken up by Liz first of all misunderstanding *unhappily/happily married*. Eventually Hollie makes it clear by emphasising the **prefix** *UN* in *UNhappily*. But she is careful not to offend her friend by directly telling Liz that she was mistaken. In fact, Hollie adds *yeah* after a pause when Liz echoes her response and says *UNhappily*.

You can also see the two friends **co-operating** to create meaning when Liz **overlaps** with *to the rescue*, showing she understands the kind of romantic story where the heroine has had wrong done to her (*her husband cheats on her*).

Both friends **affirm** and **support** each other's utterances by offering **non-verbal feedback – back-channel signals** such as *mm, oh, mm hmm*. Research studies such as those by Jennifer Coates and Deborah Tannen suggest that this sort of **supportive** behaviour is more typical of women's speech than men's. And my experience suggests that young women use more **emphatic stress** (*massive/tragic*) on individual syllables, probably to make their utterances more interesting and dramatic.

Link

→ Chapter 11 Language and the self (Paper 4, Section B)

↑ **Figure 9.1** Women use more politeness and co-operation strategies, including speaker support and paralinguistic features.

Link

→ You will be able to use an approach like this when you answer exam-style questions (Paper 3, Section B) on child language acquisition.

This student has used terminology well to show an understanding of linguistic concepts relevant to analysis of spoken language, and has paid attention to the **dynamics** of the **interaction**.

You can see how the analysis starts with a general comment on the interaction, then identifies specific details from the transcription, and finally moves on to introduce terms and concepts from wider study.

Transcription conventions

Even in that short section of transcribed spoken language in Activity 9.2, you will have noticed that the conventions of written transcription are not the same as the 'normal' conventions of written language.

In the transcriptions of spoken language which you will have to deal with, the most obvious convention is that 'normal' sentence punctuation is not used. And this is quite logical because in spontaneous spoken language people don't use 'normal' (i.e. grammatically complete) sentences. So the term 'sentence' is not useful in analysing spoken language: it's more helpful to think of an **utterance.**

We are not shocked or horrified when we receive an email or a text message without capital letters for proper nouns or quotation marks for titles. The conventions for instant electronic communication are different, or **non-standard**.

When some people compose emails, they apply the same standards of **formality** which they were used to when they wrote formal business letters. Other people accept **informal** standards when they write and receive emails. Think about your own email style(s): if you were sending an email to a teacher, would you use a similar **register** and a similar standard of 'correctness' as if you were emailing a friend?

Your own language development in childhood

The following activity is going to take some serious thought, and you may find it easier at the start to share your thinking with a partner.

You might also need the assistance and the memory of older family members. Read the instructions carefully and decide who you'll ask to help you follow them.

Activity 9.3

1. Think about the influences on your own language development from the earliest age you can remember. For most people this is around the age of 4; some people can remember being 3 or even 2. Then take this effort of memory forward in time, up to the age of 8.

2. Using a format that gives you plenty of space, construct a chart – like the one on the next page – dividing that time into stages. Some of these stages may match transferring from one school-stage to another. Divide the stages into smaller units if you like.

3. Work out some significant 'milestones' – points of development when you can identify some change in how you used language.

    For example:

    ■ Think about how **stories** which you have had read to you – or have read for yourself – have affected your language. Can other family members help to prompt your memory here?

    ■ You might remember the point at which you started to listen to **jokes** and tell your own jokes with friends. Jokes mostly depend on understanding something about how language works – **puns** are a good example, because they depend on **homophones** and **ambiguous** meanings.

    ■ You might remember a time when you didn't understand that a particular usage of language was **figurative** and not **literal**. Understanding **metaphor** is a significant milestone in a child's language development.

    ■ Other milestones might be to do with your ability to use **electronic communication devices**. Make lists of words and phrases which have come into your vocabulary from websites or instant messaging.

Exam tip

Don't look at transcriptions of spoken language as inferior versions of standard, edited written language. What would be 'mistakes' in written communication – uncorrected features of language, aspects that are considered 'wrong' or non-standard – may simply be ways of representing what was said in a spoken interaction as truthfully as possible.

One point that some students repeat over and over again is that written language is different from spoken language because there is usually time for language in the written form to be checked: it may have been composed spontaneously, but errors or inconsistencies can be corrected before it is 'published'. This is true, but you don't need to tell it to the examiner (or your teacher!) every single time you analyse a transcription of spoken language.

You could complete a table like the one below.

Age/stage	Situation	Learning to ...	Developmental stage
3 years old or less	nursery school? play-school?	• name objects • count	• can play 'pretend' games?
4 to 7		• read • write	
8 years old		• distinguish between literal and metaphorical?	

Using your memory of your own language development is difficult. So ask members of your family if they have recorded this aspect of your growing-up. There may be some video or audio footage of you talking as a 2-year-old or you on your 4th birthday.

Alternatively, there may be young children in your family or among the families of friends. Pay attention to features of their language behaviour. People in general may see the developing language skills of young children as 'cute' or 'sweet' or comical; but a linguist needs to observe with a more informed ear and eye, and think about how a child's language use is linked to stages of development.

Different kinds of research

In Activity 9.3, you used your own memory to explore (as far as you could) some features of language development. Some of the things you will have discovered will be things that you knew – though you didn't know you knew them!

But you can't rely on your current knowledge. You need to do further research – what the syllabus and exam questions call 'wider study'.

Your research into child language acquisition should cover three main areas:

- the main **stages** of early development of child language
- the different **functions** of children's language
- **theories** of how children acquire language, and **research studies** undertaken by theorists

Exam tip

It is obviously a good thing if you reach the final examination with secure knowledge and understanding of these three aspects of CLA, and with some detailed examples from research studies which you can use to support your discussion of the spoken language transcript which you are given. But you need to be flexible and to respond to the specific text on the question paper: you can't simply write all you know about child language acquisition.

Stages of early child language development

The following activity is a test of your current knowledge of concepts and theories in the field of child language acquisition. Answer as much of it as you can, on the basis of what you already know. Then leave the rest: you can keep coming back to the questions later on in the course, when you've added to your knowledge of the topics.

Activity 9.4

Copy and complete the table below. Use it to set out what you know about the stages of early development in child language acquisition.

Stages of early child language development	Features of language	Examples
Pre-linguistic	'vocal play' 'babbling'	
Holophrastic (one-word) stage: 9–18 months		*doggie* (for 'dog')
Telegraphic	Utterances are similar in style and construction to a telegram. 'Functional' items (words that build grammatical constructions) are absent but 'content' words (lexical as opposed to grammatical items) are present.	
Post-telegraphic		

Reflecting on Activity 9.4

Look back at the table you've compiled for the stages of early development in CLA. Look especially at the third column, where you should have listed examples of holophrastic, telegraphic and post-telegraphic speech. I will be very surprised if you and your friends don't use such language when you text each other or communicate online, or whenever you speak to each other. (You're more likely to notice it when it's on a screen.)

For example, telegraphic speech leaves out 'unnecessary' words – so it creates **elliptical** expressions and constructions.

Sometimes, for a joke, you probably do the opposite: you expand your normal, **casual** (elliptical) speech style into a more **formal register**, using grammatically complete constructions and more 'elevated' vocabulary.

Link

→ Go back to your recording and transcription at the start of this chapter in Activity 9.1. You are certain to find some elliptical and/or telegraphic constructions there. And if you can't, I'm willing to bet it's because you tidied them up when you wrote the transcribed version: the habit of checking and editing is almost automatic when we write or type.

→ Shifting the register of a text is a skill you will remember from AS Level – for example, Activity 2.17 on page 37.

Functions of children's language

As well as looking at the **stages** of CLA, we can also examine children's language development from a different angle.

The linguist Michael Halliday – in a very influential book called *Learning How to Mean: Explorations in the Development of Language* (1975) – identified seven **functions** that language has for children in their early years.

He argued that a child is motivated to develop language because it serves certain purposes or functions for her/him.

The first four functions help the child to *satisfy physical, emotional and social needs*:

- **instrumental** function: language used to fulfil a need – obtaining food, drink and comfort
- **regulatory** function: asking, commanding, requesting
- **interactional** function: language that develops social relationships
- **personal** function: language that expresses personal opinions.

The next three functions are to do with helping the child to *come to terms with her/his environment*:

- **representational** function: relaying or requesting information
- **heuristic** function: language that is used to explore the world and to learn and discover (e.g. by asking questions – especially the question *'Why?'*)
- **imaginative** function: using language to tell stories and create imaginary worlds.

Analysing a transcript of children's spoken language

You are now going to look at a transcript of language spoken by a child. You should be ready to cope with the twin demands that you will face in Section B of Paper 3:

- dealing with a transcript of spoken language
- applying what you've learned about child language acquisition.

Activity 9.5

On the next page is a transcription of part of an interaction between a three-year-old child (Tamsin) and her mother. They are playing a game in which Tamsin is putting her toy bear to bed. She has given the bear a smaller toy bear of its own.

Read the transcription twice.

- On your first read, just make sure you follow what's happening between the two speakers, and the toy bear!
- On your second read, make notes on:

  (a) features of Tamsin's language

  (b) ways in which Tamsin's mother speaks to her daughter.

Transcription key

(1)	= pause in seconds	underlined	= stressed sound/syllable(s)
(.)	= micropause	[italics]	= paralinguistic features
//	= speech overlap	UPPER CASE	= words spoken with increased volume

[Tamsin puts pillow under bear's head]

Tamsin: lift your head up

[Tamsin tucks bear in]

Tamsin: there (.) lay down (.) here's YOUR bear (.) there (.) now

Mother: cover his feet up too (.) his feet are sticking out (1) there you go (1) I know what he needs now

Tamsin: WHAT?

Mother: a story (.) better get him a storybook (.) over there (.) and read him a story

Tamsin: NO [but Tamsin gets a book]

Mother: come over here and sit [mother holds book]

Tamsin: i just don't know how to read it

Mother: here (.) what (.) what's the ducky saying to the birds?

Tamsin: quack quack

Mother: and what are the birdies saying to the duck? (1) what do birdies say?

[Tamsin shrugs]

Mother: what do birds say?

Tamsin: tweet tweet

Mother: yeah

Reflecting on Activity 9.5

Look at the notes you've made about features of Tamsin's language.

Then look back at Activities 9.3 and 9.4. What links can you see between:

- features of Tamsin's language and the stages of early child language development
- Halliday's functions of children's language?

Link

→ Later in this chapter – on page 176 – we will also consider more complex theories and concepts of child language acquisition, and add them to our analysis.

Looking at how adults speak to children

Look back at the second set of notes you made in Activity 9.5(b): the ways in which Tamsin's mother speaks to her daughter in the extract.

Like any other speaker, she uses a range of different **utterance types** which have different **functions.** The terminology for utterance types is the same as it would be for sentence types in written language:

- **declarative utterance/sentence** = a statement that communicates information
- **interrogative utterance/sentence** = a request for information
- **imperative utterance/sentence** = an instruction or command to do something
- **locutionary act** = obvious/surface function of an utterance
- **illocutionary act** = underlying intention of an utterance
- **perlocutionary act** = eventual effect of an utterance.

Activity 9.6

Copy and complete the table below – or design one of your own – to look at each of Tamsin's mother's turns in the interaction in Activity 9.5.

- Try to work out what **type of utterance** she has formulated in each case.
- Think about its **function** in this context: the obvious/surface intention, and the underlying/ulterior motive.

Turn	Utterance form or type	Obvious (locutionary) function	Underlying (illocutionary) intention
I know what he needs now	declarative	mother telling Tamsin that she knows what he wants/needs	getting Tamsin to ask a question
better get him a storybook (.) over there		telling Tamsin where the books are	
come over here and sit	imperative		
what do birdies say?	interrogative		

Reflecting on Activity 9.6

Whenever we speak, we **perform** a **speech act**. Most of the time, the person/people to whom we are speaking will understand the **illocutionary force** of that speech act. For example, if you're talking to one of your parents and you use the **interrogative** utterance *'Are you using the car tonight?'* you might seem to be simply asking a question (a request for information). But your parent understands that what you really mean is *'Can I borrow the car tonight?'*

Link

→ We will return to **politeness strategies** in Chapter 11 Language and the self.

Your apparently interrogative utterance is really a **politeness strategy**. It has the same **illocutionary force** as the **declarative** utterance *'I want to borrow the car tonight'* or the **imperative** utterance *'Lend me the car tonight!'*

But I'm sure you can see that, in this context, your best chance of being allowed to borrow the car is to use the most polite utterance type.

The likely outcome of using the imperative *'Lend me the car tonight!'* is that you will receive a **dis-preferred response** – for example, 'You must be joking!' – another utterance whose illocutionary force is not the same as its surface meaning.

This is becoming a complicated discussion. Surely it can have nothing to do with child language acquisition?

You might think not. But even at the age of three, Tamsin understands that when her mother asks *'what do birds say?'* for a second time, it would be a good idea to reply *'tweet tweet'* and not to [*shrug*] for a second time.

For now, it's important to recognise how sophisticated a child's linguistic understanding is at the age of three. Think about what you could do with language when you were three. You could, for example, play make-believe games in which you could pretend to be another person or an animal.

Link

→ Chapter 1 Introduction to AS Level English: Am I ready?, pages 5–7

Exam tip

Don't underestimate what young children can do with language. When you're dealing with a transcript of children's spoken language in the exam, don't go looking for 'mistakes' and 'correcting' them.

The acquisition of language "is doubtless the greatest intellectual feat any one of us is ever required to perform." (Leonard Bloomfield, 1933)

"WHAT'S THE BIG SURPRISE? ALL THE LATEST THEORIES OF LINGUISTICS SAY WE'RE BORN WITH THE INNATE CAPACITY FOR GENERATING SENTENCES."

At the end of this chapter on pages 177–8 you will find what one student wrote as an answer to the following exam-style question.

> Analyse ways in which Tamsin and her mother are using language in this conversation. In your answer, you should refer to specific details from the transcription, as well as to ideas and examples from your wider study of child language acquisition.

If you are already feeling confident that you have understood the stages of early child language development, the functions of children's language and a range of concepts and theories related to CLA, then now would be a good time to look at this response on page 177. If you're not so sure, carry on reading here.

Child-directed speech (CDS)

When a parent speaks to a child, there's often an underlying attempt to help the child develop her/his language skills. Tamsin's mother combines different utterance types in order to engage and interest her daughter and to encourage her to respond.

She gives Tamsin instructions, either as straightforward imperatives (*cover his feet up too/come over here and sit*) or indirect suggestions (*better get him a storybook (.) over there (.) and read him a story*).

Then she asks a series of **'closed' questions** – questions to which she already knows the answer. Tamsin responds immediately (and 'correctly') to the first of these questions (*what's the ducky saying to the birds?*) but not to the second (*and what are the birdies saying to the duck?*) so her mother has to prompt Tamsin to respond with the 'right' answer.

All of these features, together with other strategies and habits used by parents and other adults in speaking to children, are referred to as **child-directed speech.**

You don't have to be studying A-level English Language to notice that people speak to young children rather differently from the way they speak to their peers or to older children. The range of ways in which we vary our language when speaking to infants has been the subject of much research, and is sometimes called **caretaker/caregiver speech**, **parentese** or **motherese**.

Another term is **baby-talk** – but this has attracted some **pejorative** associations.

Some people think that using features of 'baby-talk' (such as exaggerated stress and intonation) is unhelpful in encouraging language development; others argue that infants respond well to exaggerated sounds.

Exam tip

When we look at evidence of how children speak, we also need to look at how adults (and other children) speak to them.

Link

→ Chapter 8 Language change: Semantic pejoration, page 136

Activity 9.7

As a developing linguistic researcher, you are perfectly capable of looking up research findings on this subject. But first you need to explore your own language use and the language use of those around you.

- Collect as many examples as you can of language used to speak to babies and young children.

- Copy and complete the table below – or devise your own – to apply your linguistic knowledge to the data you collect. A few ideas have been provided for you.

Strategy/technique	Example	Intention
speaking slowly		
speaking in short utterances		
employing lots of pauses		
	birdies moo-cows	
playing 'peek-a-boo'		
		teaching child new words

Reading academic articles and researching research

Several times already in the A-level section of this book you have been advised or invited or instructed to 'look up' or 'search' for some piece of information. As you know, you can easily look up <u>anything</u> on the internet! But you need to be careful about how far you trust some sources to be accurate.

You may feel confident about conducting your own research. However, it is still worth reading the guidance below, which takes you step-by-step through how to explore the academic research of other linguists.

STEP 1 Finding something reliable and worth reading

When you look up a linguistic topic or concept on the internet, you have to make some quick decisions about the results you get. For your research purposes at A Level, you need:

- a basic (but accurate) understanding of the concept
- some idea of the theory (and the theorist behind it)
- some idea of research studies into the concept.

Exam tip

For accurate knowledge in English Language and Linguistics, Wikipedia is usually very reliable, because other linguists keep checking and correcting entries. Similarly, websites belonging to the English Language and Linguistics faculties of universities can be very helpful; and some, like the University of Lancaster, have excellent pages where you can check and test your knowledge.

However, some sources are not so reliable. Websites claiming to offer you help with exams and essays can actually contain some very <u>un</u>helpful and wrong information. Be careful!

Learning to research ⟷ Researching to learn

Any simple internet search will throw up a range of sources:

1. primary sources – complex academic studies, possibly the original theory and/or research

2. secondary sources – summaries of original sources and studies, possibly from university departments of linguistics which provide reliable course materials for their students

3. general-interest sources – news and magazine articles, possibly reporting on new research studies but presenting them in a simplified way for the average reader.

You need to be able quickly to tell the difference: type 1 sources might be too detailed and complicated; type 3 will probably lack accuracy.

And there's one more problem: internet sources get moved or disappear altogether, so a source that you found really useful three months ago might be unobtainable tomorrow.

That's exactly what happened with the next text we were going to look at.

STEP 2 Finding the information you need from careful reading

I have completed Step 1 for you: I have found what I believe is a reliable source.

On the following page is a small section from a much longer report which was compiled for the Department for Education and Skills in 2003. This report belongs to a **genre** called a **literature review**, a very useful type of document which is often the first stage of a longer research process. The authors look at all the research literature which has been published on a certain topic, and then write a summary of it as a kind of platform on which to build their new research.

This particular literature review was part of a government project on the care and education of children from birth to the age of three. The section here reviews some of the most important theories of child language acquisition.

Now you need to do Step 2 yourself:

■ Read the first five paragraphs of the article and see if you think it's pitched at about the right level of difficulty: enough detail for you to feel you're learning something new, but not so much that you feel overwhelmed.

■ Step 3 will follow after you've finished your first reading. The CLA concepts which you might find most useful have been highlighted.

Exam tip

The authors follow the usual practice of referring to a researcher by name, followed by the date(s) of publication of the research – e.g. *Chomsky (1965; 1975)*.

This is a convention of writing academic articles, and it allows you to look up the original research for yourself. It's a simple convention, and one you can use to identify any author or research study you refer to.

The earliest theory about language development assumed that children acquire language through imitation. While research has shown that children who imitate the actions of those around them during their first year of life are generally those who also learn to talk more quickly, there is also evidence that imitation alone cannot explain how children become talkers. For example, in the English language, young children will say 'We goed to the shops' – they are very cleverly inventing the past tense of 'go' based on the rules they have absorbed.

Skinner, the Behaviourist theorist, suggested that children learn language through reinforcement. In other words, when a parent or carer shows enthusiasm for something a child tries to say, this should encourage the child to repeat the utterance. But again, even though reinforcement may help, this theory cannot account for children's inventions of language.

Some argue that it is not just hearing language around them that is important, it is the kind of language – whether it is used responsively (for example, following a baby's input, such as the baby making a noise or doing something). It is also clear that babies need to hear language to develop this themselves. This point is of great importance in relation to young children with impoverished language experience (see for example Ward 2000). The idea of motherese (Snow and Ferguson 1977; Trevarthen 1995) – using tuneful, accentuated speech to babies, and repeating their own language (often extended) back to young children – was put forward as a basic human requirement.

However, other research (see Bee 1989) indicates that while motherese can be used to explain how aspects of individual children's environments help or hinder them from talking, it does not explain the underlying causes of language acquisition. We can at least suggest that talking in motherese attracts and holds babies' attention and that it allows the infants themselves to take part in enjoyable turn-taking exchanges, the beginnings of conversations.

Chomsky (1965; 1975) proposed that babies are born with an inbuilt Language Acquisition Device (LAD). He suggested that language then simply emerges as the child matures. Slobin (Ferguson and Slobin 1973; Slobin 1985) continued this line of thought, proposing that just as newborns come into the world 'programmed' to look at interesting, especially moving, objects, so babies are pre-programmed to pay attention to language. Research has shown that treating babies as if they understand talk and involving them in conversational exchanges are essential experiences on which later abilities are founded.

STEP 3 Selecting the information you need and making it your own

Research into how students learn shows that with any information you have to go through a stage of 'making it your own'. The usual way to do this is by making notes in your own words. If you use some sort of visual aid as well, the information then becomes easier to remember. That's why this book uses so many lists and charts and tables: the visual part of your memory will help you to 'see' the information when you're in the exam.

The same process will work in your exam revision. If you create visual aids yourself, as part of your revision strategies, you will be able to 'see' them – and all the information they contain – when you're in the exam.

So give yourself 20 minutes to do that now. Re-read the five paragraphs on page 167 and record your understanding of the information in your words and in your format.

Activity 9.8

Below are the last three paragraphs of the extract from the literature review on CLA theories. There are some very complex ideas here about how the human brain works and how children develop various abilities. As you read them, try to think of examples from your own experience of the processes that are being explored here.

Piaget argued that language is an example of symbolic behaviour, and no different from other learning. One of his colleagues, Hermine Sinclair (1971), proposed that a child's ability to nest a set of Russian dolls uses the same cognitive process as a child needs for understanding how sentences are embedded in one another. Nelson (1985) and others, using this **cognitive processing** explanation, think language is an extension of the child's existing capacity for making meaning. This seems to fit with the fact that children will generally begin to engage in **pretend play** at about the same time as their first words are expressed, indicating that they are using symbols in the form of words and also symbolic pretend objects (for example using a block as a pretend cake).

Following on from Vygotsky's social learning tradition, Bruner (1983) stressed the importance of opportunities for babies and children to interact with, and observe interactions between, others. As we explained above, this idea is supported by research showing that mothers who behave as if their babies and young children understand language right from the start, make eye contact with them and engage in dialogue, responding to their babies' reactions (kicking, waving arms, smiling, etc) are laying the foundations of conversation.

Karmiloff and Karmiloff-Smith (2001) argue that none of these theories about language is, on its own, adequate in explaining language development and learning in the first three years of life, and that we need to take account of each of them for their ability to explain part of the story.

Source: *Birth to Three Matters: A Review of the Literature* (Department for Education and Skills)

Reflecting on Activity 9.8

Did you find those last three paragraphs difficult? It would be very surprising if you didn't. But perhaps if you are studying Human Biology or Psychology or Child Development as well as English Language, you might have come across these ideas before.

You can probably see how the ideas of the different theorists connect with each other:

Imitation → Reinforcement ← Motherese → Turn-taking

The child interacts with a parent or other adult or older sibling, and hears examples of motherese (or child-directed speech). The child then imitates some of these words and phrases, and receives positive reinforcement (*that's it! well done!*) from the older speaker. **Turn-taking** begins to emerge as the child and adult respond to each other.

The adults and older siblings in the child's environment act as a **language acquisition support system** (LASS).

Language acquisition device → Pretend play ← Cognitive processing

As the child learns about the world from playing, concepts such as size and shape and time – which you will recognise as **abstract nouns** – begin to make sense.

Piaget suggested that language emerges at the same time as understanding. For example, a child playing a shopping game might be able to put into words the idea that the shopping bag had become heavy; a child playing with a shape-sorting toy might be able to identify colours or shapes, and eventually will recognise both. (*It's that one! → Oh, it's the big square yellow one!*)

How awake are you? Did you notice that in the example above the child is also learning about the right order in which to put adjectives? Shape (*square*) comes before colour (*yellow*), but size (*big*) comes before all of them. You might like to try this out on classmates and family members, to see if there's a convention or rule about the order in which we put different kinds of adjectives in English.

Activity 9.9

Like almost all theories, ideas about child language acquisition (CLA) make better sense when we look at specific examples. So here is another transcription of a spoken interaction between a child and a parent.

- Read through the transcript, paying attention to how the mother helps her child to communicate as well as to play. As you did last time, look especially at how she uses different utterance types.
- Make notes as you go. Use some of your new CLA knowledge!

On the next page is a transcription of an interaction between Amit, a three-year-old boy, and his mother. They have been playing with his toy train set.

Exam tip

Don't worry! Even in an exam, you can't expect to understand every idea in every text you meet. The trick is to make the most of what you *do* understand, and to apply your linguistic skills and knowledge in an intelligent way to the parts you *don't* understand.

And as we're not in an exam now, you will have the chance to come back to all of these ideas and the theorists who are associated with them.

Exam tip

The transcription key and the wording of the introductions and instructions are very similar to what you will be given in your Paper 3 exam. You should now be familiar with these. By the time you get to the exam, responding to the question-wording should be almost automatic for you. Even so, read the question carefully each time and be certain that you know exactly what you are being asked to do.

Transcription key

(1) = pause in seconds   [*italics*]   = paralinguistic features

(.) = micropause   UPPER CASE = words spoken with increased volume

// = speech overlap

Mother:	is that a piece of the bridge as well?
Amit:	yeah (.) don't matter
Mother:	shall we put that one on (.) yeah?
	//
Amit:	that
Mother:	there we go (.) there
Amit:	here.
Mother:	where're you gonna put the bridge (.) the tunnel? (1) that's it (1) we'll have to try and get you some more of these pieces (.) won't we (.) to match this train? (1) see if auntie sue can get you some for your birthday
	//
Amit:	yeah
Mother:	what would you like? (1) what else do they do?
	//
Amit:	birthday (.) got this
Mother:	got that
Amit:	who put the heater on?
Mother:	I did (.) earlier (1) it was cold
Amit:	hot
Mother:	mm hmm?
Amit:	these ones (1) these ones like (1) these ones are (1) these ones are
Mother:	what?
Amit:	these ones are a car ones
Mother:	there? (1) shall we put them there?
Amit:	yeah (1) leave the tunnel up
Mother:	leave it up a bit?
Amit:	yeah (1) LOOK (1) both trains coming (.) can put it that way
Mother:	okay
Amit:	done that (.) hother one?
Mother:	other one? (1) behind you (.) there it is (1) put that one like that (1) yes .

Amit:	got no trains
Mother:	what darling?
Amit:	got no trains (.) that one pushing that one is pushing that bit (.) cause that bit (1) got no trains
Mother:	you have got lots of trains (.) haven't you?
Amit:	I go get some more

Reflecting on Activity 9.9

You may have noticed that you were not given a table or chart for Activity 9.9, nor even invited to devise one of your own.

So here is a list of features of language from the interaction between Amit and his mother.

- ✓ There is regular **turn-taking** – and Amit's turns are mostly shorter.
- ✓ Mother's **mean length of utterance** (MLU) is greater.
- ✓ Mother asks Amit a range of questions (**interrogatives**).
- ✓ Some of these are **closed** questions inviting just a yes/no answer (*'is that a piece of the bridge as well?'*).
- ✓ Others are suggestions or prompts to encourage Amit to respond – for example the **tag question** *'won't we?'*
- ✓ One question is quite open (*'what would you like?'*) and is followed almost immediately by another open question (*'what else do they do?'*) perhaps because his mother thinks Amit needs more prompting.
- ✓ Mother sets the **agenda**: she is the **topic manager**, directing the conversation in ways which will help Amit to enjoy his playing time and help him to develop his language and his thinking.
- ✓ At one point, Amit introduces a new topic – *'who put the heater on?'* – and shows he understands the concept of heat and cold.
- ✓ Amit's next utterance shows him struggling to convey a new idea: *'these ones (1) these ones like (1) these ones are (1) these ones are … '*
- ✓ And when his mother prompts him with *'what?'* his reply is not in Standard grammatical English (*'these ones are a car ones'*).
- ✓ But his mother does not correct him – perhaps she judges that it will be too difficult for him to learn a more grammatically complex way of saying what he means here.
- ✓ Mother does correct Amit when he adds an unnecessary **initial aspirate** (an *h-*) to the beginning of a word (*'hother'*)
- ✓ But she does it tactfully by simply repeating the correct pronunciation *'other'*, thus **modelling** the correct form of the word and acting as his **language acquisition support system**.
- ✓ There are examples of **deixis** – simple words like *this* and *that* which refer to objects or actions in their immediate environment.
- ✓ When his mother asks *'shall we put them there?'*, Amit can see what *'them'* are and where *'there'* is.
- ✓ These are examples of **context-dependent language**: if you are physically present in the situation, you can understand their meaning.

What no table?

Exam tip

In the exam, you can do most of your note making and possibly some of your essay planning on the question paper itself.

You should remember that in most situations you won't be handing in your question paper to be marked – though more and more often the question-paper is being combined with the answer booklet.

But don't forget the simple table. Or, simplest of all, the two-column list. All exam essays need a planning stage, and a list is the handiest planning device ever invented.

Activity 9.10

Up to this point, key terms and their definitions have been provided for you. This time you're going to create your own.

- Create a new document – on screen or on paper.

- Look through the lists of points in *Reflecting on Activity 9.9*.

- Each time you come across a piece of terminology, write it down. This should be easy: they are mostly highlighted anyway.

- You can include terms which occurred in earlier key terms lists in the book. It doesn't matter if you've got them more than once: research on learning suggests that the more often you 'rehearse' something, the more firmly it lodges in your memory.

- Try to organise your list into groups or categories. For example, some of your key terms will be the names of simple features of language (like tag questions or deixis) while some will be labels for complicated processes like imitation and reinforcement.

- Finally, when you have your categories sorted out, compile your own glossary of key terms, each with a definition in language you can understand.

Exam tip

This will be a fantastic revision aid for you. And you will be the envy of all your friends!

Theories and theorists need examples

It's tempting just to learn a list of the names of theories and theorists. Making a reference in an exam essay to '*Skinner's work on operant conditioning*' might seem like the kind of thing that would earn you extra marks.

But examiners are not stupid: they can always tell when something has been memorised but not understood.

Theories are important and useful when you can use them, when they shine a light on something and make it easier to understand. So you need to get used to providing at least one good example to back up every reference you make to a theory or a concept. The interaction between Amit and his mother is a rich source of examples.

Activity 9.11

- Look back at the table you created in Activity 9.7. If you left any gaps, you could fill them now with examples from the interaction between Amit and his mother.

- Look also at the following table of theorists and their theories/concepts. Copy and add to it. In the course of your research, you may find other theorists with interesting ideas and concepts related to CLA. In all cases try to add <u>examples</u> from your own knowledge and/or from the interaction between Amit and his mother.

Theorist/theory	Concept – and how it works	Examples
B. F. Skinner 'operant conditioning'	• behaviourism • imitation and reinforcement (with repetition)	Child: I falled down the step. Adult: You fell down the step, did you? Child: Yes, I fell down the step.
Piaget 'cognitive development'	• stages of development • idea that language development depends on psychological maturity	abstract ideas, e.g. times and future occasions, like birthdays
Chomsky 'language acquisition device'	• innate ability to acquire language • grammatical/syntactic structures are innate: child only has to learn vocabulary	Errors arise from **over-generalising** a rule, e.g. the rule that plurals are formed with -s and past tenses are formed with -ed, so child says '*I goed to see the sheeps*'.
Vygotsky 'zone of proximal development'	• actual (unaided) developmental stage *as opposed to* • potential (assisted) developmental stage	Teachers and parents provide help for children to progress beyond their current stage, e.g. by modelling a structure.
Bruner 'language acquisition support system' (LASS)	• adults provide 'scaffolding'	The 'peek-a-boo' game is an early introduction to conversational turn-taking.

Reinforcement and revision

For this section, you need a human resource.

Find a classmate, friend or family member who is prepared to help you revise the main elements of knowledge about child language acquisition covered in this chapter. The neatest solution would be a reciprocal arrangement where you and a classmate take it in turns to test each other's knowledge and understanding.

Activity 9.12

Main stages of early child language development

As you test each other on your knowledge of these stages, see if you can both come up with some new examples.

1. **Pre-linguistic**. Parents sometimes infer/imagine that the child is trying to communicate a particular meaning. Coo-ing and babbling sounds.

2. **Holophrastic**. Single words – often concrete nouns – used to stand for whole phrases. 'Drink!' = 'I would like a drink' OR 'I have spilled my drink' OR ...

3. **Telegraphic**. Elliptical utterances: *function* words (*grammatical items*) left out, *content* words (*lexical items*) used. 'Want drink juice' = 'I want to drink my juice' OR 'Do you want me to drink my juice?' OR ...

4. **Post-telegraphic**. Beginning to use utterances with more than one clause. Words which were missing in the telegraphic stage are now present: determiners, auxiliary verbs, personal possessive pronouns.

Activity 9.13

Halliday's functions of children's language

Read the following list of definitions of functions of language, then match each one to the correct terminology (listed below the definitions) as used by Halliday:

(a) Language used to fulfil a basic need – food, drink, comfort.

(b) Language used to influence the behaviour of others – persuading/commanding/requesting.

(c) Language used to help social interaction.

(d) Language used to express identity and personal preferences.

(e) Language concerned with relaying or requesting information.

(f) Language used to explore the environment (e.g. the child keeps up a 'running commentary' on what she/he is doing during play).

(g) Language used to explore the world of the imagination.

Halliday's functions:

interactional   *representational*   *regulatory*   *heuristic*

personal   *imaginative*   *instrumental*

Exam tip

As you know, it's useful to know the terminology, but much more important to understand the idea or concept and to be able to explain it with examples. Don't just drop the terminology into an exam essay and then think you've done all you need to do.

Activity 9.14

Applying Halliday's functions to transcript evidence of children's talk

If you read carefully – and you should always read carefully! – you should be able to *identify* examples of each of Halliday's functions.

But being able to find, identify and 'label' features of language is only ever the start of useful linguistic analysis. One danger with applying Halliday's 'framework' is that (because it is quite complicated) you may feel you have done your work when you finish what I'm calling the 'labelling' stage.

This is a risk with any theory or framework that you use. If you work through a text carefully, making a catalogue of features, you still haven't discussed the effect that they have on meaning.

With your revision partner, take another look at the first 15 lines of the interaction between Amit and his mother in Activity 9.9. Think about how you might apply knowledge of Halliday's functions to the dynamics of their conversation. Try to avoid the danger outlined above.

Now look at the commentary below:

In answer to his mother's first question – *'is that a piece of the bridge as well?'* – Amit gives first of all a **minimal response** (*'yeah'*) but then goes on to employ the **personal** function to express an opinion (*'don't matter'*). The effect is that his mother can tell he understands her question but is prepared to go on with the game.

Amit offers another minimal response to his mother's next long utterance – *'where're you gonna put the bridge (.) … see if auntie sue can get you some for your birthday'.* Then he follows it up by mentioning *birthday*, combining the **interactional**, **personal** and **representational** functions. He is thus engaging with his mother's topic on a **personal** level by **interacting** with her in terms of how children receive presents for their birthday, all the time building their relationship and **representing** his understanding of the world.

Amit's sudden **topic-shift** – *'who put the heater on?'* – shows signs of the **heuristic** and **regulatory** functions, because his response to his mother's explanation (*'it was cold'*) is the holophrastic utterance *'hot'*, which may imply a request that the heater be turned off again.

The aim in this commentary was to use knowledge of Halliday's functions to reach a deeper understanding of the **dynamics of interaction** between mother and child.

You may think that this approach – some linguists and teachers might call it a 'framework' – has only had limited success here. Other approaches, concepts and theories might have been more fruitful.

For example, you might analyse the lengths and types of utterance (e.g. one-word responses and interrogatives).

Or you might consider the **pragmatics** – the meanings which are implied. When Amit's mother explains that it was she who put the heater on, she seems to think it's necessary to defend herself by adding (after a pause) *'earlier'*, and then (after a longer pause) a justification: *'it was cold'*.

Activity 9.15

The following table contains some of the best-known theories and concepts of child language acquisition. Copy the table, and give yourself 20 minutes to complete it without looking back at Activities 9.8 to 9.11.

For each theory/concept, give a brief explanation in your own words. You should use linguistic terminology which you know and understand.

Theory/concept	Explanation	Theorist, and any significant research findings
behaviourism/ 'operant conditioning' (reinforcement and imitation)		B. F. Skinner
social interactionist	Parents/caregivers act as a language acquisition support system (LASS).	Jerome Bruner
nativist (innate ability)	Children have an innate language acquisition device (LAD).	Piaget Vygotsky 'zone of proximal development'
cognitive development		
child-directed speech		

Conclusion

Child language acquisition is an interesting and complicated subject. Researchers disagree about the processes involved, and new studies are going on all the time. If you do an internet search for current research into CLA, you are quite likely to find work by neuroscientists and computer scientists as well as linguists.

You now have a solid basis from which to develop your own knowledge, and you will revisit some of these ideas when you come to work on Section B of Paper 4: Language and the self.

In this chapter you have:

- looked at ways of representing spoken language in a written form
- considered the main stages of children's early development in language
- explored some of the functions of children's language
- analysed transcripts of children's spoken language
- developed your understanding of concepts, theories and research studies in child language acquisition (CLA)
- undertaken some revision and reinforcement exercises.

Student response

Below is what one student wrote as an answer to the exam-style question based on the transcription on page 161. Here is a reminder of the question:

> Analyse ways in which Tamsin and her mother are using language in this conversation. In your answer, you should refer to specific details from the transcription, as well as to ideas and examples from your wider study of child language acquisition.

Note: Key terms used are highlighted.

> Tamsin is playing with her toy bear. Her imaginative play has developed to a point where she can behave towards her toy (*here's YOUR bear*) in the way that her mother or another care-giver might play with her. She imitates the kind of language she has heard being used by her mother as she tucks her bear into its bed: *there* (.) *lay down*

There are signs of B. F. Skinner's ideas about imitation and reinforcement in Tamsin's mother's language too. She uses a range of utterance types to communicate with her 3-year-old daughter. Some of these are directives (*over there*) or imperatives (*come over here and sit*) but not all of them result in co-operation from Tamsin. At one point she replies to her mother's suggestion that she should read her bear a story with a dis-preferred response (*NO*) though she does actually follow the instruction and [*gets a book*].

Tamsin's mother uses interrogative utterances to get her daughter's attention and to engage her in the activity of sharing a book. When she asks '*what's the ducky saying to the birds?*' it's not a request for information. The mother is reinforcing the child's knowledge of animal sounds. It's much more sensible to help a 3-year-old to learn how to classify animals by the sound they make than by trying to teach her that *duck* is the common name for a large number of species in the waterfowl family which also includes swans and geese! Knowledge like that might be interesting when Tamsin is 10 or 12.

It's interesting to see that the mother uses 'baby-talk' (or 'motherese'/'parentese') versions of duck (*ducky*) and birds (*birdies*) as well as the standard version of each word. Some adults couple the sound the animal makes with the standard name for the animal when talking to children, saying *moo-cow* or *baa-lamb*.

We can use the term diminutive for the process where a standard word is altered, usually by adding an /i/ sound at the end, and with a variety of spellings: horse to *horsey*, dog to *doggy*, cat to *kitty*. Although the effect is to connote something smaller (diminutive) the word actually becomes longer. Some parents and some linguists might argue that using this particular form of child-directed speech actually slows down or damages the language development of young children, and insist on using the standard form. But Tamsin's mother uses both forms here, and it's clear that Tamsin understands. She also uses another feature of child-directed speech: she puts emphatic stress on speech-sounds and syllables (*a story*) which she might not stress if she were talking to an adult or an older child. There is some research evidence to suggest that parents do this in other languages too when talking to very young children.

English in the world

This chapter will:

→ look at the historical development of English as a global language

→ consider the changing role and status of the English language in the world

→ explore different varieties of English – standard and non-standard – including the varieties used by first-language users outside the UK

→ examine issues and problems which result from the influence of English as a global language

→ end by providing some revision and reinforcement exercises.

A reminder

In Section A of Paper 4, you will be given approximately 400–500 words of text on the topic of 'English in the world'. There will be one question, and you will be expected to:

- write an essay discussing the most important issues the text(s) raise(s) in relation to a particular aspect of the topic

- refer to specific details from the text(s) and relate points to ideas and examples from your wider study of the topic.

This is a pattern you're used to: it's the same pattern for all four of the Paper 3 and Paper 4 topics.

You're soon going to practise the skills needed for the first stage of answering an exam question on English in the world.

But first, some essential terminology:

lingua franca

a common language which can be used by different groups whose native (first) languages are different

global language

a language spoken across different countries who:

1. use it as their <u>first</u> language or mother-tongue OR

2. have adopted it as their <u>official</u> (second) language OR

3. teach it as their <u>foreign</u> language of choice in schools.

mutual intelligibility

people being able to understand each other despite having different native (first) languages

language contact

the changes that happen when speakers of different languages (or different dialects of the same language) interact with one another, leading to a transfer of linguistic features

linguistic imperialism

imposing a dominant language on native speakers of another language

English in the world: the global language?

The following activity features part of an article written by David Graddol in 2005 for the Open University about English as a global language.

> ### Activity 10.1
>
> Read the text carefully, then:
>
> - copy and complete the table at the top of the following page to make a list of the possible advantages and disadvantages of having a language which can act as a **lingua franca**
> - add the ideas which are put forward in the text about **English as a global language** – it might not be obvious whether they are advantages or disadvantages.

The development of English as a global language is one of the most remarkable phenomena of the late 20th and early 21st centuries.

For the first time in the history of human society, a single language has become sufficiently universal that it can be used as a global lingua franca for communication between speakers of many languages.

The history of English has traditionally been divided into three main phases: Old English (450–1100 AD), Middle English (1100–circa 1600 AD) and Modern English (since 1600). But it seems that Global English represents a new and fourth phase in which its main use around the world is between non-native speakers – a phase of its history which has only just begun and in which both the status and linguistic form of the language are rapidly developing.

In the next 10–15 years we may witness a situation that has been much discussed since the nineteenth century, in which the majority of the world's population can speak English.

Although Global English is largely a product of economic globalisation and very recent developments in communications technology (and indeed has helped accelerate both), the wider roots of English as a world language lie much further in the past.

Some point to the first English colonies in Wales and Ireland in the 12th century, or to the late 17th century when English-speaking settlements were established in North America and the slave trade brought cheap labour from Africa. But it was largely the British colonial expansion in the 19th century which helped establish the large communities in which English now serves as a second language – in West and East Africa, South and South-East Asia.

New varieties of English – often referred to as New Englishes – quickly emerged from contact with local languages. Indeed, by the end of the nineteenth century there was concern that these New Englishes were diverging so much from native-speaker varieties that English would become a group of mutually unintelligible languages – in the same way as Spanish, French and Italian evolved from Latin.

In other words, World English might have been no more than a celebration of diversity, like World Music, rather than the global lingua franca which it has also become.

www.open.edu/openlearn/history-the-arts/culture/english-language/global-english

Effects of English becoming a global language		
Advantages	**Neutral**	**Disadvantages**
mutual intelligibility from having a **lingua franca**	**borrowing** of lexical items and syntactic structures from **local** language into **dominant** language	damage to local language(s) – even **language death**
culture (e.g. film and popular music) becomes more 'portable'	possibility that soon the majority of the world's population may speak and/or understand English	loss of cultural variety
	helps to accelerate economic globalisation and developments in communications technology	
	new **varieties** of English ('New Englishes') emerge from **contact** with local languages	

Reflecting on Activity 10.1

There are many articles, research papers and indeed books on the subject of English as a global language or 'Global English'. Sometimes the terminology varies – the term used may be 'World English' or 'International English' – and each of these terms may carry **connotations** with it. These **associations** may be **ameliorative**, **pejorative** or **neutral**.

For the purposes of the exam, as you know, the topic is called **English in the world**. As a developing linguist, you may have noticed that this is rather a clever formulation.

■ English is 'qualified' (defined) with the **adverb phrase** *in the world* which seems to tell us a fact in a neutral way – English is out there in the world.

■ English is thus <u>not</u> qualified by an **adjective** – e.g. Global or International – and therefore the title avoids **connotations** and **cultural baggage**.

As well as a variety of **terminology**, there is a range of **attitudes** in the many texts written (and spoken) about English in the world.

Did you notice that the text you studied in Activity 10.1 is fairly **neutral** in tone? Would you say it was also **balanced** in **content**? And how far can you explain its tone, style and content by looking at the **context** in which it was produced?

An example of the neutral/balanced stance is that '*the British colonial expansion in the 19th century*' is mentioned, but no opinion is expressed or implied about its effects.

As we explore many aspects of English in the world in the rest of this chapter, we will find many opinions, both expressed and implied, about the effects of the spread of English.

Borrowing

Linguists use the term **borrowing** to mean the process during **language contact** by which a word from one language is adapted for use in another language. The word that is borrowed is called a **loanword**.

We could take a cynical view of the lending/borrowing process, and point out that the essence of the transaction is that the borrower eventually gives back to the lender what she/he has borrowed. Both verbs usually have positive connotations.

Link

→ If you've forgotten the meaning of these terms, look back at Chapter 8 Language change: Semantic change, pages 135–6

People who are critical of the spread of the English language – and Western customs and attitudes – sometimes express concern and anger about the ways in which Britain and America (in particular) have not just **borrowed** words (and traditions and ideas) but **appropriated** them.

Such critics refer to the concept of **cultural appropriation** – a process in which members of the dominant culture adopt elements of a minority culture. You can easily see how this happened throughout times when European nations were colonising less developed nations, especially in Africa and Asia.

The associated concept of **linguistic imperialism** was formulated by the British linguist Robert Phillipson. In his book of 1992 he writes:

> 'The dominance of English is asserted and maintained by the establishment and continuous reconstitution of structural and cultural inequalities between English and other languages.'

Other writers have used the metaphor of a Trojan Horse to describe the way that English may be welcomed initially in a country but then later causes concern as it dominates the 'indigenous' (native) language(s) and cultures.

We are now going to explore some examples of borrowing and loanwords.

Loanwords you use every day

As with some other activities, your research resource for Activity 10.2 is your own memory.

> **Activity 10.2**
>
> - If your first language is not English, make a list of words from your first language that are used in modern English.
>
> - Make a second list of words from other languages which you are aware of as being used in English. When you've used all the examples you know of, ask friends and family for their ideas.
>
> - Now you can do an internet search for further examples.

> **Reflecting on Activity 10.2**
>
> Look at the columns and/or lists you've compiled. You have another mini corpus of linguistic data. What are you going to do with it?
>
> You could further organise your data according to:
>
> - word–classes – I would guess that most of the words will be nouns, and more concrete nouns than abstract nouns
>
> - origin – you'll probably find that those words which were borrowed a hundred or more years ago were from countries and cultures which were part of the British Empire
>
> - mode of transmission (the route the word travelled from its origin into English usage) – you'll probably find that those words which were borrowed more recently have been communicated by computer technology.
>
> The following table offers three columns to correspond with these three categories: word-class; origin; mode of transmission. You can use the fourth column to record anything that occurs to you as linguistically interesting. Copy and complete the table with as many of your own examples as you can.

If you don't know what the Trojan Horse was, look it up! You can also look up articles on **linguistic imperialism** and **cultural appropriation**, but you may find they are written at a level suitable for students doing courses at university rather than A Level.

Loanwords and their sources			
Word and word–class	Meaning, origin and etymology	Mode of transmission	Anything else of interest
catamaran concrete noun	Tamil word *Kattumaram* which means 'logs tied together'	English adventurer William Dampier in his *A New Voyage Round the World* (1697)	– often abbreviated to *cat* – looks as if its origin would be Ancient Greek (κᾰτᾰ), with the prefix *cata-* being quite common

By analysing your data, you'll be able to see how far my predictions are supported (or not) by the evidence.

The second and third of my predictions refer to two more language issues closely connected with the global spread of English:

- cultural imperialism – the way in which a more powerful civilisation imposes its values (including language) on a less powerful civilisation
- electronic/computer technology – the effects of the internet and mobile communications technology on the development of the English language.

We've already seen how the first of these arouses strong feelings. And we'll see in the following pages some of the ways in which each of those factors has produced variation and change in the English language.

Before we move on to look at some aspects of the historical development of English as a global language, read what the Language Contact Working Group at the University of Manchester has to say about borrowing. (And for once you only need to read – though you might want to make a few notes.)

> While speaking in our own language, sometimes we use words which originally derive from other languages. These words are called "Borrowings". Another term for borrowing is "Loanword". Words can be borrowed because a language needs to designate new objects, products, or concepts; an example are the English words for "coffee" (originally from Arabic *qahwe*) and for "tea" (originally Chinese *cha*). Sometimes words are borrowed to introduce finer distinctions of meaning which are not available in native words [...] Smaller languages tend to borrow many words from more dominant, majority languages. This is because of the role that "major" languages have in technology, media, and government institutions, and in public life in general.
>
> Content words – words representing certain concepts, or objects, or products – are usually borrowed most easily and most frequently. But borrowing can also affect the grammar of a language. Words such as *and* or *but* are often borrowed by smaller languages in contact with majority languages. These are what we call "Function words"; you cannot for instance draw a picture of what they represent, and yet they play an essential role in the structure of sentences and especially when we combine sentences into conversations.
>
> Language Contact Working Group, University of Manchester

Historical development of English as a global language

The next text is an extract from a *Memorandum on (Indian) Education*, written by the British historian and politician Thomas Babington Macaulay (1800–1859).

He was writing just before the Council of India introduced the English Education Act (1835). You can look up the background if you want to – but read the text first, and see what you can **infer** about the attitudes of the writer.

Exam tip

You should have accumulated many examples of loanwords from your own experience in doing Activity 10.2 and completing the table following the Reflection. Memorise these examples: they are exactly the kind you will need in the exam.

Exam tip

Don't forget or neglect your AS Level reading skills. So far at A Level the texts you've dealt with (for language change and child language acquisition in Paper 3) have provided you with language data rather than linguistic attitudes; but in this Paper 4 topic you'll need your ability to detect implied meaning and explore how a writer's beliefs shape argument.

Look at Macaulay's use in that *Memorandum* of a series of sentences beginning '*It is …*'. What is the effect of this succession of declarative sentences? What is '*It*'?

And what about the first person plural pronouns? Who exactly are '*we*'?

In India, English is the language spoken by the ruling class. It is spoken by the higher class of natives at the seats of Government. It is likely to become the language of commerce throughout the seas of the East. It is the language of two great European communities which are rising, the one in the south of Africa, the other in Australia, —communities which are every year becoming more important and more closely connected with our Indian empire. Whether we look at the intrinsic value of our literature, or at the particular situation of this country, we shall see the strongest reason to think that, of all foreign tongues, the English tongue is that which would be the most useful to our native subjects.

Other Englishes

Fifty years before Lord Macaulay was advising the Governor-General of British India to direct financial support to schools that taught a Western curriculum with English as the teaching language, the use of English had already become a topic of interest in America.

Activity 10.3

Read the following texts, all written after the American Declaration of Independence from Britain (1776). As you read, identify and make notes on:

- the context in which the text was created
- linguistic issues and concepts related to the status of the English language
- attitudes to the use of English.

Text A and Text B are written by John Adams, taken from *The Adams Papers*, Papers of John Adams, vol. 10, *July 1780–December 1780*, ed. Gregg L. Lint and Richard Alan Ryerson. Cambridge, MA: Harvard University Press, 1996, pp. 127–130.

Text A is an extract from *A Letter to the President of Congress* written by Adams in 1780. Adams later became the second President of the United States (1797–1801) but during the 1780s he travelled as an ambassador from Congress (the American government) to France, the Dutch Republic and Great Britain.

Here he is recommending that Congress should create an Academy to protect the use of the English language in the same way that the *Académie française* protects the French language.

Text A

Most of the nations of Europe have thought it necessary to establish by public authority institutions for fixing and improving their proper languages. I need not mention the academies in France, Spain, and Italy, their learned labors, nor their great success. But it is very remarkable, that although many learned and ingenious men in England have from age to age projected similar institutions for correcting and improving the English tongue, yet the government have never found time to interpose in any manner; so that to this day there is no grammar nor dictionary extant of the English language which has the least public authority; and it is only very lately, that a tolerable dictionary has been published, even by a private person, and there is not yet a passable grammar enterprised by any individual.

The honor of forming the first public institution for refining, correcting, improving, and ascertaining the English language, I hope is reserved for Congress; they have every motive that can possibly influence a public assembly to undertake it. It will have a happy effect upon the union of the States to have a public standard for all persons in every part of the continent to appeal to, both for the signification and pronunciation of the language. The constitutions of all the States in the Union are so democratical that eloquence will become the instrument for recommending men to their fellow-citizens, and the principal means of advancement through the various ranks and offices of society.

In the last century, Latin was the universal language of Europe. Correspondence among the learned, and indeed among merchants and men of business, and the conversation of strangers and travellers, was generally carried on in that dead language. In the present century, Latin has been generally laid aside, and French has been substituted in its place, but has not yet become universally established, and, according to present appearances, it is not probable that it will. English is destined to be the next – and, in succeeding centuries, more generally the language of the world than Latin was in the last or French is in the present age. The reason of this is obvious, because the increasing population in America, and their universal connection and correspondence with all nations will, aided by the influence of England in the world, whether great or small, force their language into general use, in spite of all the obstacles that may be thrown in their way, if any such there should be.

It is not necessary to enlarge further, to show the motives which the people of America have to turn their thoughts early to this subject; they will naturally occur to Congress in a much greater detail than I have time to hint at. I would therefore submit to the consideration of Congress the expediency and policy of erecting by their authority a society under the name of *"the American Academy for refining, improving, and ascertaining the English Language."*

Exam tip

You're reading these texts for what they tell you about the historical development of the English language in America. In other words, you're increasing your knowledge. But don't forget to practise your A Level skills too:

- noticing aspects of language change

- using your reading skills of inference.

Text B is an extract from another letter written by John Adams in 1780, just a few weeks after the letter in Text A. Here he is writing about the difficulties of carrying out his diplomatic mission to the Dutch Republic without a common language.

Text B

This business must be conducted with so much secrecy and caution, and I meet so many difficulties for want of the language, the gentlemen I have to do with not understanding English and not being very familiar with French, that it goes on slower than I could wish. Commodore Gillon, by his knowledge of Dutch and general acquaintance here has been so useful to me as he has been friendly. I never saw the national benefit of a polished language generally read and spoken in so strong a light as since I have been here. The Dutch language is understood by nobody but themselves; the consequence of which has been, that this nation is not known with as profound learning and ingenuity as any people in Europe possess. They have been overlooked because they were situated among others more numerous and powerful than they.

I hope that Congress will profit by their example, by doing what they have lost so much reputation and advantage by neglecting; I mean by doing everything in their power to make the language they speak respectable throughout the world. Separated as we are from the British dominion, we have not made war against the English language any more than against the old English character. An academy instituted by the authority of Congress for correcting, improving, and fixing the English language would strike all the world with admiration and Great Britain with envy. The labors of such a society would unite all America in the same language, for thirty millions of Americans to speak to all nations of the earth by the middle of the nineteenth century.

Text C

These are three extracts from the writings (1781) of John Witherspoon, when he was President of Princeton University in America.

Witherspoon was originally from Scotland, and had suffered criticism from English writers for his use of 'Scotticisms' – terms that someone from Scotland might use when writing or speaking in English. This experience led him to be interested in 'Americanisms'.

1.   The first class I call *Americanisms*, by which I understand an use of phrases or terms, or a construction of sentences, even among persons of rank and education, different from the use of the same terms or phrases, or the construction of similar sentences in Great-Britain. It does not follow, from a man's using these, that he is ignorant, or his discourse upon the whole inelegant; nay, it does not follow in every case, that the terms or phrases used are worse in themselves, but merely that they are of American and not of English growth.

   The word *Americanism*, which I have coined for the purpose, is exactly similar in its formation and signification to the word *Scotticism*. By the word *Scotticism* is understood any term or phrase, and indeed any thing either in construction, pronunciation or accentuation, that is peculiar to North-Britain. There are many instances in which the Scotch way is as good, and some in which every person who has the least taste as to the propriety or purity of a language in general, must confess that it is better than that of England, yet speakers and writers must conform to custom.

2.   I have heard in this country, in the senate, at the Bar, and from the pulpit, and see daily in dissertations from the press, errors in grammar, improprieties and vulgarisms, which hardly any person of the same class in point of rank and literature would have fallen into in Great Britain.

3.   The vulgar in America speak much better than the vulgar in Great-Britain, for a very obvious reason, viz. that being much more unsettled, and moving frequently from place to place, they are not so liable to local peculiarities either in accent or phraseology. There is a greater difference in dialect between one <u>county</u> and another in Britain, than there is between one <u>state</u> and another in America.

Text D

Link

→ Chapter 2 A toolbox for textual analysis: Lexis and diction, page 33.

This is an extract from a 1789 work entitled *DISSERTATIONS ON THE ENGLISH LANGUAGE: with NOTES, HISTORICAL and CRITICAL – to which is added, BY WAY OF APPENDIX, an ESSAY on A REFORMED MODE of SPELLING*.

The author was Noah Webster (1758–1843), most famous for *A Compendious Dictionary of the English Language* (1806) and *An American Dictionary of the English Language* (1828).

As an independent nation, our honor requires us to have a system of our own, in language as well as government. Great Britain, whose children we are, and whose language we speak, should no longer be our standard; for the taste of her writers is already corrupted, and her language on the decline. But if it were not so, she is at too great a distance to be our model, and to instruct us in the principles of our own tongue.

It must be considered further, that the English is the common root or flock from which our national language will be derived. All others will gradually waste away – and within a century and a half, North America will be peopled with a hundred millions of men, all speaking the same language. Place this idea in comparison with the present and possible future bounds of the language in Europe – consider the Eastern Continent as inhabited by nations, whose knowledge and intercourse are embarrassed by differences of language, then anticipate the period when the people of one quarter of the world, will be able to associate and converse together like children of the same family.

Compare this prospect, which is not visionary, with the state of the English language in Europe, almost confined to an Island and to a few millions of people; then let reason and reputation decide, how far America would be dependent on a trans-Atlantic nation, for her standard and improvements in language.

Reflecting on Activity 10.3

There was a huge amount of text to read and absorb in Activity 10.3.

It may be a good idea to leave it now, and come back to this Reflection on another day. When you do return, copy and complete the following table with your ideas.

Attitude/belief	Idea	Concept/terminology
	Text A – reference to *'a tolerable dictionary'* – presumably Dr Samuel Johnson's 'Dictionary of the English Language' (1755)	**codification** = classifying language – giving it a stable **definition** and official **status** (e.g. by putting it in a dictionary)
Text C (2) – things we hear and read which don't conform to our expectations are Bad English – *'errors in grammar, improprieties and vulgarism'* → **prescriptivist attitude**	**Text C (1)** – the idea of one form of language being <u>better</u> – *'every person who has the least taste as to the propriety or purity of a language in general, must confess that it is better than that of England, yet speakers and writers must conform to custom.'*	**prescriptivism** = language is subject to rules and should not change **descriptivism** = <u>usage</u> is what matters: we should observe how language is used and try to explain that usage in linguistic terms
Text A – English will become the world language – *'the increasing population in America, and their universal connection and correspondence with all nations will, aided by the influence of England in the world, whether great or small, <u>force</u> their language into general use'*		**linguistic colonisation** = colonising power imposing its language on native speakers of another language **exonormative stabilisation** = language becomes established according to the 'norms' (standards and customs) of the colonising country
Text B – a common language is needed – *'I never saw the national benefit of a polished language generally read and spoken in so strong a light as since I have been here.'*		**lingua franca** =
Text D – America needs to develop its own 'standard' form of English **–** *'America would be dependent on a trans-Atlantic nation, for her standard and improvements in language'*		**nativisation** and **endonormative stabilisation** = language takes on the 'norms' (standards and customs) of the native/local area/country

Exam tip

All of the attitudes and beliefs, ideas and linguistic concepts/terminology implicit in the texts and made explicit in the table emerged from the context of America at the end of the 1700s. They can all be applied to other situations, times and places – for example, to the *'two great European communities which are rising, the one in the south of Africa, the other in Australia'* (Macaulay's *Memorandum*). If you can develop links like these in the exam, you will be earning high marks.

The big difference between the varieties of English which have emerged in these three contexts – American English, South African English and Australian English – and other African, Asian and Australasian varieties of English is that all three have achieved **endonormative stabilisation**. We will explore reasons for that difference in the next section.

Models of World English(es)

A number of linguistic theorists have put forward diagrammatic 'models' to illustrate and explain linguistic processes relating to English in the world. For example, Anne Pakir has developed a theory of *expanding triangles of English expression by English-knowing bilinguals in Singapore*. (You can look it up!)

Perhaps the best-known diagrammatic model to illustrate the global spread of English is Braj Kachru's **three circles** theory, which he first put forward in 1982.

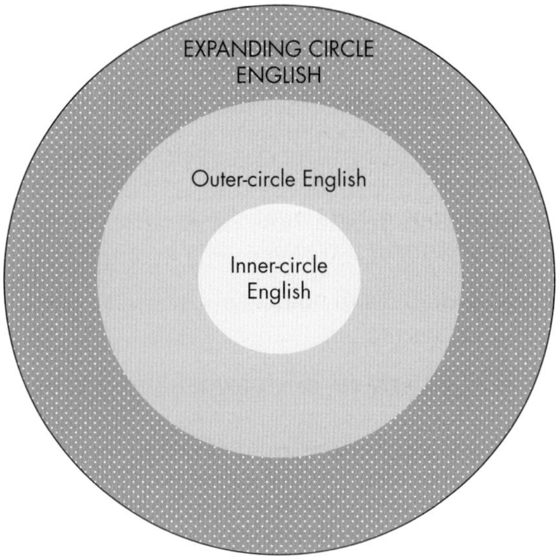

In this model the spread of English is imagined in terms of three concentric circles of the language:

↑ **Figure 10.1** Kachru's model of three concentric circles

- the **inner circle** – a spread from the United Kingdom to countries where native English speakers have settled down in large numbers (Australia, Canada, New Zealand, South Africa, and the United States) where English is a **first language** for many
- the **outer circle** – where English is a **second language** for many (e.g. Hong Kong, India, Bangladesh, Singapore, the Philippines, Nigeria, Ghana) and where English has current status as an official language, and/or has had such status in the past, and/or has 'subsidiary language' status
- the **expanding circle** – where English is a **foreign language** (e.g. Germany, Hungary, Poland, Egypt, China, Korea and Japan).

Activity 10.4

Find a willing work-partner – classmate, friend, family member – and between you try to list as many countries as you can according to which of Kachru's circles you think they belong to.

Where you're not sure which circle a particular country belongs to, think about relevant factors that would have influenced that country's linguistic history. For example, has it ever:

- been invaded
- taken in large numbers of immigrants
- been part of the British Empire or Commonwealth
- been a colony of another European country?

If you have the skill and the time, you might want to create a world map and see what else that tells you about the spread of English.

Activity 10.5

Think about your local context. Which of Kachru's concentric circles does your home country belong in?

Think also about your own consumption of English-language culture. Do you watch American films at the cinema, on DVD, or as downloads? How much of your time online involves dealing with the English language?

Once you've had time to think about the impact on your local context of the international status of English, give yourself 40 minutes to do the following:

- Make a list of points about your own country in terms of Kachru's three circles model.

- Make another list of points – this time about the status of English in your country – e.g. is it an official language? Is it used in law courts or in parliament?

- Write two paragraphs, one based on each of those lists, in which you try to explore and develop your points by referring to other aspects of English in the world which we've covered in this chapter.

Reflecting on Activity 10.5

I'm going to offer you some personal and autobiographical details.

I was born and went to school in what is now referred to as the United Kingdom (UK), which at the time was more often called 'Great Britain'. But I was not born in England: I was born in Wales – which is one of the countries that make up Great Britain or the UK.

Wales has its own language (Welsh) which is not like English, but more like French in vocabulary and grammatical structures. For example:

- the Welsh for 'wall' is *mur*, the same spelling as the French *mur* but a different pronunciation

- the Welsh for 'bridge' is *pont*, the same spelling as the French *pont* but a different pronunciation

- in Welsh, as in French, the adjective generally comes after the noun, whereas in English the adjective usually comes first: 'black cat' in English, *cath ddu* in Welsh, *chat noir* in French.

The population of Wales is about 3.1 million, that of England about 55 million. Of that 3.1 million, about 20% can speak Welsh as well as English. And about half of that 20% are fluent in Welsh; the other 10% can speak *some* Welsh.

You might ask the question: Are there any people in Wales who speak *only* Welsh (i.e. people who are monoglot or **monolingual** in Welsh, speaking no English)?

The answer is that there may be some people over the age of 80 or more, living in isolated rural communities, who were brought up as Welsh-speakers and have never needed to learn English; and there may be some children under 5, being brought up in Welsh-speaking families and attending a Welsh-speaking nursery school, who haven't been exposed to English yet. Otherwise, everyone who lives in Wales can speak some English; and many people who live in Wales can speak no Welsh.

Exam tip

Think about your government's attitude to the status of any 'local' varieties of English compared to Standard English. Some specific examples of this attitude would be useful in an exam essay to illustrate a discussion of **prestige.**

Exam tip

You may find that some of the reasons and explanations you have used are more practical than linguistic. And this can happen in dealing with the topics of language change and English in the world.

Reasons which are not strictly linguistic might be to do with the structure of society; they might be to do with economics or employment; they might be to do with technology or communications. It's quite acceptable to consider non-linguistic explanations for linguistic phenomena; but don't forget to focus back on factors to do with language as soon as you can.

Activity 10.6

Think about the situation I've just outlined about the position (and the **status**) of the Welsh language.

- Look back at Activity 10.5.

- Then make a list of possible reasons and explanations for the facts and figures about the Welsh language. Give yourself 5 minutes to do this.

- Finally, develop the points in your list into a single paragraph, making sure that you use linguistic terms and concepts where they are needed. Give yourself 10 minutes for that.

Historical factors and government attitudes: language planning

The UK is made up of four countries: England, Wales, Scotland and Northern Ireland. Although there is a central government for the whole of the UK, based in London (England!) there are levels of 'devolved' government in Wales, Scotland and Northern Ireland. So the Welsh Government has the power to make some laws and regulations, and has a certain amount of control over government spending in Wales.

Like many governments all over the world, the Welsh Government has plans for the development of the language. In 2016, an announcement was made of a 'vision' for the future: a target of reaching a million speakers of Welsh by 2050. Welsh is taught in schools; road-signs and some government communications have to be in Welsh as well as English.

You're not very likely to be given a chart of quantitative linguistic data for a question on English in the world, but you can never be quite sure … It's good to practise your chart-reading skills for Paper 3, so consider Figure 10.2 below from the Welsh Government.

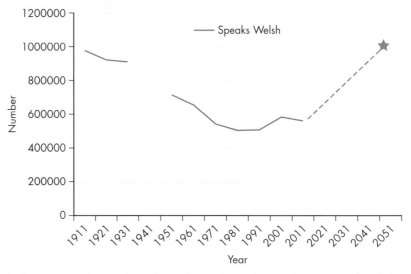

↑ **Figure 10.2** The number of people aged 3 and over who can speak Welsh. *Source of data:* Census 1911–2011, as well as the government's ambition for 2050 (Note: no census was conducted in 1941)

An Asian example of government language planning

As you saw on the previous page, the Welsh Government's policy concentrates on boosting the use of Welsh rather than trying to limit the use of English – which would be impossible and wasteful of time and money.

Other governments have other language-planning policies. Some seek to limit the spread of English and others encourage it. For example, the government of Singapore believes that the country's economic success depends on international communication in English. For that reason, it promotes the *Speak Good English Movement*.

At the same time as promoting **Singapore Standard English**, the government wants to raise awareness of the differences between Singapore Standard English, broken English and the **local variety**, **Singapore Colloquial English** known as **Singlish**. However, the movement recognises the importance of Singlish as a cultural marker.

↑ **Figure 10.3** Advert promoting the Speak Good English Movement in Singapore. There is an emphasis on correctness and on Standard English

Finding ideas and examples

You need to keep remembering the two requirements of all exam questions in the A Level Papers 3 and 4:

- refer to specific details from the text and data given to you in the exam
- relate points in your discussion to <u>ideas</u> and <u>examples</u> from your wider study of the topic.

So far, we've mainly concentrated on the <u>ideas</u> element of that second point, because these ideas are linguistic concepts that are new to you, and you have to understand them fully if you're going to use them in any sensible way.

But you also need to approach the exam with some good examples. Some of these will come from research studies which you've explored. Others will need to be found by you closer to home.

You, your friends and your family will be your linguistic resource for this investigation. There will be no data – *yet* …

Research method

Look at the list of Key Terms below. They provide you with <u>concepts</u> and <u>terminology</u> to describe the different varieties of language you use and hear.

You're going to apply them to your own local context – your country and/or your local area. The way to show you understand these terms and concepts is to find <u>examples</u> that make good sense to you.

✓ **variety** = form of language in a country – either a Standard form or a non-Standard form, e.g. there are two main varieties of English in Singapore: Singapore Standard English (SSE) and Singapore Colloquial English (SCE or Singlish)

✓ **Standard English** = form of English used in formal and public contexts in an English-speaking country; the accepted/approved form, especially in writing, e.g. Standard American English (SAE or StAmE)

✓ **non-Standard English** = features of language that don't conform to the norms of the Standard, e.g. using multiple negatives: 'I didn't hear nothing' instead of 'I didn't hear anything' or 'I heard nothing'

✓ **dialect** = a <u>regional</u> or <u>social</u> (non-Standard) variety of a language: dialect is a to do with the choice of words and structures, e.g. people who live in the north-east of England in casual conversation will speak in a dialect called Geordie which uses the word *pet* as a term of affection: 'You're not looking too well today, pet.'

✓ **accent** = the speech-sounds associated with a particular area, e.g. people who live in the north-east of England will pronounce the word *bath* as /bæθ/ while people who live in the south-east of England will pronounce the word *bath* as /bɑ:f/

✓ **colloquial** = forms of language found in casual/informal everyday speech

✓ **vernacular** = the dialect spoken by the ordinary local people of a country or region

Activity 10.7

Copy and complete the chart below. If it looks a bit more empty than usual, that's because you will be filling it with examples from close to home – features of language which you genuinely understand because you use them or hear them all the time – though you may not have subjected them to linguistic analysis before now.

My varieties of English			
Standard English (my local variety)	Non-Standard features that I use	My local (English) dialect	My local (English) accent

Exam tip

Don't try to use examples you don't fully understand in your exam responses. For example, there's no point in using an example of accent or pronunciation if you can't actually hear or distinguish the speech-sound.

Reflecting on Activity 10.7

There are no 'right answers' to Activity 10.7: the details and examples with which you have filled your chart will depend on where you live, and the presence of varieties of English in your **linguistic environment**.

The purpose of the activity was to get you to think about the different situations in which you speak and hear different varieties of English.

You are more likely to hear or use a mostly Standard form when you're:

- talking to the head teacher or principal of your school or college
- listening to a news bulletin on a 'serious' radio channel.

You are more likely to use or hear non-Standard features when you're:

- talking to friends or family
- listening to a music radio channel.

Your friends would be puzzled or amused if you insisted on Standard forms in a casual conversation; your family would be surprised – even hurt – if you consciously avoided features of dialect and/or accent with which you'd grown up.

Similarly, the principal of your college would be surprised (and perhaps annoyed or insulted) at being greeted using non-Standard or dialect terms. It's not that the principal is ignorant of these forms – she/he may use them at home, or to other teachers in casual settings – but that they are not part of the appropriate linguistic **variety** (or **code**) for the situation.

Linguists sometimes refer to a variety as a **code**, and talk about code-switching. You probably do it dozens of times every day. You may not notice how easily and skilfully you switch from one variety to another. If you live in a bilingual environment, where English is just one of the languages being spoken around you, you may not just be **code-switching** between varieties of English but into and out of English altogether.

Many of the language choices we make are related to the image we want to project of ourselves. The public **self** we display to the world is **constructed** more by language than by the clothes we wear. And one of the most important aspects of how language achieves such construction is the concept of **prestige**.

Prestige

In English-speaking countries, the variety which has **overt prestige** will be a form of Standard English: it may be British Standard English or American Standard English or Australian Standard English or South African Standard English or any other local Standard.

Link

→ Chapter 7 Introduction to A Level English Language, page 132

Link

→ Chapter 11 Language and the self: Playing a series of parts, page 221

Exam tip

Don't forget that the variety with overt prestige is still a **dialect**: it just happens to be the dialect which has been adopted as the Standard. This dialect may be reinforced by a matching **accent** which also has overt prestige. Traditionally in the United Kingdom, this was Received Pronunciation (RP), which was often said to be the accent of the Queen and the BBC. However, this has changed over time, as you can clearly hear by listening to sound-clips of broadcasts from twenty, thirty, forty, fifty and sixty years ago.

Link

→ Chapter 9 Child language acquisition, Activity 9.3

Link

→ Chapter 11 Language and the self: Language varieties and identity, page 233

Exam tip

Be careful not to view non-Standard features as 'wrong' or 'mistakes'. The speaker may have a wide **linguistic repertoire**, including the ability to code-switch, but in this situation is employing the variety that she/he thinks is appropriate.

Standard forms of English carry high overt prestige: using a Standard variety of English in a formal or educational setting is likely to give you high status.

On the other hand, using non-Standard forms with close friends – especially friends who come from the same area as you – can earn you status through **covert prestige**.

As children develop language skills, they are being influenced in two opposite directions:

- probably at school, and possibly at home, towards a Standard form with overt prestige, which will be the expected variety in education
- by social and friendship groups which they belong to, towards non-Standard forms.

It's natural for humans in informal settings to **downwards-converge** to the 'norms' of their peers, and to modify their choices of words and speech-sounds to match the more casual aspects of their environments. **Colloquial** language has covert prestige: older children and teenagers use slang to demonstrate their membership of social groups and to separate themselves from parents and teachers.

This can happen with racial as well as social groups. And the process can become more complicated when people deliberately **diverge** away from the **speech norms** of their upbringing in order to join a **marginalised** group and construct for themselves a rebellious image or identity.

Such a wish for a different identity – a different sense of **self** – is often strongest amongst teenagers. So, for example, some white teenagers in the United States converge to aspects of **African-American Vernacular English** (AAVE) – a low-status and **stigmatised** variety – because it has associations with rap and hip hop music and allows them to assert their identity against other groups in society.

How does covert prestige work? You display your membership of a group by using the same kind of language as other members of that group. This might include dialect forms with regional features which are different from the Standard – e.g. speakers in some parts of the North of England don't distinguish between *was* and *were* in some constructions, so might say 'You was' or 'I were' when the Standard forms are 'You were' and 'I was'.

Some studies (e.g. by the linguists William Labov in America and Peter Trudgill in the UK) also suggest that women seek overt prestige in conversation more than men. They do this by **hyper-correcting** – that is, reformulating non-Standard utterances to **upwards-converge** closer to the Standard English form.

The researchers who suggest that women seek overt prestige through hyper-correction also suggest that men gain covert prestige from using non-Standard forms, which in some situations are seen as more 'manly'.

All of the concepts in the last few pages will be useful in your work on the second Paper 4 topic, Language and the self, as well as to English in the world.

But we now need to look at some more of the issues and problems which result from the influence of English as a global language.

Language contact: pidgins and creoles

What happens when speakers of one language come into contact with speakers of another language but they have no common language?

One result can be a **pidgin** – a made-up language with **lexis** (vocabulary) from one language and **grammatical structures** from the other. A **pidgin** has no native speakers: it just exists to allow communication for a specific purpose (which, historically, was usually colonial trade).

A **creole** occurs when a pidgin lasts long enough or extends far enough to develop some native speakers. This can happen when a pidgin which has been developed by adults for use as a second language becomes the native and primary language of their children. This process is known as **nativisation**.

Where English is involved as the language providing the lexis/vocabulary for the creole (the **lexifier** language) it is known as the **superstrate** language. The lower-prestige language (providing the syntax/grammar) is known as the **substrate** language.

The **lectal continuum** is a concept formulated to explain the relationship between and non-Standard forms of English in, for example, Malaysia and Singapore. This model consists of:

- an **acrolectal** form – Malaysian Standard English (MySE) or Singapore Standard English (SSE) – which has high prestige and is very similar to Standard British English and/or Standard American English (Figure 10.4a)

- a **mesolectal** form – similar to MySE and SSE but with some variations from the Standard in grammar – e.g. leaving out the indefinite article or leaving verb-forms unmarked for tense or person (*He always go there* instead of *He always goes there*) (Figure 10.4b)

- a **basilectal** form – Malaysian Colloquial English (Manglish) or Singapore Colloquial English (Singlish) – having low prestige but high popularity in casual settings as a marker of group and national identity (Figure 10.4c).

↑ **Figure 10.4** Examples of where **a** acrolectal, **b** mesolectal and **c** basilectal forms of English are used

Negative effects of the spread of English in the world

Look back at the third column of the table you created in Activity 10.1. You should be able to see there a number of disadvantages resulting from English becoming a global language.

Activity 10.8

Take ten minutes now to add to that list of disadvantages, using the knowledge you've gained from this chapter and from your wider study.

What are, in your opinion, the most serious disadvantages of the spread of English and its place in the world?

Exam tip

You can look up these concepts and look for research findings. There is plenty of material on the internet, but some of it is not directly relevant to the effect of English. So be careful.

For example, there is a famous study (1979) by Susan Gal, who investigated language shift among bilingual people living in Oberwart, a town near the Austrian-Hungarian border. The study is a very interesting one in terms of which language (Hungarian or German) developed higher status and prestige – but it didn't involve English at all.

Reflecting on Activity 10.8

Most linguists would list the following concepts:

- language attrition
- language shift
- loss of indigenous culture
- language death.

You can see these as three increasingly dangerous steps and a fatal conclusion: each of the first three is a warning sign that the fourth might actually happen.

Language attrition (wearing away) takes place first at an individual level, as speakers of a native language begin to learn English and gradually lose their original language as they use English more and more. For example, they may concentrate on improving their English in order to pass an entrance exam for a university course.

Language shift takes place at the level of groups or whole populations. It happens when the individual process of language attrition begins to involve significant numbers of native speakers.

Loss of indigenous culture is likely to follow language attrition and language shift. For example, seeing that English has higher prestige, speakers may become consumers of books, films and other media productions in the English language, spending less time and money on productions from their own culture.

Language death (or **extinction**) is defined as taking place when the last native speaker of that language dies.

Figure 10.5 below shows the proportion of languages that are currently endangered, according to data from the United Nations Educational, Scientific and Cultural Organization (UNESCO).

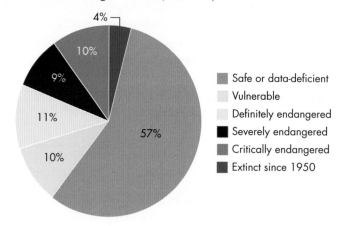

↑ **Figure 10.5** UNESCO chart of endangered languages

How to approach an exam-style question on English in the world

STEP 1

Read the question and make sure you know what you're being asked to do.

> Read the following two texts. Text A is an extract from a research paper published in 2006 on 'The Impact of Global English on Language Diversity'. Text B is from a BBC World Service series (2015) about 'The Future of English'.
>
> Discuss what you feel are the most important issues raised in the texts relating to the spread of English around the world. You should refer to specific details from the texts as well as to ideas and examples from your wider study of English in the world.

You should treat the text(s) which you are given in Section A of the Paper 4 exam as a free gift. The 400–500 words of text will offer you material that will allow you to display your knowledge and skills. It's not the sort of gift you can refuse to accept altogether, but the purpose is to help you, not to give you problems.

- In the real exam there may be more than one text.
- If there are two or more texts, they may offer different perspectives on the issues they raise, relating to English in the world.

STEP 2

Read the texts and annotate them on the question paper itself.

- Look at the introductions to the text(s). You will usually be told the source of each text – and that may offer a clue to the 'angle' taken towards the topic.
- If any ideas occur to you as you're reading the question, jot them down straight away! It's easy to forget good ideas when you're under pressure of time.
- Read and annotate Text A first. Try to pick out references to issues and linguistic concepts which relate to English in the world.
- Then do the same with any other text. If there are two or more texts, try to make connections – by simply drawing lines or arrows from relevant points in one text to relevant points in the other.
- Start thinking about how to group ideas in a way that would help you create a paragraph plan for your essay.
- Give yourself 15 minutes to do Step 2.

The two texts you will be working with are on the next two pages.

Exam tip

Once you're in the exam room, the question paper belongs to you and you can do anything with it that helps you. Some students (and some teachers) are reluctant to write on the question paper, but the best way to read a text in an exam is with a pen in your hand. That way, even in your first read-through, you will be ready to pick out features which you can use in your answer.

You won't usually be handing the question paper in at the end of the exam with your answer paper, unless the question paper and answer booklet have been combined into one document. So you won't actually get any marks just for making the annotations. But students who make a good job of the annotations stage give themselves a much better chance of doing well when they come to write their essay answer.

Text A

Excerpt from a research paper by Constantine Lendzemo Yuka, published in 2006, on *The Impact of Global English on Language Diversity*.

English is gradually becoming a mass language. The more speakers the language attracts, the more the language is becoming diversified along regional lines. It is spoken around the world with different varieties existing and evolving across the globe. For most of these 'new converts', English is either the second or third language which they speak with mother tongue interference. Some of these varieties are so distinct that linguists have suggested they be considered as separate (though related) languages. During the 2004 Tsunami disaster, the American cable news network CNN found it necessary to subtitle responses from disaster victims despite the fact that the two interlocutors employed *English*.

The difference between the standard and some of these varieties is beginning to impede intelligibility. Such linguistic substrata are often evident not only in pronunciation but in sentence structure as well as in the expression of ideas. More varieties are emerging as the language continues to reflect local articulation. The speakers of these varieties live in environments where multilingualism is the norm. Even where English is the official language, the syntactic, lexical and phonological systems of the indigenous languages are evident in the variety of English spoken in such multilingual contexts.

Africans are becoming contemptuous of their languages. A good number among the young people consider their languages as uneducated, primitive and non-prestigious. Young people in search of economic opportunities are leaving their villages into cities where they gradually speak less and less of their languages and more of English. The cosmopolitan cities provide them with an opportunity to intermarry. It often turns out that these mixed couples have no common language apart from the language of wider communication – like English, or Pidgin in Nigeria or Cameroon. Most of the children of such mixed marriages grow up to speak the majority language as their first and only language.

'The Impact of Global English on Language Diversity', 2006

Text B

Text B is from the website of the BBC World Service.

Can English remain the 'world's favourite' language?

English is the world's favourite *lingua franca* – the language people are most likely to turn to when they don't share a first language. Imagine, for example, a Chinese speaker who speaks no French in conversation with a French speaker who speaks no Chinese. The chances are that they would use English.

Five years ago, perhaps. But not any more. Thanks to advances in computer translation and voice-recognition technology, they can each speak their own language, and hear what their interlocutor is saying, machine-translated in real time.

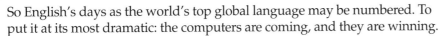

So English's days as the world's top global language may be numbered. To put it at its most dramatic: the computers are coming, and they are winning.

You are probably reading this in English, the language in which I wrote it. But with a couple of clicks on your computer, or taps on your tablet, you could just as easily be reading it in German or Japanese. So why bother to learn English if computers can now do all the hard work for you?

www.bbc.co.uk/news/world-44200901

STEP 3

Look at your annotations from Step 2. They should show what you thought were significant issues arising in Texts A and B, relating to the spread of English around the world.

In the exam, you will need quickly to organise these points into groups of ideas which would lead to a paragraph structure for an essay.

- Take a fresh sheet of paper and try to organise the points emerging from your annotations about English in the world into groups which could be developed into paragraphs of sensible discussion. (Drawing a quick table of columns or rows might help.)

- Give yourself 10 minutes to write an opening paragraph, and then stop. Go and do something else for 24 hours!

Reflecting on the exam-style question

Look back at Steps 2 and 3 for approaching the exam-style question.

You should have some notes on English-in-the-world issues, organised into groups which can easily become a paragraph plan.

You should also have an opening paragraph, but we'll leave this aside for the moment.

The writers of Texts A and B mention a number of issues and concepts relating to what the exam-style question calls 'the spread of English around the world'. If all you do to start with is list them, you should still have the bones needed to assemble the skeleton of an essay-plan – and then you will put the meat on the bones by adding ideas and examples from your wider study. Consider the points in the table below:

from Text A	from Text B
mass language	'world's favourite' language?
diversified along regional lines	*lingua franca*
different varieties	Why bother to learn English? (computers can now do all the hard work)
mother-tongue interference	
intelligibility	
official language	
uneducated, primitive and non-prestigious	
pidgin	

Exam tip

An opening paragraph can be very important, but not always for the reason that some people believe. Its main importance is to help you set off in the right direction. Sometimes two lines can be enough to do that. You don't have to write a summary of everything that's going to be in the rest of the essay.

Now it's time to look again at your opening paragraph. What does it actually <u>do</u>?

■ Does it 'announce' a subject for your essay – a subject any more specific than *issues raised*?

■ Does it mention a number of the issues/concepts listed in the table?

■ Does it signal clearly to you as the writer (and to an examiner as a reader) where the essay is going next?

Look at the sample student response below. It is quite simple, but it manages to do all of those things in just eight lines.

The two texts take quite different views of the spread of English – perhaps because they are separated by almost ten years (2006 and 2015) and a lot can happen in a decade, especially in technology. It might not have been possible to let 'computers ... do all the hard work for you' in 2006. Whether or not this is true, the writer of Text B doesn't seem to think that intelligibility is a problem, whereas the writer of Text A is concerned that 'different varieties of English are becoming so distinct that linguists have suggested they be considered as separate (though related) languages.'

Language revitalisation

As you saw earlier in the chapter, language attrition, language loss, language shift and language death continue to happen. But there are some encouraging examples of language revival and revitalisation.

Exam tip

The most useful thing you can do is research some examples, and settle on one or two which you genuinely understand. There is no point in spending time trying to learn examples which are very far away from your own linguistic experience.

You may live in or near a country where there has been the threat of language loss and/or subsequent language revival. These processes may still be going on. If that's true for you, then learn whatever detail you can, and apply your knowledge of linguistic concepts and theories.

Link

→ Activity 10.5, page 189

Reflecting on Activity 10.5

As I told you before, I was born in Wales – and in fact in a village called Rhosllanerchrugog where almost everyone spoke Welsh, as either their first or their second language. When I was four, I moved to a town just a few miles away where hardly anyone spoke Welsh. At the time, the Welsh language was declining: road signs and place names and official letters were all in English.

In the years since then, the Welsh government has made sure that signs and letters are written in both languages.

There have been many other initiatives to promote the Welsh language and Welsh culture. I know about language revitalisation in Wales from personal experience, and can give reliable examples.

However, if you were to do an internet search of news items and surveys on the use of the Welsh language now, you would find that people disagree: some would argue that the Welsh language was still declining, and others would put forward evidence for the opposite **point of view**.

You may find differences of opinion on such issues in your local area. So I repeat my earlier advice: find some examples of this linguistic issue which you understand and which you feel confident about.

Professor David Crystal

No chapter on the spread and influence of the English Language would be complete without some contributions from David Crystal. He is described by the *Guardian* newspaper as:

> 'The foremost writer and lecturer on the English language, with a worldwide reputation and over 100 books to his name. He is honorary professor of linguistics at the University of Wales, Bangor, and in 1995 was awarded the OBE for services to the English language.'

↑ **Figure 10.6**
Professor David Crystal, OBE

Activity 10.9

Below is part of a 2001 question-and-answer web-chat at Wordsmith.org, in which members of the public from across the world were invited to put their concerns to Professor David Crystal.

Read the questions and answers. For each one:

- pick out any linguistic concept which emerges
- write a short explanation of that concept in your own words.

 Bingley – Indonesia

Prof. Crystal, what do you think is the reason for prescriptive grammar arousing such strong feelings?

David Crystal

Language raises the strongest feelings in everyone. Accent and dialect differences in particular. And most people have something conservative inside them, which makes them always look back with regret to an imagined golden age. This turns up as prescriptivism in language. I think maybe everyone has a tiny bit of the prescriptivist inside them.

 Gillian – Scotland

Hello David. Do you think the globalisation of English diminishes language as a 'cultural tool'?

David Crystal

Hi, Gillian. Yes and no. On the one hand, the impact of English on other languages has been pretty disastrous in places – like all major languages which have travelled around the world. On the other hand, as we see English spreading, we see it beginning to reflect local cultural practices. When people adopt English they immediately adapt it. So there is a case for saying that cultural variation is being maintained, but in new ways.

Pasargada – USA

English is the new universal Lingua Franca. Isn't that an awesome burden?

David Crystal

Absolutely. And there are no real precedents to go on. We just don't know what happens to a language when it is spoken by so many people in so many places. A quarter of the world's population use English now. On the other hand, that means the burden is shared, to some extent. No-one 'owns' English now. What happens to it is on the shoulders of all of us.

Marilena – Italy

Hello David, I'm reading your book *English as a Global Language*. English is now the most important language, but the development of computer communication, artificial intelligence can replace this leadership?

David Crystal

Hello Marilena. It's very difficult to predict what Artificial Intelligence will bring. My next book is on 'Language and the Internet' – it's not out until September, but when I was researching it last year, I learned two things. First, all the AI people tell me *'you ain't seen nothing yet'*! Second, the internet is ceasing to be a purely English-language medium, as it was when it started. I found over 1500 languages on the Net. And my estimate is that the Net is now down to about 65% English, and still falling. That's much lower than the figure I give in *English as a Global Language*.

Marilena – Italy

Do you consider that as world economic change and countries such as India or China begin to dominate that English will lose its place as the only global language?

David Crystal

If that happens, then yes. A language becomes a world language for one reason only – the power of the people who speak it. Power means political, economic, technological, and cultural power, of course. For historical reasons, English has achieved the position it has. But it could be knocked off its path if some major shift in world power were to take place. I think it's unlikely in the immediate future – but who dares predict very far ahead? Who would have predicted, 1000 years ago, that Latin would be negligible today?

Majika

What do you think about the trend of accepting faults of international English?

David Crystal

Depends what you mean by a "fault". When English settles in a new part of the world, local people adapt it, and may speak it with errors. Some of these errors then come to be used by everyone, including the most influential people in the country. At that point, even the native speakers in that country start using those 'errors' – and they cease to be errors anymore. For instance, 'gotten' was thought of as an error a long time ago – but not any more. And when I was in Egypt last year, I found everyone said 'Welcome in Egypt' – a usage which is now recognised in one of the English grammars published there. I would be cautious about accepting a change until there is clear evidence that it is really widespread – including its arrival in the written language. But such changes will always happen.

Indira

Will the usage of Email all over the world impact on the language creativity?

David Crystal

Yes, and for the good, I feel. All domains of the internet – email, the Web, chat groups, and the fantasy games that people play – are introducing new styles and possibilities into the language. Every new technology does this. The arrival of printing brought an amazing range of new forms of expression. Broadcasting brought another. And now we have internet technology, also adding a fresh dimension to language. And don't forget that e-mail is changing. It's only been around a few years, and its original 'speedy language' – lacking punctuation, capitals, careless spelling – is now being supplemented by more formal e-mail writing. Many people write to me these days and begin 'Dear David', and so on, just like a letter. Its style is changing.

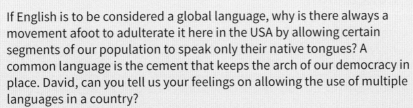

Jack – USA

If English is to be considered a global language, why is there always a movement afoot to adulterate it here in the USA by allowing certain segments of our population to speak only their native tongues? A common language is the cement that keeps the arch of our democracy in place. David, can you tell us your feelings on allowing the use of multiple languages in a country?

David Crystal

I know there is a confrontation on this one in the US, probably because the rate of change has been so rapid this century. But there isn't any need for confrontation. Three-quarters of the world's population are naturally bilingual. It's perfectly possible to maintain the role of a standard language as a lingua franca and at the same time maintain local languages – the standard guarantees intelligibility; the local expresses identity. In my ideal world, everyone would be bilingual, with the two languages being used for different purposes. I'm speaking from Wales, and Welsh is my other language – but I wouldn't use that in this chat room!

Atnes – Slovenia

Professor Crystal, do you think that a 'lingua franca' of such an impact as is the case with English today can seriously threaten languages of limited diffusion – languages spoken by a relatively small number of people?

David Crystal

Yes – this has already happened in Australia and North America, where most of the indigenous languages have gone down under the English steamroller. But it isn't just English. In South America, Spanish and Portuguese have been the steamrollers. Any powerful language is a danger. Which is why smaller languages need our respect and often protection.

Bingley – Indonesia

Has the fact that you live in Wales influenced your work on language death?

David Crystal

Very much so. I've lived through a period when Welsh was on its way out, seen the activism which led to its turnaround. It now has two Language Acts protecting it, and a Welsh TV channel, for example. And we've now seen an upturn in the number of speakers, at the last census. So I do have a certain emotional sympathy which might otherwise have been lacking. On the other hand, the plight of languages which have only one speaker left, or very few, is nothing like the situation here in Wales. So I can see that there are many other stories out there.

Source: https://wordsmith.org/chat/dc.html

Conclusion

English in the world is an ever-changing subject. Governments and the media are keen to show interest, but their attitudes and comments are not always well-informed by genuine linguistic knowledge or proper research.

You, however, do now have a sound understanding of the issues. Some of these – such as the concepts of prestige and varieties of English – will appear again in the next chapter on Section B of Paper 4: Language and the self.

In this chapter you have:

- looked at the historical development of English as a global language
- considered the changing role and status of the English language in the world
- explored different varieties of English – Standard and non-Standard – including the varieties used by first-language users outside the UK
- examined issues and problems which result from the influence of English as a global language.

This chapter will:

→ study the degree to which language is innate, learned, or both

→ look at the ways in which language and thought are both interwoven with, and separable from, each other

→ explore how language allows us to communicate our sense of self to others

→ consider the role played by language in constructing, determining and developing that self

→ examine ways in which we use language, both consciously and unconsciously, to construct and maintain social identities

→ end by providing some revision and reinforcement exercises.

A reminder

In Section B of Paper 4 you will be given approximately 400–500 words of text on the topic of 'Language and the self'. You will be given one question and be expected to:

▪ write an essay discussing the most important issues the text raises in relation to a particular aspect of the topic

▪ refer to specific details from the text and relate points to ideas and examples from your wider study of the topic.

This is a pattern you're used to: it's the same pattern for all four of the Paper 3 and Paper 4 topics.

You're soon going to practise the skills needed for the first stage of answering an exam question on language and the self.

But first, a reminder of what you learned about child language acquisition in Chapter 9.

Link

→ Chapter 9 Child language acquisition

Exam tip

You're about to encounter some frightening-looking **polysyllabic** words, most of them ending in the **suffix** -ism or -ness. Remember that most polysyllabic words can be broken down into separate **morphemes** which, by themselves, have quite simple meanings.

un- = **prefix** meaning 'not'

happy = **adjective** meaning 'contented'

-ness = **suffix** meaning 'state'/'condition'

unhappiness = state of not being content

hippopotomonstrosesquippedaliophobia

(n.) the fear of long words

Child language acquisition and the self

As we saw in Chapter 9, theorists who follow Noam Chomsky's **innateness** (or **nativist**) theory of CLA believe that children are born with an inbuilt **language acquisition device** (LAD). This enables them to apply what is in their minds from birth to the language they experience. So, for example, they hear adults forming the **past tense** of verbs by adding the **suffix** *-ed*, and they then do the same. That is why (according to Chomsky) a child might go through a stage of saying *I go-ed* instead of *I went*.

"I always thought that meant the time after students returned from Spring Break."

When Chomsky formed his LAD theory, he was disagreeing completely with theorists like B. F. Skinner, who believed in **behaviourist** explanations for CLA. Skinner argued that children achieved competence with language by responding to the stimulus of speech from parents/care-givers/adults and getting feedback in the form of positive reinforcement or correction.

Skinner's ideas can be traced back to the English philosopher John Locke (1632–1704). He argued that when a child is born its mind is a blank slate (in Latin, a *tabula rasa*) or white/blank sheet of paper. Children, he believed, are born without **innate** ideas: they only acquire knowledge from experience; and experience is derived from the perceptions of our senses. This is now known as **empiricism**.

Perhaps you can see from this explanation how Locke was able to come up with what was, at that time, a very new way of looking at the **self**. If the child's mind is a blank slate at birth, then the individual human being is free to be the 'author' of her/his own **identity**.

In modern terms, we could say that aspects of our identity are **constructed** by society and through the use of language.

Innateness/nativism *versus* behaviourism/empiricism

You will need someone who is not studying English Language for the following activity: a non-linguist classmate or friend, or a patient family member.

Activity 11.1

On the next page is a chart which summarises some of the main features of child language acquisition in the debate between **innateness** and **behaviourist** theories of learning.

Your task is to explain each point in the simplest possible terms to your non-linguist assistant, and to provide enough specific examples to make that explanation clear.

Innateness/nativist theories a 'nature' view of language development	Behaviourist/empiricist theories a 'nurture' view of language development
language acquisition device	Fundamentals of language are developed through *operant conditioning*.
Child is able to identify speech sounds.	*Imitation* leads to formation of good language habits.
Child is able to categorise linguistic data.	Infant 'vocalisations' (e.g. babbling) are rewarded by giving the infant attention.
Child is able to refine these categories and classifications over time.	Child learns politeness principles from adults.
Child is able to establish acceptable linguistic structures.	Child learns about **pragmatic** aspects of language (e.g. implied meaning).
Child is able to cope with linguistic structures which deviate from those previously known.	Child imitates accents and dialect forms of their parents or other adults (and older children) around them.
Child is able to keep streamlining the details of the emerging language system.	Child learns lexis by copying adults' usage, and by being corrected.

Applying Halliday's functions of language to ideas of the self

As you'll remember, Halliday identified seven functions and divided them into two groups.

According to Halliday, the first four functions (**instrumental**, **regulatory**, **interactional**, **personal**) help the child to *satisfy physical, emotional and social needs*; and the next three functions (**imaginative**, **representational**, **heuristic**) are to do with helping the child to *come to terms with her/his environment*.

Link

→ Look back at the two appearances in Chapter 9 of Halliday's functions of children's language (pages 160 and 174).

Activity 11.2

Copy and complete the table below, with two purposes:

- to remind yourself of how each function works by adding a specific example of what a child might say to fulfil that function

- to apply Halliday's categories to ways in which developing language allows the child to communicate a developing sense of her**self**/him**self** to others.

Function	Example of language use	Sense of self?
instrumental	'me milk' 'Tanya bed'	refers to self with pronoun (*me*) or own name
regulatory		
interactional		
personal		expressing feelings and opinions → establishing individual identity
imaginative		
representational	'Asif at school'	aware of self as separate and of independence of others as 'selves'
heuristic		

Reflecting on Activities 11.1 and 11.2

You will have realised that Activities 11.1 and 11.2 'revisit' concepts you covered in Chapter 9. It's always helpful to revisit knowledge and skills that are still quite recent: each time you apply a concept it becomes more securely embedded in your understanding.

However, you should have been doing much more than simply repeating what you already know. You are now looking at the child's **language** as evidence of a developing **self**.

We have one other concept (**egocentric speech**) and two other theorists (Piaget and Vygotsky) to consider.

In everyday speech and writing, *egocentric* is an adjective with some **pejorative** (negative) connotations.

The Oxford Dictionaries website offers this definition of how the word is used in British and World English: *thinking only of oneself, without regard for the feelings or desires of others; self-centred.*

The example given is '*egocentric loners with an over-inflated sense of self-worth*' – which is as clear a sign of pejoration as you're ever likely to get! And this is how the word is generally used in modern English.

However, the Oxford Dictionaries website does give a second definition – what seems to be a more specialised usage: *centred in or arising from a person's own individual existence or perspective* and the example is: '*egocentric spatial perception*'.

This second (more precise, technical – even scientific) usage is much closer to what Piaget and Vygotsky suggest. You may wonder if there is a linguistic explanation for the phenomenon of a word having a pejorative sense in everyday usage but a neutral meaning in scientific discourse – it's something to think about!

Egocentric speech – Piaget and Vygotsky

On the following page you will find information about Piaget's and Vygotsky's theories of **cognitive development** (= how children think and learn). This is very 'dense' information: there's a lot to digest and understand, and not all of it is just about egocentric speech.

Activity 11.3

- Study the information – taking just one of these theorists at a time. Give yourself at least 10 minutes simply to read and absorb each one.

- Next, make yourself a two-column plan or chart. Using your own words – a certain way to make sure you've understood something – make notes on the two theorists' concepts of egocentric speech. Make sure you understand the similarities and the differences. Use your plan or chart as a way to organise these notes in a helpful order.

- Using only your notes, and not the information on page 209, write a paragraph explaining in simple terms what each theorist believed about egocentric speech. Give yourself 30 minutes to do this.

- Check through what you've written for accuracy – spelling and punctuation. Look actively for mistakes! Don't just read what you think you've written.

1. Jean Piaget's concept of egocentric speech

- Piaget's **stages of cognitive development**

  - **sensori-motor** (birth to 2 years): the child experiences his or her own world through the senses and through movement → understands that her/his actions can cause other actions → goal-directed behaviour; can reverse actions, but cannot yet reverse thinking; understanding of object permanence

  - **pre-operational** (2 to 7): still does not have the ability to think through actions; assumes others share her/his point of view → **egocentric** → engages in collective monologues (other children are talking, but not interacting); acquires understanding of <u>conservation</u> (= understands that the amount of something remains the same even if its appearance changes); but still hasn't developed 'reversible' thinking

  - **concrete operational** (7 to 11): develops reasoning processes → learns that a person or object remains the same over time (identity) → learns concepts of <u>seriation</u> (ordering objects by certain physical aspects) and <u>classification</u> (grouping items by focusing on a certain aspect of them)

  - **formal operational** (11 years to adulthood): able to think abstractly → develops inductive and deductive reasoning abilities → develops complex hypothetical thinking skills → can imagine the best possible solutions through the ability to think ideally → acquires skills of meta-cognition (thinking about thinking).

- In the **pre-operational** stage (2 to 7) children also develop <u>schemes</u> (mental <u>representations</u> of people, objects, or principles). Schemes can be altered through **assimilation** and **accommodation**:

  - **assimilation** is information we already know

  - **accommodation** involves adapting existing knowledge to what is perceived

  - **dis-equilibrium** occurs when new knowledge does not fit with existing knowledge

  - when **equilibrium**, assimilation and accommodation have occurred → new cognitive stage (**concrete operational**).

- In the **pre-operational** stage, the child begins to learn how to speak → talks to him/herself without addressing anyone in particular; the child almost always uses loud speech in these cases.

- This happens because the child has not learned to be **social** yet – and being social involves the need to take others' viewpoints into consideration.

- If unable to communicate effectively with others, the child resorts to egocentric speech. It's all 'internal' to the child – what he/she is thinking.

- As the child grows, she/he learns to be a part of the 'social arena' → develops proper means of communication → **egocentric** speech fades away and is replaced by **social** speech.

2. Lev Vygotsky's concept of egocentric speech

- It appears about the age of 3 or 4 and disappears a few years later.

- The child is a **social** creature to begin with and does not become social with time.

- Social speech (a development from the child communicating his or her needs through crying, babbling and cooing) is initially learned as an integral part of interaction with caregivers.

- **Egocentric speech** (speech for oneself) develops as a part of the gradual **differentiation of the self** from the collective and the transition from other-control to **self-control**.

- Vygotsky organised trials to develop and demonstrate his theories → activities similar to those of Piaget, but added obstacles and difficulties.

- Vygotsky observed a relationship between **egocentric speech** and the activity the child was participating in: in difficult problem-solving situations, egocentric speech almost doubled.

- Vygotsky argued that egocentric speech did not last long: it appeared to be a release of tension and a strategy for problem-solving.

- Vygotsky theorised that egocentric speech is related to **inner speech** (e.g. verbal memorisation of a poem).

A note on terminology

In recent years, the term **egocentric speech** has often been replaced by '**self-talk**', '**verbal thought**' or **private speech**.

Can thoughts occur without language?

Link

→ As you know from encountering George Orwell's writing and ideas on pages 86 and 125, he was tremendously interested in the power of language and the dangers that come from misusing words.

Reflecting on Activity 11.3

Once again, you will need a willing work-partner – classmate, friend or family member – this time to provide an objective view of how lucid (clear) your written explanations are.

Ask this person to listen to you reading aloud one of your paragraphs from Activity 11.3, then to read through the written/printed version of this paragraph. How well could they understand your explanation?

Ask them to assess two aspects:

- how accurately you communicated meaning – that is, the quality of your expression

- how fully you developed your ideas – that is, the quality of the content.

These are both aspects of AO2: *Write effectively, creatively, accurately and appropriately, for a range of audiences and purposes.*

The questions 'how accurately?' and 'how fully?' are questions an examiner has to answer when reading your work. Judgements will range from low (*limited/basic*) to middle (*clear and relevant*) to high (*fully developed and sophisticated*).

If your work-partner is a classmate, you can practise making judgements about each other's work. And if you don't find the low/middle/high categories helpful, try just describing the style of the writing or the approach to explanation.

Now, do this once more, this time with your second paragraph: read aloud first, then read the version in this book. It might be interesting to invite your work-partner to use '**self-talk**' or '**verbal thought**' – to provide a spoken commentary as they read.

This takes us neatly to the **language of thought hypothesis** (LOTH).

Language of thought hypothesis (LOTH)

LOTH was first introduced by Jerry Fodor in his 1975 book *The Language of Thought*. In simple terms, it's the idea that thoughts are like sentences in your mind. If this is true, it would mean that mental representation has a **linguistic structure**, and that thought takes place within a mental language. This is sometimes referred to as **mentalese**.

You could spend the rest of your life wondering about this. Or you could read George Orwell's novel *1984*.

Does thought depend on words?

George Orwell's novel *1984*, which was published in 1948, is set in an imagined future where a brutal government ('the Party') tries to control how people think by making enforced changes to the language.

The political **ideology** (system of beliefs) of the Party is referred to as *English Socialism* (*Ingsoc*). A new language called 'Newspeak' has been devised by the Party to support its ideology.

In an *Appendix* at the end of the book, Orwell explains how Newspeak worked. He doesn't use linguistic terminology or refer to complex linguistic concepts, but the whole idea of making changes to language in order to control how people think depends on a concept known as **linguistic determinism**.

Activity 11.4

Read the text below, which is taken from the beginning of the *Appendix* in *1984*.

When you are sure that you understand Orwell's explanation:

1. make a list of the stages by which the Party is trying to achieve its objective of making it impossible to think any *thought diverging from the principles of Ingsoc*

2. write a paragraph in which you use your knowledge of linguistic terminology and concepts to explain the linguistic processes which the Party is using and abusing.

Newspeak was the official language of Oceania and had been devised to meet the ideological needs of Ingsoc, or English Socialism … The purpose of Newspeak was not only to provide a medium of expression for the world-view and mental habits proper to the devotees of Ingsoc, but to make all other modes of thought impossible. It was intended that when Newspeak had been adopted once and for all and Oldspeak forgotten, a heretical thought – that is, a thought diverging from the principles of Ingsoc – should be literally unthinkable, at least so far as thought is dependent on words. Its vocabulary was so constructed as to give exact and often very subtle expression to every meaning that a Party member could properly wish to express, while excluding all other meanings and also the possibility of arriving at them by indirect methods. This was done partly by the invention of new words, but chiefly by eliminating undesirable words and by stripping such words as remained of unorthodox meanings, and so far as possible of all secondary meanings whatever.

To give a single example. The word *free* still existed in Newspeak, but it could only be used in such statements as 'This dog is free from lice' or 'This field is free from weeds'. It could not be used in its old sense of 'politically free' or 'intellectually free' since political and intellectual freedom no longer existed even as concepts, and were therefore of necessity nameless. Quite apart from the suppression of definitely heretical words, reduction of vocabulary was regarded as an end in itself, and no word that could be dispensed with was allowed to survive. Newspeak was designed not to extend but to *diminish* the range of thought, and this purpose was indirectly assisted by cutting the choice of words down to a minimum.

1984 by George Orwell

Here's what one student wrote in response to instruction 2 from Activity 11.4. (Useful linguistic terminology and concepts are highlighted.)

Here, Orwell is putting forward the idea that if you prevent people from using the words which refer to certain ideas, then the ideas will cease to exist: 'Newspeak was designed not to extend but to diminish the range of thought, and this purpose was indirectly assisted by cutting the choice of words down to a minimum'. This would interfere with the natural processes of semantic change, where some words acquire new or extra meanings and other words acquire positive or negative connotations – amelioration and pejoration. Orwell gives the example of how the word 'free' is stripped of its positive (metaphorical) meaning of 'politically free' or 'intellectually free'. It's easy to see how this would work 'not only to provide a medium of expression for the world-view and mental habits proper to the devotees of Ingsoc, but to make all other modes of thought impossible'. But Orwell adds: 'a heretical thought – that is, a thought diverging from the principles of Ingsoc – should be literally unthinkable, at least so far as thought is dependent on words'. And this last idea is the crucial thing. You would have to believe that 'thought is dependent on words'.

Link

→ What Orwell describes is an attempt to interfere with the natural processes of semantics which we looked at in the section on **semantic change** in Chapter 8 (pages 135–6). Newspeak would try to halt **semantic broadening** and get rid of **connotations** and **synonyms**.

Exam tip

It is very easy just to mention the Sapir–Whorf hypothesis in an exam essay and to think that you've demonstrated knowledge and understanding by doing so. You haven't really. But it would also be easy to spend a whole exam essay doing nothing else but tying yourself in knots over the Sapir–Whorf hypothesis. So, treat it with caution.

This is an intelligent discussion as far as it goes. (An examiner would be thinking of making judgements in the middle-to-high ranges that we referred to in **Reflecting on Activity 11.3**.) You can probably think of further concepts and terminology which the student could have introduced in a more developed answer. But you know very well by now that terminology on its own is of little use.

The student ends by referring to the belief/concept that 'thought is dependent on words'. This is one of the most difficult issues in linguistics, philosophy and psychology!

Linguistic relativity and linguistic determinism: the Sapir–Whorf hypothesis

The following two concepts are known as the **weak** and **strong** forms (respectively) of the **Sapir–Whorf hypothesis**:

- **linguistic relativity** = the idea that the structure of a language <u>affects</u> how its speakers see the world and understand things
- **linguistic determinism** = the idea that a language and its structures <u>limit</u> and <u>determine</u> how its speakers think and how they understand things → so people who speak different languages as their mother tongues have different thought-processes.

There has for many years been an enormous amount of discussion about this area of linguistics – and not just linguistics but anthropology, philosophy, psychology, sociology …

Views of the Sapir–Whorf hypothesis

Read the following text, which is part of an article written by Bernard Comrie from the website of the Linguistic Society of America, then complete Activity 11.5.

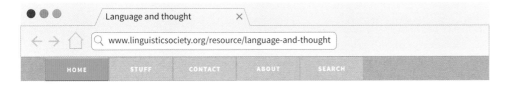

Relativity and Determinism

There are two problems to confront in this arena: linguistic relativity and linguistic determinism.

Relativity is easy to demonstrate. In order to speak any language, you have to pay attention to the meanings that are grammatically marked in that language. For example, in English it is necessary to mark the verb to indicate the time of occurrence of an event you are speaking about: *It's raining; It rained;* and so forth. In Turkish, however, it is impossible to simply say, *'It rained last night'*. This language, like many American Indian languages, has more than one past tense, depending on one's source of knowledge of the event. In Turkish, there are two past tenses – one to report direct experience and the other to report events that you know about only by inference or hearsay. Thus, if you were out in the rain last night, you will say, 'It rained last night' using the past-tense form that indicates that you were a witness to the rain; but if you wake up in the morning and see the wet street and garden, you are obliged to use the other past-tense form – the one that indicates that you were not a witness to the rain itself.

Differences of this sort have fascinated linguists and anthropologists for centuries. They have reported hundreds of facts about 'exotic' languages, such as verbs that are marked or chosen according to the shape of an object that is being handled (Navajo) or for the relative ages of speaker and hearer (Korean).

Proponents of linguistic **determinism** argue that such differences between languages influence the ways people think – perhaps the ways in which whole cultures are organized. Among the strongest statements of this position are those by Benjamin Lee Whorf and his teacher, Edward Sapir, in the first half of this century – hence the label, 'The Sapir-Whorf Hypothesis', for the theory of linguistic relativity and determinism.

Whorf proposed: *'We cut nature up, organize it into concepts, and ascribe significances as we do, largely because we are parties to an agreement to organize it in this way – an agreement that holds throughout our speech community and is codified in the patterns of our language'* (Whorf, 1940; in Carroll, 1956, pp. 213–4).

And, in the words of Sapir: *'Human beings...are very much at the mercy of the particular language which has become the medium of expression for their society. ...The fact of the matter is that the "real world" is to a large extent unconsciously built up on the language habits of the group'* (Sapir, 1929; in Manlbaum, 1958, p. 162).

Activity 11.5

Do you feel confident that you've grasped the concepts of **linguistic relativity** and **linguistic determinism**? If you do:

- do a careful internet search for two specific examples used to support each concept

- write a paragraph about each of these examples – so that's four separate paragraphs – in which you take a critical linguistic approach to the evidence.

Reflecting on Activity 11.5

Although people – even linguists! – generally refer to these concepts of **linguistic relativity** and **linguistic determinism** as the Sapir–Whorf hypothesis, Sapir and Whorf never actually put them forward in those terms.

The evidence and examples given to support either the weak or strong versions of the hypothesis are often questionable. For example, one idea is that certain languages have multiple **lexemes** for particular things which are common in their culture or their geographical location.

The Inuit have been said to have many lexemes in their language for (different types of) snow; and (according to the next text you will be given) the Baniwa tribe of Brazil has 29 words for ants and their edible varieties.

Your internet search in Activity 11.5 may already have shown you that for every source offering evidence and examples there is at least one other source criticising the first source and accusing the author of dishonesty or ignorance.

It can be quite entertaining to read columns and articles and blogs in which journalists and academics accuse each other of dishonesty or ignorance! But when you're under pressure to find reliable information and research then it can be less amusing.

You will have realised that you have to be careful as to which sources you can trust. You can trust the texts you will be given in the exam. However, you need to bear in mind that they will be of different kinds and from different sources.

Some texts will come from a more academic source – such as a research paper, or a report on a research study. With a text like this, you will need your skills of careful reading, and to show in your writing that you have understood the material.

You might do this by integrating some of the content into your answer, using:

- *linked quotation*, where you weave the words of the text into the fabric of your **sentence structure**

- *brief quotation*, where you refer to a few words of the text to support a point

- *summary* or *paraphrase,* where you provide the sense of ideas from the passage, summed up in your own words.

Other texts might have originally been intended for a more general reader. Such texts might come from newspaper or magazine articles – print or online – whose author has taken a linguistic topic and made it simple enough for the non-linguist to understand.

Link

→ Remind yourself of the different types of research resources listed on page 166.

With a text like this, you will need your reading skills of selecting and analysing ideas and examples from the texts, relating them to theories, theorists and studies from your wider study, and your writing skills of synthesising all these into a coherent analytical essay. You might do this by using:

- *a critical approach,* where you explore or challenge ideas in the text
- *linguistic terminology and concepts*, where you take an idea that appears in simplified, general-knowledge terms and 'translate' it in a way that shows a genuinely linguistic approach
- *reference to research*, where you apply your knowledge of precise, technical evidence to a situation that's only referred to loosely in the text.

In the next activity you will be given an example of this second sort of text – a newspaper article which combines reference to complex linguistic ideas with a more 'journalistic' informal style – and an exam-style question on the topics recently covered in this chapter.

In Activity 11.8 you will be given an example of the first sort of text – one written in a more academic style. Again you will have to answer an exam-style question, this time with a focus on the topics which will be covered later in this chapter.

How to approach an exam-style question on language and the self

STEP 1

Read the question and make sure you know what you're being asked to do.

> Read Text A, an extract from an article published in 2014 in the Education section of the *Guardian* newspaper.
>
> Discuss what you feel are the most important issues raised in the text relating to the ways in which language and thought are connected. You should refer to specific details from the text as well as to ideas and examples from your wider study of language and the self.

STEP 2

Read the text and *annotate* it on the question paper itself. Give yourself 10 minutes to do this step.

- Look at the introduction to the text. As usual, you have been told the source of the text – though in this case that doesn't offer much of a clue as to the 'angle' taken towards the topic.

  The *Guardian* is a 'serious' newspaper – what used to be called a 'broadsheet', as opposed to a 'tabloid'. However, it is famous for having one particular trick of style: even where the subject of the article is relatively serious and/or formal, the headline often uses a pun or some other verbal joke. Once you've read the article, have another look at how this headline begins: '*Relatively speaking …*' Does that mean anything to you?

Exam tip

Remember that the question wording will direct you to a particular aspect of the broader topic of language and the self. In this case the focus is *the ways in which language and thought are connected.*

Link

→ Look back at the Exam tips given to you in Chapter 10, page 197.

- Read and annotate the text.
    - Try to identify and pick out references to <u>issues</u> and linguistic <u>concepts</u> which relate to *the relationship between language and thought*, and to the broader topic of language and the self.
    - Try to jot down a phrase (in your own words) which summarises the content and/or purpose of each paragraph.

Text A

Excerpt from a newspaper article, published in the UK in 2014.

Relatively speaking: do our words influence how we think?

Linguistic relativity can tell us about our perceptions of reality and the relationship between language and the way we think.

The idea that the language you speak affects the way that you think sounds sort of obvious, one of those things you just assume. Speak French all day and you'll start thinking stylishly; speak Swedish all the time and start feeling really good about taxation. But what exactly is the relationship between what goes on in your head and the words you use? If, say, the Swedish didn't have a word for taxation (they do; it's *beskattning*), would they be able to conceive of it?

The principle of linguistic relativity is sometimes called the Sapir-Whorf hypothesis, or Whorfianism, after the linguist who made it famous, Benjamin Lee Whorf. Put simply, Whorf believed that language influences thought. In his 1940 essay, *Science and Linguistics*, influenced by Einsteinian physics, Whorf described his "*new principle of relativity, which holds that all observers are not led by the same physical evidence to the same picture of the universe, unless their linguistic backgrounds are similar*". His research appeared to show that speakers of different kinds of language were, as a result of those language differences, cognitively different from one another.

Whorf's hypothesis is one of those slices of 20th-century thought that embedded itself right away in the culture and then underwent an interesting trajectory, falling in and out of academic favour ever since. Ever heard the one about the people who have "no concept of time"? Inuit words for snow? All Whorf.

The time-less people were the Hopi, a Native American tribe who live in north-eastern Arizona. Whorf claimed that they didn't have any words for time – no direct translation for the noun *time* itself, no grammatical constructions indicating the past or future – and therefore could not conceive of it. They experienced reality in a fundamentally different way. The idea fascinated people: Whorf's work became popular "knowledge" but his credibility waned from the 60s onward. By the mid-80s, linguist Ekkehart Milotki had published two enormous books in two languages discrediting the "time-less Hopi" idea.

From the very first, scientific testing of Whorf's hypothesis seemed to prove him wrong. His idea that people cannot conceive of realities for which they have no words just doesn't make sense: how would we ever learn anything if that were true? We aren't born with words for everything that we understand.

Whorf was of a different time: his research came out of older traditions of thinking about language that have lost cultural traction. In the 18th and 19th centuries, writers such as Wilhelm von Humboldt believed that a culture's language encapsulated its identity, to the extent that different languages represented totally distinct worldviews. The late 19th century was the heyday for the idea that white culture was objectively the best, so you can see how this kind of theory really caught on.

STEP 3

Look at your annotations from Step 2. They should show what you thought were significant issues arising in Text A.

Can you easily see any obvious groups of ideas?

- If you can, those groups will be the paragraph structure for your essay. All you need to do is decide on a sensible order. If you have time, think about how the last point in one paragraph might lead on logically to the first point in the next paragraph.

- If you can't see any obvious groups of ideas then you might need to spend a few more minutes on creating a paragraph plan. And if you're totally stuck, you could follow the structure of the original text, creating your own argument by commenting on argument of that text.

- That's where your brief summary in your own words will be useful. You'll be able to see what that line of argument was, and you can trace it in your writing.

STEP 4

Write the essay. Give yourself 55 minutes. Make sure that you:

- focus on the question: how language and thought are connected
- use examples and ideas from the text
- add examples and ideas from wider study
- develop (most) points in detail – though some very simple points can just be left to stand on their own
- leave at least 5 minutes time to check what you've written.

After you've done that, put the essay away for another day.

Reflecting on the exam-style question

It's always easier to make a judgement about an essay you've written if you allow some time to elapse before looking at it again.

It's also always helpful to limit the number of things you're trying to focus on and improve. We'll go for <u>three</u>.

So, as we look back at your note-making (Step 2), your essay-planning (Step 3) and your final essay-writing (Step 4), we need to devise a three-point *agenda for improvement*:

- ✓ how well your basic paragraph organisation has worked – has it allowed you to cover enough points?
- ✓ how well you've managed the transition (movement) from each paragraph to the next
- ✓ how well you've integrated the elements of a good answer:

concepts ↔ examples ↔ developed discussion

If you feel confident about making these judgements for yourself, read through your essay now, with a red pen in your hand.

- Trace how you've organised the line of your argument. Use lines or arrows to show points and ideas emerging and then being developed – or not.
- Do the same for transitions from one paragraph to the next.
- Annotate your essay to show concepts ↔ examples ↔ developed discussion
- Put a BOX around concepts; put a horizontal wavy line under examples; draw a vertical wavy line down the margin to show a discussion being developed – and a question mark to show when the discussion was not developed.

Reminding ourselves what this chapter is about: Language and the self

There has been so much in this chapter already that it would be easy to forget the focus of Paper 4, Section B: '**Language and the self**'.

At the start of the chapter you were promised that you would have opportunities to:

- explore how language allows us to communicate our sense of self to others
- consider the role played by language in constructing, determining and developing that self.

So before we have any new linguistic terminology or further linguistic concepts to digest, we'll consider a very important source of knowledge: Things You Know but are Not Aware of Knowing.

Activity 11.6

This will be a short and easy activity, but the introduction is long.

Think about your life as a series of stages (the sort you have in a theatre) and yourself as an actor on those stages, playing a series of parts.

For example, the main part (or role) you play in your immediate family may be that of a son or a daughter, a sister or a brother; but in your more extended family you may also be an aunt or an uncle.

With your friends, you may be the Joker of the group, or the Organiser. In a close relationship with one particular friend, you may take on the role of Encourager or Supporter.

When you play a part for a long time, that part becomes an element of your **self**. You may not be wearing a t-shirt with JOKER printed on it, but your friends might expect you to be the one who cheers up the atmosphere when they're feeling miserable.

Some socio- and psycho-linguistic theorists would suggest that we <u>do</u> wear the equivalent of a t-shirt with a title (or a label) whenever we 'present' our selves to other people.

Actors talk about *inhabiting* a part or a role. As you can see from the way the word *inhabiting* is constructed – its **morphology** – it connotes a space that you live in. And when the space has a defined name (like a job-title) then it may become a space that limits you. Are you defined by the parts you play? Do these parts give you freedom to express your self?

- Make three lists: **(1)** of all the parts you currently play; **(2)** of all the parts you have played in the past; **(3)** of all the parts you expect to play in the future.
- Keep these lists until after you've done the next Activity and read the next Reflection.

Activity 11.7

An even shorter and even easier activity!

Make a list of compound words with the **prefix** *self-*.

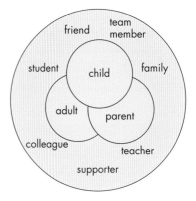

↑ **Figure 11.1** Some of the roles we play in the world

Link

→ Activity 11.8, page 221

As a developing linguist you should, wherever possible, look at the world from the point of view of language.

So it will be interesting to consider your Activity 11.7 list of compound words with the **prefix** *self-* from the point of view of **word classes** and **connotations.**

self-	Word class	Meaning → connotations
self-worth	abstract noun	a sense of yourself as being important, and worth caring for
self-pity	abstract noun	feeling of being 'sorry for yourself' → a bad thing, because to feel pity for someone else is a sign of kindness/unselfishness, but pity for yourself is selfish and frowned upon
self-satisfied	adjective	pleased with yourself → too easily pleased with yourself → complacent
self-interest	abstract noun	trying to get an advantage to yourself, especially at the expense of others
self-denying	adjective	putting other people first, especially when supplies of basic necessities are short → unselfish
self-confidence	abstract noun	the belief that you have the ability to do things well
self-image	abstract noun	the view you have of your own abilities, appearance and character → it's a positive thing to have a 'healthy' self-image

One example for you to consider and pursue:

The word *righteous* means '*morally right*' or '*good, just or fair*' – all **positive-evaluative** adjectives with **ameliorative** connotations. But when you add the prefix *self-* to create *self-righteous*, the result is an adjective with entirely **pejorative** connotations – designating someone who behaves as if certain that they are totally correct or morally superior.

Can we infer that there is a rule of semantics operating here? Does adding the prefix *self-* to an adjective with positive connotations always transform it into an adjective with negative connotations?

Look back at the three lists you made for Activity 11.6.

We're going to use them in two ways:

1. Looking at the <u>names</u> (or '<u>labels</u>') for the different parts/roles you play.

2. Looking at how the idea of playing a series of parts explains the ways in which people interact with each other.

Playing a series of parts → roles → functions

The Oxford Dictionaries website offers several definitions and examples for *part*. They include the idea of an *actor* on stage or in a film playing a *role*. The definition of role includes the idea of a *function*.

All of these nouns – *part/role/function* – involve *acting* and *performance*. And both of those two words connote an element of *pretending*.

All of this means that the **self** we show in public is the result of *imagining*, *presenting* and *performing*.

The expression to *act naturally* is therefore a **paradox** or even an **oxymoron**.

Summing-up 1: concepts concerning the self

We now have a number of concepts to keep in our minds concerning the **self**.

- The **self** develops through stages of learning (**cognitive** stages) which involve development of **language**.

- The relationship between our **language** and our **thought** is complicated: some theorists argue that language limits or determines thought.

- The idea of **self** seems to involve some aspects of acting or performing.

And we haven't yet explored the notion of **identity**.

Before we do, here are some more ideas about performance and presentation.

'The presentation of self in everyday life'

Erving Goffman (1922–1982) was an American academic – a sociologist rather than a linguist. In his 1956 book *The Presentation of Self in Everyday Life* he applied concepts from **dramaturgy** (the study of plays, and stage performance) to the ways in which people interact with each other in social situations.

> ### Activity 11.8
>
> Below is the section of the book in which Goffman introduces his ideas. He is writing a report, based on his research, for an academic audience (other sociologists) so his main focus is not language.
>
> Read this text carefully.
>
> - Pick out the terminology (which is from **dramaturgy**, not linguistics) which Goffman uses to set up his theory.
>
> - When you feel you've understood the main points, write a paragraph in your own words explaining how you could use Goffman's theory to analyse ways in which a person might communicate **self**.
>
> > *Belief in the part one is playing*
> >
> > When an individual plays a part he implicitly requests his observers to take seriously the impression that is fostered before them. They are asked to believe that the character they see actually possesses the attributes he appears to possess, that the task he performs will have

> ### Link
>
> → Think back to Activity 11.3 and Piaget's stages of development. Consider how the teenager or adult preparing for a new situation or an exam is like the child in the pre-operational stage – getting ready to *act a part* and *perform*.

the consequences that are implicitly claimed for it, and that, in general, matters are what they appear to be. In line with this, there is the popular view that the individual offers his performance and puts on his show 'for the benefit of other people'. It will be convenient to begin a consideration of performances by turning the question around and looking at the individual's own belief in the impression of reality that he attempts to engender in those among whom he finds himself.

At one extreme, one finds that the performer can be fully taken in by his own act; he can be sincerely convinced that the impression of reality which he stages is the real reality. When his audience is also convinced in this way about the show he puts on – and this seems to be the typical case – then for the moment at least, only the sociologist or the socially disgruntled will have any doubts about the 'realness' of what is presented.

At the other extreme, we find that the performer may not be taken in at all by his own routine. This possibility is understandable, since no one is in quite as good an observational position to see through the act as the person who puts it on. Coupled with this, the performer may be moved to guide the conviction of his audience only as a means to other ends, having no ultimate concern in the conception that they have of him or of the situation.

Exam tip

This student approaches the task by using **linked quotation** – taking examples of content from the text and weaving them skilfully into the fabric of her/his sentences, showing very good understanding. She/he also brings in some AS Level skills of textual analysis.

Such an approach is perfectly acceptable as long as you make it clear that you understand the quotations you're making use of. It's clear that this student does understand, because she/he comments on and explains them immediately: 'the expression *puts on his show* does suggest something that's imagined'.

Link

→ See explanation of **linked quotation**, page 214.

Have you written your paragraph? Don't read any further until you have!

Sample student response to Goffman

The student here is summarising Goffman's argument rather than explaining how she/he would use the ideas for analysis of interactions.

Goffman seems to want to emphasise that acting/playing a part is not necessarily the same as being dishonest or pretending to be something that you're not. He looks at the **performance** – the <u>presentation</u> – from the point of view first of the **audience**, then of the **actor**. However, the expression 'puts on his show' does suggest something that's imagined, and 'the impression of reality' is one step away from 'real' reality. When Goffman writes that a 'sincere' performer 'can be fully taken in by his own act', we have more language that reminds us of the un-reality of a stage performance. And the performer who is 'moved to guide the conviction of his audience only as a means to other ends' is later referred to by Goffman as 'cynical'.

Reflecting very briefly on Activity 11.8

Look back at your paragraph. You were given a different 'brief' from the student who wrote the response on page 222, but you would still need to show understanding. Do you think you managed that?

Politeness strategies and 'face'

You may have come across the concept of **face** when researching theories of spoken language.

This concept also began with Goffman, who defined it as *the positive social value a person effectively claims for himself by the line others assume he has taken during a particular contact.*

(You can probably detect a similarity in that definition to what Goffman was saying about playing a part and performance.)

Face is more-or-less equivalent to **self-image**. It refers to how speakers want to maintain their status and **self-esteem** in interaction with other speakers, and how (most of the time) they want to avoid offending other speakers.

The idea is similar to – but not exactly the same as – the English idioms 'saving face' or 'losing face'. It is also related to important cultural concepts in Chinese and Japanese culture.

The linguistic theorists and researchers Penelope Brown and Stephen Levinson took on the concept of face in their work on politeness theory (1987).

Like Goffman, they assume that speakers want to preserve their own dignity, status and **self-esteem**, and not **impose** on the self-esteem of other speakers.

Brown and Levinson's concept of face has two aspects.

- **Positive face** is our wish to have our self-image approved of by others.
- **Negative face** is our wish not to let other people impose upon us – thus preserving our freedom to act.

Thus speakers are said to have **face needs**. They will wish to **protect** these needs, and to avoid making any **threat** to the face needs of other speakers.

Face-threatening acts, and how to avoid them

A face-threatening act (FTA) is any form of words which creates a risk that our own face needs – or the face needs of anyone with whom we are interacting – will be damaged.

Younger children sometimes have to be told and taught what to do in order to avoid causing a FTA; they also have to learn how to deal with FTAs from others.

But you are a sophisticated and skilful user of language, so you will manage the following activity very well …

Link

→ This is a chance for you to practise your data-handling skills from Chapter 8 Language Change by doing a collocate search for these idioms and similar expressions with 'face'.

It's all in how you ask.

Activity 11.9

Here is a list of some types of situations in which face needs may be threatened:

- making a request – for information, for a product or service, for a change in plans, for clarification or even for money
- saying 'no' – which may suggest you don't care about the concerns of the person who made a request to you
- disagreeing/stating a preference/offering contrasting ideas
- making a complaint/demanding an explanation
- making a suggestion/giving advice
- offering help – this may seem the opposite of a FTA; but when we offer our help we may risk giving the impression that we think we have superior skills
- giving a warning.

For each type, think of a specific example with specific speakers – and if it's from recent personal experience you may need to be careful who you show it to!

Then, using the conventions you've been used to for transcriptions of spoken language, write a 'script' for two brief exchanges:

(a) one which includes FTAs

(b) one which avoids FTAs by using politeness strategies.

Reflecting on Activity 11.9

If you found it difficult to create scenarios for any of the situations above, find a classmate or friend who's willing to help, and script your interactions together. (It might be even more helpful if your work-partner is <u>not</u> studying A Level English Language. It would be a good test of your understanding if you had to explain FTAs to another person.)

This is one of those situations where learning about spoken language makes you highly aware of your own everyday interactions. You might suddenly shout out 'Face-threatening act!' while listening to a conversation between friends.

In most of the situations in Activity 11.9, you can modify your language to avoid FTAs. One way is to use **hedges** – words and phrases used to soften the force of an utterance, particularly if it's an order (**imperative**) or a question (**interrogative**).

So, when asking a stranger to tell you the way to the station, you will probably not issue an imperative: 'Tell me the way to the station!'

This would be very direct – too direct for the context, and certainly too direct for British English. It would be more polite to use a more **indirect** request, an interrogative utterance with a **modal verb** and a hedge: 'Could you perhaps tell me the way to the station, please?'

Some people would argue that other Standard varieties – for instance, Standard American English, Standard Australian English, Standard South African English – would employ fewer politeness strategies. Standard British English is thought by some to be excessively polite.

If you're interested in pursuing ideas about politeness strategies and face needs, you can look up research findings on negative and positive politeness.

As you will see later in this chapter when you consider **language and gender**, there are other popular **stereotypes** (like the notion of Standard British English having more politeness strategies than other varieties) which don't always match the research.

Co-operative principle and Grice's maxims

Before Brown and Levinson published their work on politeness theory, other theorists (including Goffman) had assumed that the **co-operative principle** was a feature of almost all conversational interactions.

Paul Grice is the theorist most associated with this idea, and it can be helpful to refer to some or all of his four **maxims** (1975).

- maxim of quantity: only say as much or as little as you need to in a situation
- maxim of quality: only say what you know to be true
- maxim of relevance: only say what's relevant to this situation, here and now
- maxim of manner: avoid being unclear/obscure or ambiguous.

A speaker might **violate** a maxim. That means breaking one of the maxims in such a way that other people don't realise it's been broken. For example, if you tell a lie you **violate** the maxim of quality. Or a speaker might **flout** a maxim. That means breaking one of the maxims in such a way that it is obvious to all concerned that it has been broken.

> **Exam tip**
>
> Like all theories, the co-operative principle and Grice's maxims can be useful if you apply them carefully, but they don't explain all interactions, and they are not a set of 'rules' which people have to follow.

Activity 11.10

Imagine a number of different situations in which Speaker A asks Speaker B the question, '**How old are you?**'

The partly completed table below explores a range of responses to that question, for different situations and contexts. Copy and complete the table, and add as many more examples as you can think of.

Context	Response	Linguistic analysis
filling in a form at the dentist's office		
chatting with friends		Question might involve sarcastic implicature, for example if you've just done something childish or silly.
being interviewed for a job		
meeting someone for the first time	'None of your business!'	Answer is **elliptical** in construction. Answer deliberately **flouts** the maxims of quantity and manner, in order to communicate that this is an impolite question in this situation.

Reflecting on Activity 11.10

As you will have discovered, even a very simple question about someone's age can generate a lot of linguistic complication.

You could, of course, argue that it's not a simple question at all. It could, for example, be interpreted as a face-threatening act.

Once again a work-partner would be very useful, either while you consider each situation, or when you've finished. She/he might interpret particular situations in different ways from you.

Finally, on Grice's maxims:

- Violating the maxim of quality suggests telling a lie; but in some social situations it might be more polite to lie than tell a truth which would be hurtful to your interlocutor. (Can you think of an example?)

- Violating the maxim of quantity by not giving enough information can be seen as being 'economical with the truth' – a famous **euphemism** for lying. (Look it up!)

- Flouting a maxim is overt, not covert – so the hearer knows it has been flouted, and knows also that she/he is meant to infer some extra meaning over and above what is said. For example, if Speaker A says he's happy, but says it in such a way that it's obvious he isn't happy, then what Grice calls 'sentence meaning' is not the same as 'utterer's meaning'. Through an obvious **flout**, a **conversational implicature** has been communicated.

Summing-up 2: questions to consider

Before you explore further aspects of language and social identity, it might be helpful to sum up some aspects of the issues covered so far which don't have clear answers and which you might go on thinking about.

- Are character and identity fixed and stable in one person at any one time? Is there a definite **self**? Or do you play many roles based on different situations?

- Was Goffman right in arguing that we display a series of masks to others? Do we enact roles, controlling and staging how we appear, and constantly trying to present ourselves in the best light? Do we have a true self or are we endlessly performing?

- Now that many people have an online 'presence', it would be possible to create for yourself a whole series of digital identities. What does this tell us about how language constructs identity?

Morphology

You have done well to get this far in the course without a section on **morphology**.

You have probably picked up most of this knowledge along the way, either before A Level or during the course. But some of the terminology will be new. And you know well enough by now that the terminology will only be helpful if you make sure you understand the concepts.

- ✓ **morphology** = the study of how words are formed – for example, how the **plural** form of a **noun** is formed from the **singular**, or the **past tense** of a **verb** is formed from the **present tense**

  cat → cats: add the **affix** *-s*

  play → played: add the **affix** *-ed*

- ✓ **morpheme** = the smallest unit of meaning that can exist in a language

  free morpheme: a unit that makes sense on its own, e.g. *cat*

  bound morpheme: a unit that makes sense, but not on its own – e.g. the *-s* **affix** used to turn singular *cat* into plural *cats*

- ✓ **stem** = the simplest form of a word – also called a **root** form or **base** form – for example, the singular form of a simple noun

- ✓ **inflection** = making a change to the **root** or **base** form of a word in order to change its grammatical meaning or function – e.g. adding *-ing* to the base form of a verb to create a present participle (*walk → walking*)

- ✓ **affix** = a unit that can be added to a **stem** or **root**

  prefix is placed before the root-word: *un + happy = unhappy*

  suffix is placed after the root-word: *happy + ness = happiness*

- ✓ **marked-ness** = the way in which one linguistic element in a group or pair is more distinctively identified (or **marked**) than another (**un-marked**) element

  - same root with affix to show gender: *lion/lion**ess***

  - completely different word: *stallion/mare; cow/bull*

  - one term in a contrasting pair is marked, and the other is (or can be) **neutral**: *mare/horse* (where *horse* can be used neutrally to mean male or female).

The question of **marked terms** begins to be controversial when you consider pairs of terms for human roles or occupations that are marked for **gender**.

At earlier stages in the development of the English language, this issue would only have been relevant to learning lists of 'correct' male/female terms for particular occupations, e.g. *policeman/policewoman; usher/usherette; comedian/comedienne*. Such learning would not have been seen as offensive or sexist. It would have been seen as similar to the learning of the 'correct' **collective nouns** for particular animals: a *swarm* of bees; a *caravan* of camels; a *pack* of wolves; a *pride* of lions.

Link

→ Exam tip on page 205: 'un-happi-ness'

Link

→ Gendered language is explored in Activity 8.1, in Chapter 8 Language change

In contemporary English, however, issues of **language and gender** are central to the study of how personal and social identities are constructed by language.

Language and gender

Link

→ Activity 11.5

1. Marked terms

Look back at the lists of roles/parts you made in Activity 11.6. Pay attention in particular to the <u>names</u> which you gave to the different roles which you inhabit.

Some of them are likely to denote the position you occupy in your family in relation to other family members. This means that in English some of them will be **marked for gender** (son, daughter, sister, brother, aunt, uncle) while others will not (cousin, parent).

It would be interesting to look at whether the names for any of the other roles you play are also **marked**.

2. Marked-ness and linguistic relativism/relativity

As we saw earlier in this chapter, the theory of **linguistic relativism/relativity** suggests that the structure of a person's native language will influence how that person sees the world.

For example, in the sentence you've just read, the **non-gendered noun** *person* was repeated when it might have been neater style to use an **anaphoric** pronoun – a pronoun that refers back to a noun which the writer or speaker has just used. But in English this causes a problem, because there are three third-person singular pronouns – *he/she/it* – two of them **gendered** and one **neutral**.

At an earlier stage in the development of the English language, that part of the sentence would have read:

> 'The structure of a person's native language will influence how he sees the world.'

This was because for centuries the male/masculine pronoun was used whenever the person to be referred to might be male or female. Traditionally, laws and other legal documents assumed that the male 'included' the female.

Even recently, this has sometimes been the case. The International Football Association Board (FIFA) introduced its 2015–16 document 'Laws of the Game' with the following statement:

> 'Male and Female:
>
> References to the male gender in the Laws of the Game in respect of referees, assistant referees, players and officials are for simplification and apply to both men and women.'

The 2018–2019 version of the document does <u>not</u> have this provision.

Activity 11.11

> 'The structure of a person's native language will influence how that person sees the world.'

Look again at the potentially controversial part of that sentence again: 'The structure of *a person's* native language will influence how *that person* sees the world.'

If we replace the second use of the noun *person* with a pronoun, we might get: 'The structure of a person's native language will influence how **he** sees the world.'

But this is a gender-biased way of using language: 50% of the human race is female, but the male pronoun and has just been used to represent *person*, who could equally well be female as male.

You could devise a series of corpus searches to generate some quantitative data about the extent to which the male pronoun was used to 'include' the female.

But your immediate task now is to explore your knowledge of how *occupation titles* are used.

- Make a list of as many job titles and titles for positions of authority as you can.

- Using a table like the one below, divide them according to whether they are **marked for gender** – that is, whether the title includes an indication or assumption that the job will be done by a male or a female or neither.

- For each term, note down what you think is the effect of the gender-marking.

Link

→ Chapter 8 Language change: Trying out some corpus data searches, page 149.

Marked: male	Marked: female	Un-marked
policeman (assumes that a figure of authority will be male?)	cleaning lady (assumes that a domestic job will be done by a woman?)	doctor (BUT is there an assumption that most doctors are male?)
		nurse (BUT is there an assumption that most nurses are female?)

Exam tip

This tendency is a clear example of what the exam syllabus refers to as 'ways in which we use language, both consciously and unconsciously, to construct and maintain social identities'. Any interesting specific examples you can find might be very useful in an exam essay.

Link

→ Chapter 10 English in the world: An Asian example of government language planning page 191.

Link

→ Chapter 8 Language change: Most people would say that language is becoming more gender-neutral. As this happens, some gender-marked terms are gradually (or suddenly) dropping out of use and being replaced by gender-neutral, un-marked terms – e.g. *policewoman* → *police officer*, or *stewardess* → *flight attendant*.

Can you think of any instances in your linguistic experience or your linguistic environment where this has happened? Once it <u>has</u> happened, it's very hard to decide whether the change was gradual or sudden.

If you're interested in sport, for example, you might want to pursue some research into what might have happened in the administration of international football to cause shifts in attitudes to language and gender stereotyping.

Reflecting on Activity 11.11

As you listed and considered examples, you probably found many examples of gender **stereotypes** – situations where we <u>assume</u> that men or women are more suited to a particular occupation, and where our language reflects that belief.

Official language policies

Decisions and attitudes in public life can lead to shifts in language use in private life.

Sometimes the people who make official and/or public policies are following a trend in society; sometimes they are trying to create a trend, in order to shift behaviour and attitudes.

When the policy is going to affect speakers of other languages as well as speakers of English, the position is complicated by the different structures of those languages.

Sample exam-style question

Read and answer the following exam-style question.

> The following text is taken from the *Gender-Neutral Language Guidelines (2018)* of the European Parliament.
>
> Discuss what you feel are the most important issues raised in the text relating to the ways in which language can shape and reflect social identity.
>
> You should refer to specific details from the text as well as to ideas and examples from your wider study of language and the self.

> ### GENDER-NEUTRAL LANGUAGE IN THE EUROPEAN PARLIAMENT
>
> #### Multilingual context
>
> In the multilingual environment of the European Parliament, the principles of gender neutrality in language and gender-inclusive language require the use of different strategies in the various official languages, depending on the grammatical typology of each language.
>
> As far as grammatical gender is expressed in the official languages of the Union, a distinction can be made between three types of languages and the accompanying strategies to achieve gender neutrality:
>
> **Natural gender languages** (such as Danish, English and Swedish), where personal nouns are mostly gender-neutral and there are personal pronouns specific for each gender. The general trend here is to reduce as much as possible the use of gender-specific terms. In these languages, the linguistic strategy most usually used is neutralisation. In order to avoid gender references, one can use gender-neutral terms, i.e. words that are not gender-specific and refer to people in general, with no reference

to women or men ('*chairman*' is replaced by '*Chair*' or '*chairperson*', '*policeman*' or '*policewoman*' by '*police officer*', '*spokesman*' by '*spokesperson*', '*stewardess*' by '*flight attendant*', '*headmaster*' or '*headmistress*' by '*director*' or '*principal*', etc.). This gender-neutral trend has led to the disappearance of the older female forms, with the previous male form becoming unisex (e.g. '*actor*' instead of '*actress*'). Gender-inclusive language is also used, replacing, for example, '*he*' as a generic reference by the terms '*he or she*'.

Grammatical gender languages (such as German, Romance languages and Slavic languages), where every noun has a grammatical gender and the gender of personal pronouns usually matches the reference noun. As it is almost impossible, from a lexical point of view, to create widely accepted gender-neutral forms from existing words in those languages, alternative approaches have been sought and recommended in administrative and political language.

Feminisation (i.e. the use of feminine correspondents of masculine terms or the use of both terms) is an approach that has become increasingly used in these languages, in particular in professional contexts, such as job titles when referring to women. Because most occupations have been, by tradition, grammatically masculine, with only a few exceptions, typically for traditionally feminine jobs such as '*nurse*' or '*midwife*', the feeling of discrimination has been particularly strong. Therefore female equivalents started to be created and increasingly used for virtually all functions of masculine gender ('*Kanzlerin*', '*présidente*', '*sénatrice*', '*assessora*', etc.). Also, replacing the generic masculine with double forms for specific referents ('*tutti i consiglieri e tutte le consigliere*') has gained acceptance in many languages.

Thus, the use of generic masculine terms is no longer the absolute practice, even in legislative acts. For example, in the German version of the Treaty of Lisbon, the generic term '*citizens*' appears also as '*Unionsbürgerinnen und Unionsbürger*'.

Genderless languages (such as Estonian, Finnish and Hungarian), where there is no grammatical gender and no pronominal gender. Those languages do not generally need a particular strategy to be gender-inclusive, save for the very specific cases that are discussed in the particular guidelines for those languages.

Reflecting on the exam-style question

This exam-style text is an example of the type of text that is very information-rich.

A text like this gives you (as an exam candidate):

- a very obvious 'aspect' (namely **gender-neutral language**) of the language topic 'Language and the self'
- multiple repetitions of key concepts: gender-inclusive language … gender-neutral

In an exam, you should take all the help you're offered!

→ **Don't** simply/automatically re-use the structure of the exam text in planning your essay – be prepared to plan something different.

→ **But** if the exam text provides a structure that would work for you – as this text does – then it's fine to work your way through that text in both your note-making AND your writing.

- a structure that you could mirror in your answer: Introduction; focus on English; many specific examples; comparison with other languages.

You will of course be adding ideas and examples, as you go, from your wider study.

And you may find that you have enough material on the particular question-focus (**gender-neutral language**) to keep you going for the whole essay. As long as you provide enough material of your own to add to what is in the text, that is fine.

If you haven't enough material on the narrow focus, you will need to venture beyond gender-neutral language and move your discussion on to other areas of language and identity.

These other areas will form the rest of this chapter.

Stereotypes, covert sexism and 'deviance'

Fewer than 10 years ago, a dictionary definition of *business**man*** was *a person who works in commerce, especially at executive level*. You will immediately see that this is a male-gender-marked term, yet the definition involved the neutral term person. In addition, it included the *connotation* of being senior and successful.

The current dictionary definition is different in being gender-specific ('*a man who works in commerce, especially at executive level*') but retains the rest of the older wording.

Interestingly, when the dictionary goes on to offer examples, it provides sentences which use the plural (business**men**) as well as the singular. And it becomes clear then that in the plural the term is being used as if it were gender-neutral – e.g. '*I've always said that we needed to look at it as businessmen always look at high-risk business investments.*' This is to some extent logical: we can't know how many of these *businessmen* might actually be women. But it's another instance of **covert sexism** in the use of the English language, because of the assumption that the general/vague reference will be to the masculine and not to the feminine.

This argument is linked to the notion of the **deviant** term. As you know, some roles and occupations (for example, nursing) attract stereotyped gender expectations and so to show **deviation** from the norm, the nouns are 'modified' to show this difference. Examples of this **overt marking** include *female* doctor, career *woman*, *male* nurse.

Not all overt marking is aimed at 'deviant' women: some examples of overt marking are aimed at 'deviant' men. The point is that the marked form is the one which stands out as different or deviant from the norm. Another example is 'priestess'. The unmarked form 'priest' is seen as the norm; and it is the norm which marked lexical items are measured against.

Research into sexist language

Sexist language is a popular area for linguistic research. Recent research includes an investigation of sexist terms in common proverbs and idioms in English and an analysis of the reduction in sexist language in newspapers, decade-by-decade, between 1965 and 2015.

The developing linguist is entirely capable of carrying out her/his (!) own research using the corpus linguistics skills he/she (!!) learned in Chapter 8.

Language varieties and identity

As you saw at the start of the chapter, one of the ways that children pick up language habits is likely to be by **imitation** from their immediate environment and **reinforcement** from parents and carers of 'good' language use.

As they grow older and spend more of their time at school and with friends, other influences may take over.

It's likely that lessons in school and interactions with adults in educational settings will favour 'correct' and 'formal' uses of language. Children will learn to seek **overt prestige**: this is the respect or status given by society to a particular variety of language. Children may **upwards-diverge** to more formal choices of lexis, grammar and syntax. They may also **upwards-diverge** from their regional accent; or they may strongly resist doing so.

As you saw in Chapter 10, the variety which has overt prestige in English-speaking countries will be a form of Standard English: it may be British Standard English or American Standard English or Australian Standard English or South African Standard English, or any other local Standard.

Activity 11.12

In Chapter 10, you explored the varieties of English in your local linguistic environment. You looked at:

- Standard English – your local variety
- non-Standard features that you use
- your local (English) dialect
- your local (English) accent.

Remind yourself of what you discovered about your own uses of language.

If you can now see aspects that you couldn't see at the time, try to add to the examples there.

Link

→ Chapter 8 Language change: pages 144–149.

Link

→ Activity 11.1

Link

→ Chapter 10, Activity 10.7

Exam tip

It's much easier to try to generate good examples from your own linguistic environment when you have time and leisure to do that – i.e. now! During the exam is too late.

Conclusion

You have worked your way through some extremely complex concepts in this chapter. Many idioms in English reveal the connection between language and the self: we express our selves; we embarrass our selves; we present our selves; we even advertise our selves.

Most of the time this is automatic: we don't stop to think about it. Sometimes it's more careful and deliberate, requiring preparation, practice and rehearsal.

But examining the language we use to do all of this is hard. So you should be pleased with yourself … and think about whether that's different from being pleased with your self.

To remind you of what you have to be pleased about, let's review what you've done.

In this chapter you:

■ studied the degree to which language is innate, learned, or both
■ looked at the ways in which language and thought are both interwoven with, and separable from, each other
■ explored how language allows us to communicate our sense of self to others
■ considered the role played by language in constructing, determining and developing that self
■ examined ways in which we use language, both consciously and unconsciously, to construct and maintain social identities.
■ undertook some revision and reinforcement exercises.

Next steps

The next chapters of the book will take you through a further series of revision and practice activities to prepare you for your A Level exams.

Even the most conscientious of developing linguists can sometimes find aspects of their work that they haven't done quite as thoroughly as they thought they had. So do go back over Chapters 7, 8, 9 and 10 before you go further on.

Going forward isn't always progress. And although the topics you've studied for Papers 3 and 4 will be tested separately, there are connections everywhere. Almost everything involved in a proper study of how the English language works is connected to language and the self and language and identity.

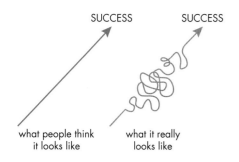

↑ **Figure 11.2** Success isn't a straight line. Revisiting concepts from previous topics and striving to make connections will be the key to your success in this course

This chapter will:

→ begin with an overview of how practice and preparation work

→ remind you of the format of the Paper 3 and Paper 4 exams

→ look at how the questions match the Assessment Objectives

→ revise strategies for effective reading, note-making and essay-planning

→ provide you with practice in combining your response to the question paper material with examples and ideas from your wider study.

A question of balance

Soon you will get to the days of your Paper 3 and Paper 4 examinations.

You will want to feel:

✓ ready to perform, but not in a panic

✓ a little nervous, but not paralysed by fear

✓ reasonably prepared for any question, but flexible enough to respond to what's put in front of you

✓ in control of your time and organisation.

You will want to avoid:

✗ feeling under-prepared

✗ being surprised or shocked by anything you're faced with

✗ being distracted.

It's all a question of balance.

If you're interested in sports psychology, you will know that 'performing' in the pressurised situation of an examination room is in some ways similar to a sporting performance.

Top performers in a range of sports visualise themselves succeeding. Sometimes they prepare by going into the arena or stadium when it's empty, so that they know what it feels like and are familiar with the surroundings. Then when they come to the real performance they can concentrate on what they're doing and forget everything and everybody else.

Can you prepare yourself for an English Language examination in this way?

Activity 12.1

1. Try to visualise the front cover sheets of your Paper 3 and Paper 4 question papers. Give yourself 5 minutes to remember and write down:

   ■ the total amount of time you have for each paper

   ■ the names and topics of the sections in each paper

   ■ what order the questions come in.

Link

→ If you're not sure that you've remembered correctly, look back at how you will be assessed on page 131 of Chapter 7.

2. Now try to visualise the two sections of Paper 3. Try to 'see' the layout of question and texts. Try to remember the requirements of the tasks.

- Imagine you have a classmate who is not as well prepared as you are for this exam. In your own words write down some simple instructions that would help this classmate. She/he needs a list of the steps to follow in order to deal with the language data – the texts – and the question-wording in both sections of the paper.

- Give yourself 10 minutes to do this.

- Check what you've written. Does it make sense? Are there any parts you're not sure of?

Now check again, looking back at Chapter 7: How will I be assessed?

Reflecting on Activity 12.1

Be honest with yourself: How well were you able to do the two parts of that Activity?

If you were mostly sure about what's in Paper 3, try out your instructions on a real classmate.

Now try the same with Paper 4. Follow the same instructions as in 2 above.

Exam tip

Remember that AO1 ('*Read and demonstrate understanding of a wide variety of texts*') is worth 10 marks out of 25 in both sections of Paper 4, and 5 marks out of 25 in Section B of Paper 3.

AO1 is not assessed in Section A (Language Change) of Paper 3. But *textual understanding* is still important in that paper: it's assessed as AO5 ('*Analyse and synthesise language data from a variety of sources*') and is worth 15 marks.

Responding to a text in an exam (1): text-types, grouping and planning

Earlier in the book, for example in Chapter 8, you were told that the texts in the exam are a free gift for you to use as a resource. These texts will contain *ideas* and *examples* related to the aspect of the topic which the question targets. You can add these to the ideas and examples you have prepared from your wider study of the whole topic.

For the first of the two Paper 3 topics – Section A: Language change – the range of **prose text-types** which you might be given as **Text A** is the same as the range for Reading and Writing in Papers 1 and 2.

Text-type classification

Activity 12.2

In the lists below, these text-types have been put into groups which have features in common. Have you thought before now about considering the text-types in groups? If not, spend a few minutes now thinking about what the items in these groups have in common:

- advertisements, brochures, leaflets
- editorials, news stories, articles, reviews
- blogs, investigative journalism

- letters, biographies, autobiographies, travel writing, diaries, essays
- podcasts, scripted speech
- narrative writing and descriptive writing.

The process above is called **classification**, and it's one of the basic cognitive processes which our human brains develop. It's natural for humans to try to understand anything new in terms of what they already know.

So, for example, the 2-year-old who knows that the family pet – a four-legged animal – is called *dog* might see another four-legged animal and call it *dog* even if it's a cat. Later, the child's developing brain creates a **class** or **category** of four-legged animals, each with a separate name – *dog*, *cat*, *horse*, *cow*, *lion*. And eventually the child develops a series of mental sub-categories: four-legged animals that can live in houses, four-legged animals that live on farms, four-legged animals that you can ride, four-legged animals that live in the wild, four-legged animals that are dangerous …

This is the process which you can use at Stage 2 of most of your exam essays – the point where you've read and annotated a text, and you're ready to put your ideas and examples into an order which will allow you to create a coherent essay-plan.

So … have you worked out what some of items in the text-type categories might have in common?

The groups of text-types listed in Activity 12.2 are not rigid or fixed categories. For example, *letters, biographies, autobiographies, travel writing, diaries* and *essays* all have a strong personal element, so we could categorise them as personal writing. But *travel writing* is also likely to be narrative and descriptive – so already there is some overlap between items in that particular classification of groups.

This is an advantage to you when you plan and write an essay. You can use the overlaps from one group or category of ideas and examples into another to create links from one paragraph to the next. This technique will work for ALL of your Paper 3 and Paper 4 questions and essay answers.

Responding to a text in an exam (2): quantitative language data

As you know, Texts B and C for Section A (Language change) on the Paper 3 question paper will consist of **quantitative language data**. There will be two particular types of texts:

- **n-gram graphs** representing changes in language use over time – such as comparisons of related words, parts of speech (word classes), inflections, collocations
- **word tables derived from corpus data** – such as collocate lists and synonym lists.

Either of these texts might be interesting if you just found it by itself – especially if you like interpreting statistical data.

Link

→ Chapter 9, Child language acquisition, and Chapter 11, Language and the self.

Exam tip

AO2 (*'Write effectively, creatively, accurately and appropriately, for a range of audiences and purposes'*) is worth 5 out of 25 marks in Section A (Language change) of Paper 3 and in both sections of Paper 4. This may not seem like a high proportion of the total marks available. However, experienced examiners often report that the single most important skill in an examination is the ability to plan and write clearly.

But the reasons why Texts B and C are important in the exam are that:

- they give you extra information about examples of language used in Text A
- they offer some hints about which examples of language use you should be looking at in Text A.

Look back at Texts A, B and C in Chapter 8 (pages 138–9). You can see that Texts B and C pick up just two examples of language use in Text A which are different from ways we would use language in modern English. They are not the only differences, but if you had read Text A and at first couldn't find any interesting examples of language change, then the ones highlighted by Texts B and C would at least give you a start.

This is another way in which the exam texts are a 'free gift'. There is an old English idiom that advises you not to look a gift horse in the mouth …

Responding to a text in an exam (3): transcriptions

As discussed previously, you won't know in advance what type of text you'll be given as Text A in Section A (Language change) of Paper 3.

The same is true in both sections of Paper 4 – English in the world and Language and the self. You know that you'll be given *400–500 words of text*, but you don't know what text-type or how many different texts.

This means that for those sections you need to practise dealing with lots of different text-types, so that you become confident and comfortable dealing with any kind of text.

But for Section B of Paper 3 – Child language acquisition – you do know what type of text you'll be given. It will be a *transcript(ion) featuring language spoken by a child or children between the ages of 0 and 8, possibly alongside other speakers.*

You also know that you will have to:

- analyse ways in which the speakers in the transcript use language
- refer to specific details from the transcription
- relate your analysis to ideas and examples from your wider study of child language acquisition

In Chapter 9, Activity 9.6, you were advised to read the transcription twice:

- first read: just make sure you follow what's happening between the speakers
- second read: make notes on features of the child(ren)'s use of language and ways in which any adult(s) speak(s) to the child(ren).

That's still the best advice you can follow.

But before the exam, you can help yourself a bit more. As you noticed throughout Chapter 9, written and printed transcriptions of spoken language don't look like other printed texts. They have their own conventions, designed to make them a more accurate and truthful way of representing how words are really spoken, and to make them easier to follow.

Exam tip

Remember that the most important Assessment Objective for the Language change question (15 marks out of 25) is AO5: *'Analyse and synthesise language data from a variety of sources'.* To get the highest marks you have to include data from all three Texts (A, B and C) in your essay answer.

Link

→ Chapter 9, Activity 9.6 (page 160)

One way in which some students go wrong in dealing with transcriptions of language spoken by and to children is by taking a 'deficit approach'. That means looking for 'mistakes' and treating non-standard usages as 'wrong'.

DON'T treat them like a written text and don't look for mistakes.

You now know enough about language to realise that it's more interesting to explore and explain how language is used than to try to apply fixed rules. So, when a child says '*me looking at them sheeps*', what linguistic concepts can you use to analyse the use of language here? Remember, the most important Assessment Objective for this question (15 marks out of 25) is AO4: 'Demonstrate understanding of linguistic issues, concepts, methods and approaches'.

Responding to a text in an exam (4): 400–500 words of text in Paper 4

For both Paper 4 topics (English in the world and Language and the self) you know in advance that you will be given *400–500 words of text on an aspect of the topic* which the question focuses on.

You don't know how many texts you'll have to deal with; and you don't know what types of text they might be.

So you need to prepare in such a way that you can cope with any kind of text, and any combination of texts.

What skills and knowledge have you already developed, to help you respond to whatever you're given?

- From your AS Level studies:

  Paper 1 – responding to a very wide range of unseen texts

  Paper 1 – identifying points of comparison between texts (the unseen text and your own directed-writing response)

- From your A Level studies:

  Paper 3 – working on language change, you have developed your skills of identifying significant features of language in different texts, and combining these with ideas and examples from wider study

  Paper 3 – working on child language acquisition, you have developed your skills of dealing with transcriptions of spoken language

You also know that your linguistic environment is full of texts: signs, notices, leaflets, online forums, emails, text messages, advertisements. These texts have all been written by someone, even if that someone is anonymous or 'hidden'. And whenever anyone composes a text, she/he is using **language** to communicate a sense of her-/him-**self**.

And what about **English in the world**? If you live in a place where English is not the native or first language, or if you live amongst people for whom English is a second or third language, you will still be surrounded by English-language films, songs, signs, advertisements.

Link

→ There are some notes at the end of the chapter on *me looking at them sheeps* on page 243.

Exam tip

Remember that AO1 ('*Read and demonstrate understanding of a wide variety of texts*') is worth 10 marks out of 25 in both sections of Paper 4.

It doesn't stop at texts and linguistic artefacts. The world is also full of opinions about language use, and especially about the use (and abuse) of the English language. Discussions in online forums and 'Comments' sections following articles in online newspapers and magazines often turn into arguments about the language one person has used to express her/his view.

Responding to a text in an exam (5): multi-purpose texts and 'overlap'

As you know, each of the sections in each of the A Level papers has a separate topic. And each of the texts you will be given in the exam papers will be suitable for the particular section/topic and question.

However, there is some 'overlap' between these topics. For example:

- you were able to explore some concepts and theories of child language acquisition (Paper 3, Section B) in greater depth when you studied innateness and behaviourist theories of learning at the start of Chapter 11 (Paper 4, Section B: Language and the self)
- the topics of language change (Paper 3, Section A) and English in the world (Paper 4, Section A) will overlap if you are given a text about what the English language will be like in the future.

So you have to be careful if the text you are given in any one of the exam questions contains ideas which seem to 'belong' to another topic.

The next activity contains this kind of multi-purpose text.

The future of English

The following text is an article written in 2015 by Simon Horobin, Professor of English Language and Literature at the University of Oxford. In this article he looks back at the 20th century and forward into the 22nd.

Activity 12.3

- Read the article.
- Pick out any ideas and examples which you think could be used in an exam essay on language change.
- Do the same for ideas and examples which you think could be used in an exam essay on English in the world. You'll have to work harder on this, because the ideas for this topic are <u>implied</u> rather than directly stated; and you may find no examples at all.

What will the English language be like in 100 years?

In the 20th century, it was feared that English dialects were dying out with their speakers. Projects such as the Survey of English Dialects (1950–61) were launched at the time to collect and preserve endangered words before they were lost forever. A similar study undertaken by the BBC's Voices Project in 2004 turned up a rich range of local accents and regional terms which are available online, demonstrating the vibrancy and longevity of dialect vocabulary.

But while numerous dialect words were collected for "young person in cheap trendy clothes and jewellery" – *pikey*, *charva*, *ned*, *scally* – the word *chav* was found throughout England, demonstrating how features of the Estuary English spoken in the Greater London area are displacing local dialects, especially among younger generations.

The turn of the 20th century was a period of regulation and fixity – the rules of Standard English were established and codified in grammar books and in the New (Oxford) English Dictionary on Historical Principles, published as a series of volumes from 1884–1928. Today we are witnessing a process of de-standardisation, and the emergence of competing norms of usage.

In the online world, attitudes to consistency and correctness are considerably more relaxed: variant spellings are accepted and punctuation marks omitted, or repurposed to convey a range of attitudes. Research has shown that in electronic discourse exclamation marks can carry a range of exclamatory functions, including apologising, challenging, thanking, agreeing, and showing solidarity.

Capital letters are used to show anger, misspellings convey humour and establish group identity, and smiley-faces or emoticons express a range of reactions.

Getting shorter

Some have questioned whether the increasing development and adoption of emoji pictograms, which allow speakers to communicate without the need for language, mean that we will cease to communicate in English at all? ;-)

The fast-changing world of social media is also responsible for the coining and spreading of neologisms, or "new words". Recent updates to Oxford Dictionaries give a flavour: *mansplaining*, *awesomesauce*, *rly*, *bants*, *TL;DR* (too long; didn't read).

Clipped forms, acronyms, blends and abbreviations have long been productive methods of word formation in English (think of *bus*, *smog* and *scuba*) but the huge increase in such coinages means that they will be far more prominent in the English of 2115.

Whether you 👍 or *h8* such words, think they are *NBD* or *meh*, they are undoubtedly here to stay.

Exam tip

There will always be some overlap between linguistic topics, but the texts in the exam papers will be chosen particularly for their focus on the topic in that particular question. If you find yourself writing about language change for half a paragraph in an essay on English in the world, that's all right. But you need to get back to the main topic of the section and the question as quickly as you can.

Reflecting on Activity 12.3

Look back at the ideas and examples you found in Professor Horobin's article. You should have found some on language change and some on English in the world.

■ If any of the examples were new to you, look them up now. For instance, did you know the abbreviation *TL;DR*?

■ Write <u>two</u> opening paragraphs based on those ideas and/or examples:

  – one which would work as an introduction to an essay on language change

  – one which would be suitable as an introduction to an essay on English in the world – although you may need to provide some examples of your own.

This exercise of writing just an opening paragraph is one of the most useful pieces of exam practice you can do. It makes you think quickly under pressure; and when you find that an opening paragraph hasn't worked well you can usually see quite easily what you could have done differently.

Conclusion

This chapter began with the notion of successful preparation being a question of balance. One very important aspect of balance is how to combine ideas and examples from the text(s) with ideas and examples from your own wider study.

In any question, you could start with the text, or you could start with your own ideas. The risk of starting with your own ideas is that you may spend too long in setting out all that you know on the subject and then find that you haven't time to discuss the main points of the question or to use the material you've been given.

This is always a danger with an examination which involves learning material and examples as part of your preparation. You've worked hard to learn the information, so now you want to use it. But dumping a lorry-load of information straight into an essay answer doesn't work. You have to sort through the contents carefully and only unload the items you really need for the question which you've been asked.

Every year, many students are disappointed with their examination grades. Those who later see their examination answers often realise that this is what they had done: they'd written everything they could remember about child language acquisition or English in the world, but ignored what the question had asked them to do.

Traditionally, witnesses in court cases swear an oath to be truthful. They promise that their evidence will be 'the truth, the whole truth, and nothing but the truth'. It can help to apply this guidance to what you write in an examination answer: you should answer 'the question, the whole question and nothing but the question'!

When planning an essay answer, it's always best to start with the text you've been given.

- Make sure you know exactly what the question is asking you to do.
- Read and annotate the extract.
- Underline or highlight key concepts, and jot down links to examples from your own studies as soon as you think of them.
- Decide on a helpful order in which to discuss the ideas, and then start writing.

In Chapter 13, you will have the chance to try out some more exam-style questions, and to see some examples of student answers.

Below you will find a response to that example of child language from page 239.

Responding to a text in an exam: transcriptions

Analysing language use when a child says 'me looking at them sheeps'

- Younger child refers to self by name or as *I/me*, but doesn't become consistent in saying *'I'* until she/he is older.
- Leaving out the **copular verb** – not saying 'I *am* looking' or 'Paolo *is* looking' – is a normal feature of telegraphic speech in a young child, and a normal feature of some non-Standard dialects, such as African-American Vernacular English (AAVE).
- *Them sheep* is a **dialect** form in parts of Britain – in **Standard English** it would be *those sheep*, but *them* is a **dialectal variant**, not a mistake.
- *Sheep***s** is an example of the child applying the general rule for creating a plural by adding the suffix *-s* – it's just that *sheep* doesn't follow that rule.

You can give yourself a Good Linguist Gold Star if you noticed that there's a joke there in that last point that depends on the **connotations** of *sheep*.

Link

→ Chapter 11 Language and the self, page 225.

You will have noticed that this guidance is very close to Grice's maxims. The maxims are excellent advice for anyone writing an examination essay:

- ✔ Be clear and unambiguous.
- ✔ Be relevant.
- ✔ Write what you know to be true – and if you add some possibilities, make sure you support them with evidence.
- ✔ Only write as much or as little as you need to – go into detail where it's necessary; make briefer references where detail isn't needed.

Papers 3 and 4: Exam-style questions and student answers

This chapter will:

→ provide you with an exam-style question on each of the Paper 3 and 4 topics

→ give you a chance to practise all of the exam techniques from the previous chapter and from earlier in the book

→ show you a sample answer for each exam-style question

→ offer examiner comments on the sample answers

→ remind you of good habits.

Link

→ Chapter 7 How will I be assessed?, page 131.

Link

→ Chapter 8 Language change: How to approach an exam-style question on language change, page 137.

Paper 3, Section A: Language change

Remind yourself of how this section of Paper 3 works:

- 5–10 minutes to read the question, and then to read and annotate the texts
- 5 minutes to list ideas and examples from the texts
- 5 minutes to link these to a list of ideas and examples from your wider study
- 45 minutes to write a coherent essay
- 5 minutes to read, correct and add to your essay

  = 65 minutes

Read Texts A, B and C.

Analyse how **Text A** exemplifies the various ways in which the English language has changed over time. In your answer, you should refer to specific details from **Texts A**, **B** and **C**, as well as to ideas and examples from your wider study of language change.

Text A is taken from an advertisement for coffee from the 1650s, when it was first introduced into London.

Text A

THE VERTUE OF THE COFFEE DRINK first made and publicly sold in England by Pasqua Rosee.

The grain or berry called coffee, groweth upon little trees only in the deserts of Arabia. It is brought from thence, and drunk generally throughout all the Grand Seignour's dominions. It is a simple, innocent thing, composed into a drink, by being dried in an oven, and ground to powder, and boiled up with spring water, and about half a pint of it to be drunk fasting an hour before, and not eating an hour after, and to be taken as hot as possibly can be endured; the which will never fetch the skin off the mouth, or raise any blisters by reason of that heat.

The Turks' drink at meals and other times is usually water, and their diet consists much of fruit; the crudities whereof are very much corrected by this drink.

The quality of this drink is cold and dry; and though it be a drier, yet it neither heats, nor inflames more than **hot posset**. It so incloseth the orifice of the stomach, and fortifies the heat within, that it is very good to help digestion; and therefore of great use to be taken about three or four o'clock afternoon, as well as in the morning. It much quickens the spirits, and makes the heart lightsome; it is good against sore eyes, and the better if you hold your head over it and take in the steam that way. It suppresseth fumes exceedingly, and therefore is good against the head-ache, and will very much stop any deflexion of **rheums**, that distil from the head upon the stomach, and so prevent and help consumptions and the cough of the lungs.

It is excellent to prevent and cure the dropsy, gout, and scurvy. It is known by experience to be better than any other drying drink for people in years, or children that have any running humours upon them, as the king's evil, &c. It is a most excellent remedy against the spleen, hypochondriac winds, and the like. It will prevent drowsiness, and make one fit for business, if one have occasion to watch, and therefore you are not to drink of it after supper, unless you intend to be watchful, for it will hinder sleep for three or four hours. It is observed that in Turkey, where this is generally drunk, that they are not troubled with the stone, gout, dropsy, or scurvy, and that their skins are exceeding clear and white. It is neither laxative nor **restringent**.

hot posset	hot drink used as a remedy for colds
rheums	tears or watery discharge
restringent	binding

Text B

Figure 13.1 is an *n*-gram graph for the words *watchful*, *wakeful* and *awake* (1650–2000)

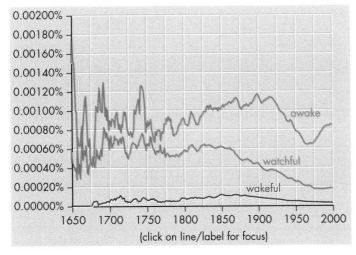

↑ **Figure 13.1** A comparison between *watchful*, *wakeful* and *awake* for the years 1650–2000

Text C

Figure 13.2 is a table of the top five synonyms for *simple* and *innocent* from the British National Corpus (1980s–1993)

'simple'	'innocent'
easy	simple
regular	safe
plain	pure
modest	naïve
straightforward	harmless

↑ **Figure 13.2** Top five synonyms for *simple* and *innocent* from the British National Corpus (1980s–1993)

Sample student response

Immediate focus on a specific example of language change.

> The first significant feature of language change in Text A is in the title: 'The Vertue of the Coffee Drink'. In modern English, the word 'virtue' is an abstract noun with the denotative meaning of a 'good quality', used in an expression like 'she has many virtues'. The word usually has connotations of moral goodness or innocence.

Correct knowledge of word-class – and a comment worth making.

Understands 'connotations', and uses the concept to create a link to the start of the next paragraph.

> These associations connect with the descriptions of 'the grain or berry called coffee as a simple, innocent thing'. The writer is telling a mid-17th century audience about something they have possibly never seen or experienced before, so is explaining three things: the origins of coffee, which 'groweth upon little trees only in the deserts of Arabia'; how the drink is made 'composed into a drink, by being dried in an oven, and ground to powder, and boiled up with spring water'; and how it is good for you if you follow a set of instructions which make it sound like a medical treatment 'and about half a pint of it to be drunk fasting an hour before, and not eating an hour after, and to be taken as hot as possibly can be endured; the which will never fetch the skin off the mouth, or raise any blisters by reason of that heat'.

Understands the audience and purpose of the text – an AS Level skill, but still relevant because it leads to a realisation about how the writer 'makes it sound like a medical treatment'.

Detailed discussion of just one word reveals wide knowledge of linguistic concepts and approaches. Good development.

> The abstract noun 'heat' seems to have had more layers of meaning in mid-17th century English than it has in modern English. We use the word in its simple denotative sense of high temperature – the opposite of cold. We also use it in connotative and metaphorical senses, for example to suggest anger or other strong feeling, e.g. 'the heat of passion'. But in 1650 it seems to have some wider meanings to do with medicine and health 'fortifies the heat within, that it is very good to help digestion'. It must have undergone slight semantic narrowing, perhaps losing some of the older medical meanings as new discoveries were made about how digestion works.

Neat link to a new paragraph, using the concept of 'semantic narrowing'.

> Another word in Text A which seems to have undergone slight semantic narrowing is 'watch', when used as a verb. In the sentence 'It will prevent drowsiness, and make one fit for business, if one have occasion to watch and therefore you are not to drink of it after supper, unless you intend to be watchful, for it will hinder sleep for three or four hours'. Here it seems to mean 'stay awake'. We still use the word 'watchful' to mean wide-awake and paying close attention; and sailors refer to periods of night duty as 'watches'.

Clever choice of a significant word which allows the answer to move on to Text B.

> Text B shows the decline of 'watchful' compared to 'awake' over the years 1750–2000. The n-gram also shows a comparison with wakeful, but that adjective also has the negative connotations of 'being unable to sleep'. It also has a neutral usage in collocation with 'night staff', in which case it refers to a night-

Good use of wider knowledge about how the word is used in collocations in modern English.

time job with no opportunity to have any sleep, as opposed to a night-time 'on-call' job where you can sleep until you are needed.

Text C goes into more detail about synonyms in modern English for 'simple' and 'innocent'. Experience of everyday usage would suggest that 'simple' is more often used for objects or processes, and 'innocent' for situations of people. A 'simple plan/idea' is not quite the same as an 'innocent plan/idea'. When used to describe a person, the adjective 'innocent' has the ameliorative meaning of 'morally good' as it is the opposite (antonym) of 'guilty'. 'Naïve' has some negative associations: it suggests a person who lacks experience and therefore makes unwise/foolish decisions.

'Simple' and 'pure' are interesting synonyms. Both have ameliorative meanings in contemporary English in the discourse of food advertising and packaging, where they connote good-quality ingredients without additives or chemicals. This connects back to the way coffee is constructed as health-giving in the descriptions in Text A.

Single words in Text A display other kinds of language change as well as semantic change. The morphology of present tense verbs shows the suffix -eth in 'groweth', 'incloseth', 'suppresseth'. In modern English the present tense would end in -s or -es. Sentence structure is different too, with a number of compound strings (and ... and ... and), longer than we would have in modern English: 'composed into a drink, by being dried in an oven, and ground to powder, and boiled up with spring water, and about half a pint of it to be drunk fasting an hour before, and not eating an hour after, and to be taken as hot as possibly can be endured'.

The most obvious differences between the English of 1650 in Text A and contemporary English are to do with changes in medical knowledge rather than purely changes in language. You would have to be expert in the history of health and medicine to understand fully what some of the terms meant: 'deflexion of rheums ... consumptions and the cough of the lungs ... the dropsy, gout, and scurvy ... running humours ... the king's evil ... the spleen, hypochondriac winds'. But it is interesting that coffee is described as a cure for all of these.

> Moves on to morphology – not such an obvious feature as meaning (i.e. semantics).

> And then moves on to a relatively simple feature of syntax. Gives a long example, but it's correct.

> Helpful summary of how Text A is 'different' to the modern reader.

> Candidate has devised clever way of dealing with the limits of her/his knowledge. She/he could have speculated about what each of these terms meant, but might have spent a long time on that and got nowhere. So she/he has decided instead to group them together and summarise how the writer has used them: to show that 'coffee is ... a cure for all of these'.

This answer is shorter than the other sample responses in this chapter but it's well-structured and has ended neatly with that summary.

Link

→ Chapter 7 How will I be assessed?, page 131.

Paper 3, Section B: Child language acquisition

Remind yourself of how this section of Paper 3 works:

- 5 minutes to read the question, then the transcription key, and then to read the transcription once to make sure you understand what's going on in the interaction
- 5 minutes to read the transcription a second time, picking out interesting features of language
- 5 minutes to link these features to concepts of child language acquisition from your wider study
- 45 minutes to write a coherent essay
- 5 minutes to read and correct and add to your essay
  - = 65 minutes

> Read the following text, which is a transcription of a conversation between Nathan (age four years and two months) and his mother. (James is Nathan's older brother.)
>
> Analyse ways in which Nathan and his mother are using language in this conversation. In your answer, you should refer to specific details from the transcription, as well as to ideas and examples from your wider study of child language acquisition.

Transcription key

(1) = pause in seconds   underlined = stressed sound/syllable(s)

(.) = micropause   [*italics*] = paralinguistic features

// = speech overlap   /əm/ = phonemic representation of speech sounds

↗ = upward intonation   ↘ = downward intonation

Mother: how come you're playing with barbie more than action man↘

Nathan: dont like action man
//

Mother: you dont like action man↗ (1) do you like barbie↗

Nathan: yeah

Mother: mm hmm (.) i see

Nathan: what one you like (1) [*picks up toy*] this one↗ what one↘

Mother: i used to play with them (.) sindies (.) when i was little (.) i used to have sindies a lot
//

Nathan: sindies

Mother: mm (.) she was like that (.) called sindy

Nathan: big or not↘

Mother: no the same (.) same size as her she was

Nathan: bit bigger↗

Mother: no (.) about the same

Nathan: no big
　　　　 //
Mother: she had long blonde hair
Nathan: a girl or boy↘
Mother: a girl
Nathan: girl
Mother: mm
Nathan: and /əm/ got /əm/ get lot and /əm/ get lot hair↗
　　　　　　　　　　　　　　　　　　 //
Mother: 　　　　　　　　　　　　　yeah lots of hair she had
Nathan: lots
Mother: long hair
Nathan: lots like <u>this</u>↗
Mother: mmm yeah
Nathan: that have <u>loads</u>
Mother: she <u>did</u> have loads
Nathan: real (.) real loads really (.) <u>really</u> loads↗
　　　　　　　　　　　　 //
Mother: 　　　　　　　 well about the same as she had (.) it
was quite long (2) <u>your</u> hair needs cutting
Nathan: not day
Mother: not today↗
Nathan: morrow
Mother: going tomorrow↗
Nathan: yeah
Mother: you're going <u>out</u> tomorrow night
Nathan: who↘
Mother: <u>we</u> are
Nathan: me↗
Mother: and you
Nathan: james↗
Mother: yeah and james
Nathan: where we going↘
Mother: football presentation
Nathan: what is it↘
Mother: its /kəz/cause james is getting a a trophy
Nathan: what↗
Mother: for playing football (1) <u>you'll</u> get one next year if you keep playing (.)
won't you↗
Nathan: yeah i have now

Mother: you <u>did</u> play (.) didn't you (.) yesterday (1) are you gonna go every week↗

Nathan: yeah

Notes: *action man* = a type of male doll in combat dress
sindy and *barbie* = types of dolls representing conventionally attractive young women

Sample student response

Short but effective opening. Introduces the idea of child-directed speech, and realises that parents/care-givers don't consciously employ CDS in every interaction with a child.

> Nathan's mother manages to keep this interaction going by using various features of child-directed speech – although it is probably automatic for her to speak to her son in this way, and she is not necessarily making conscious efforts at CDS.

Not a sharply linguistic comment, but a sensible observation: being spoken to or treated in obviously 'gendered' ways might well be an aspect of child development and language acquisition.

> It is interesting to see that the notes at the end of the transcription explain the toys Nathan is playing with in stereotypically 'gendered' ways. Nathan's mother seems not to be concerned about his preference for *barbie* over *action man,* and simply responds with an affirmation: *mm hmm (.) i see*

Comments on Mother's expectations of Nathan's language skills, but doesn't link this to wider study of developmental stages.

> At the start of the interaction, she clearly expects that he will be able to respond to a question asking for an explanation: *how come you're playing with barbie more than action man* ↘ Nathan completes the adjacency pair with an elliptical response (*dont like action man*). He omits the first-person pronoun (which

Confident and accurate use of linguistic terminology. Candidate clearly understands these terms: they're not just there for 'show'.

> might have been *I* or *me*) but the sense is entirely clear.

Uses concept of 'ellipsis' to create a link to this new paragraph. This allows the argument to be developed.

> Some of Nathan's other responses also show ellipsis, which can be characteristic of the telegraphic speech stage: *what one <u>you</u> like ... big or not ... where we going ...* However, his age suggests he would typically be beyond the stage of telegraphic speech; and his mother does not alter her speech style to accommodate any limitations in Nathan's. In fact her speech reveals two

Notices aspects of Mother's speech, and explains them in terms of linguistic concepts. Again the linguistic analysis is linked to an understanding of how the two speakers are interacting.

> instances of reverse/inverse syntax, when she says *same size as her she was* and *yeah lots of hair she had.* Nathan seems to have no difficulty in understanding these utterances.

> We can see a typical feature of child-directed speech (CDS) when Nathan's first utterance (*dont like action man*) is echoed by his Mother with the full (grammatically Standard) *you don't like action man* ↗ *(.) do you like barbies* ↗

Notices Mother's 'echo' utterance and how Mother 'models' full/Standard/grammatically correct language for the child.

> Although his Mother controls the topics of the interaction, Nathan is capable of making inferences from what his Mother says and introducing ideas of his own. He repeats the word *sindies* after his Mother uses it twice – though he may not yet associate it with its referent (the toy figure) – and he understands the concepts of relative size (*bit bigger* ↗), quantity (*lots ... loads*) and length.

Skilful integration of a good deal of accurate linguistic knowledge here. Shows understanding by weaving concepts (e.g. topic control) and terminology (e.g. 'referent') into the fabric of the sentence rather than stopping to explain each element.

Nathan also understands concepts of time, and the words to represent these concepts, as we can see in this exchange:

Nathan: not day

Mother: not today↗

Nathan: morrow

Mother: going tomorrow↗

Nathan: yeah

Mother: youre going <u>out</u> tomorrow night

Again Nathan ellipts the syllable to- from today and *tomorrow*, and again his Mother models the Standard form. There is no information in the transcript about accents or speech sounds apart from the /əm/ sound in Nathan's longest and least fluent utterance (and /əm/ got /əm/ get lot and /əm/ get lot hair↗) in which he is struggling to articulate several concepts: the length and amount of hair, the colour, the gender of the toy figure. Similarly, the only word in his Mother's speech which is given in phonemic notation is /kəz/, and this is not really a sign of accent since almost everyone shortens *because* to /kəz/ in everyday speech.

Some researchers have suggested that children learn the alternating pattern of adjacency pairs from playing the "peek-a-boo" game. Nathan copes well with such a turn-structure and always responds to his Mother's turns. She seems to sense that the exchange about *lots of hair* is getting nowhere – although Nathan keeps responding – and after a longer pause (2 seconds) shifts the topic to something in the more immediate environment: *well about the same as had (.) it was quite long (2)* <u>your</u> *hair needs cutting*

The only dysfluency apparent in the Mother's utterance comes (*james is getting a a trophy*) when she needs to explain to Nathan what the abstract idea of a *football presentation* is:

Nathan: where we going↘

Mother: football presentation

Nathan: what is it↘

Mother: its /kəz/cause james is getting a a trophy

Nathan: what↗

Mother: for playing football (1) youll get one next year if you keep playing (.) wont you↘

Introduces a longer quotation by explaining in advance what it shows …

… then makes another useful comment about a specific feature of language shown in that quotation, and links this to the earlier observation about Mother 'modelling' the Standard form.

It can be extremely <u>un</u>helpful to comment on what is <u>not</u> present in a text. But here the candidate makes a useful point about speech sounds, because we might expect some indication of how well the child can articulate more difficult sounds – e.g. consonant clusters.

Candidate is not tempted to make exaggerated claims about signs of accent or 'fast' speech: she/he realises that many sounds are not fully articulated in normal everyday speech, though a parent might be more particular about 'modelling' sounds for a child to copy.

This is a rather loose concept, but it is often referred to and has some backing from research.

Not a sharply analytical linguistic point, but a sensible inference about what's going on in this interaction.

Some candidates waste time searching for and listing what they think are dysfluency features. Often these features are normal and not worth commenting on. Here, however, a good point is made about how the hesitation suggests the Mother's careful choice of vocabulary.

A complex and developed explanation about the child's cognitive development. Again, not linked to any specific named theory or theorist, but it's sophisticated knowledge of how language works.

Using a longer quotation to support the point.

Careful understanding of what's going on in terms of the interaction between the speakers. Linguistic terminology and concepts <u>are</u> being used: notions of the <u>abstract</u>, and a <u>topic shift</u>.

Accurate understanding of how the tag question is used.

Slightly abrupt ending – but candidate has covered the whole of the transcription, and possibly used all the time she/he has allowed for this question. It is much better to end with a simple linguistic observation like this one than to waste time with a long concluding paragraph which does nothing apart from repeating points already made.

A *trophy* is a concrete object which Nathan will be able to see. In cognitive terms, it's the physical representation of a reward for an achievement. Although Nathan is probably too young to use metaphorical or figurative language himself, he can understand that an object can be a symbol for an idea. For example, he has no trouble understanding that a toy figure can represent gender – though of course he doesn't use that word:

Mother: she had long blonde hair

Nathan: a girl or boy↘

Mother: a girl

Nathan: girl

Mother: mm

After mentioning the *trophy*, his Mother probably senses that staying on the abstract topic of a *presentation* is likely to confuse Nathan, so she shifts the topic slightly to Nathan's memory of himself playing football. She uses a tag question to check that he remembers: you <u>did</u> play (.) didnt you (.) yesterday (l) are you gonna go every week↗

Although there is no formal 'closing signal', the conversation has reached a kind of natural 'closure' where the transcription ends.

Overall examiner comments on the Paper 3 sample responses

1. Neither of the two sample responses offered a long introduction. This was sensible, because the paper tests language analysis, and you do that by tackling the language as soon as possible. The examiner knows what the question is, and there is no point in repeating it or saying that you're going to answer it.

2. Neither of the two sample responses offered a concluding paragraph summing up the answer. Again, this was sensible, because nothing is achieved by repeating points.

3. Both sample responses made good use of the examples provided in the exam texts, and added to these by providing developed explanations based on their wider study.

4. Both sample responses demonstrated some skill in linking points from one paragraph to the next. Both were clearly and accurately expressed.

Paper 4, Section A: English in the world

Remind yourself of how this section of Paper 4 works:

- 5–10 minutes to read the question, and to make sure you understand the 'angle' – the aspect of the topic which is being highlighted – then to write down some relevant ideas and examples from your wider study
- 5 minutes to read and annotate the text(s) – picking out the main issues
- 5 minutes to organise your own ideas and examples, and the ideas and examples from the texts, into groups which will form a paragraph plan
- 45 minutes to write a coherent essay
- 5 minutes to read and correct and add to your essay

  = 65 minutes

Link

→ Chapter 7 Introduction to A Level English: How will I be assessed? page 131.

Link

→ Chapter 10 English in the world: How to approach an exam-style question on English in the world, page 197.

Read the following two texts. **Text A** is an extract from an academic article on how the global spread of English is affecting the language situation in South Africa. **Text B** is a selection of comments made in response to an online debate on the question 'Is the global spread of English good or bad?'.

Discuss what you feel are the most important issues raised in the texts relating to the spread of English around the world. You should refer to specific details from the texts as well as to ideas and examples from your wider study of English in the world.

Text A

English in South Africa is one of the official languages and has enjoyed a special status since the re-establishment of British rule in the Cape Colony in 1806, which is generally considered as the beginning of the process of Anglicization in South Africa. This would place the country somehow on the fence between the Inner and Outer Circle (Kachru's Model).

The number of speakers of English as a Native Language (ENL) in South Africa is considerable; there are about 3.45 million native speakers of English, who comprise (using old racial divisions): 1.71 million white, 0.58 million coloured, 0.97 million Indian and 0.11 million 'African'.

South African English is divided into separate ethnolects and is naturally a continuum ranging from 'standard' to vernacular. However, there is also a large number of speakers of English as a Second Language in South Africa, and localised varieties of 'New Englishes' (the term related to Kachru's Outer Circle) are present in local cultures. Such cultural embedding of the language is a clear example of Inner Circle dynamics. On the other hand, the percentage of those ENL speakers with respect to the overall population makes them a clear minority, and the acquisition of English by new groups follows rather the creolised patterns of the Outer Circle. Therefore, South Africa appears to be a troubling combination of the elements that are characteristic of both the Inner and the Outer Circle.

Text B

Comment 1: I can see why people debate about this topic. It's good to have a mutual intelligible language, so that everyone can communicate and understand each other, but also it is bad because it feels like one language will start to dominant others risking one's native language, culture, and people.

Comment 2: For the most part, I think that it is good. Although, I believe that we should not emphasize English so much that it becomes too overbearing, having more and more people learn English is great for globalization and becoming more interconnected like the "Communication for the globalized age" point made reference to. At the same time, there is a legitimate threat to the loss of local languages, as one debater put it above. In order to have a happy medium, we need to understand how to implement English without threatening other native and local languages.

Comment 3: No, The spread of English isn't necessarily forcing people to stop speaking their heritage language. English is the lingua franca. It has facilitated many business ventures and relationships, and it has connected the world in such a major way. Some individuals might choose to not pass down their ancestral language to their children, but that is a decision made by the individual, and I don't think that English, or the spread of English is to blame.

Source: www.debatewise.org/debates/2165-is-the-global-spread-of-english-good-or-bad/comment-page-1/#comments

Sample student response

Annotation	Response
Candidate starts by identifying 'a tone of concern' in Text A – which could be linked later in the answer to problem and conflicts associated with English in the world.	Text A uses the language situation of South Africa to raise a number of concepts and problems relating to the spread of English around the world. The author of this article adopts a tone of concern: 'South Africa appears to be a troubling combination of the elements that are characteristic of both the Inner and the Outer Circle.' Meanwhile, the comments in Text B offer a range of views about English as a world language.
Candidate decides to use the 'minor errors' in Comment 1 to perform some Language Analysis. This is an acceptable approach in Paper 4 if **(a)** the analysis supports an argument relevant to the topic, and **(b)** the analysis is careful and thoughtful and <u>correct</u> – bearing in mind that there will be acceptable variations in different varieties of English.	The writer of Comment 1 may well be someone for whom English is a second (or third) language, going by the evidence of three minor errors in English usage. Firstly, the phrasal verb *debate about* is not (strictly speaking) correct Standard/idiomatic British English. (*I can see why people debate about this topic.*) In SBE, there would be no need for the preposition *about*: debate is a transitive verb and can be followed by a direct object without a preposition.
Candidate is managing to show awareness that there are acceptable variations in different Standard Englishes.	However, in many local varieties of Standard English (such as Singapore Standard English), *debate about* would be an accepted phrasal-verb form.

Minor errors in the use of prepositions are amongst the most common mistakes made by non-native speakers of English. This is not surprising, since distinctions of preposition use can be very precise, according to context. For example, in SBE a person arrives *at* a town or house, but arrives *in* a country – e.g. 'we arrived *in* Canada *at* 17.30.' Similarly, a person may be said to be *welcome in Britain* (meaning that the British people are pleased to see that person) but the greeting spoken would be 'Welcome <u>to</u> Britain.'

There are two other errors in Comment 1. The writer has used *dominant* (the adjectival form) – *it feels like one language will start to domin<u>ant</u> others –* where it should be *dominate* (the verb form). And the expression *mutual intelligible* uses a pair of adjectives where the adverbial form should be used to pre-modify the adjective: *mutual<u>ly</u> <u>intelligible</u>.*

But the important point in relation to English as a world language is that Comment 1 is <u>completely</u> <u>intelligible</u>, despite the fact that it contains three non-Standard ('incorrect') usages of English. As the author of this comment says: *'It's good to have a mutual intelligible language, so that everyone can communicate and understand each other.'* The author of Comment 3 agrees: *'English is the lingua franca. It has facilitated many business ventures and relationships, and it has connected the world in such a major way.'*

> Good use of the discussion about minor errors to prove that Mutual Intelligibility is not harmed by minor variations.

The linguist Braj Kachru put forward a 'model' of the use of English across the world in terms of three Concentric Circles: the Inner Circle, the Outer Circle, and the Expanding Circle.

> Shows understanding of the Kachru Model and knowledge from wider study, but it doesn't take the argument much further forward.

Countries in the Inner Circle are those where English is the native language: Britain, North America, Australia and New Zealand, plus parts of Canada and South Africa. The Outer Circle consists of those countries which were colonised at some point in history and adopted (or had to adopt) English as an official language for education, government and the legal system – countries such as India, Pakistan, Bangladesh, Malaysia, Singapore, Tanzania, Nigeria, Kenya and other parts of Canada and South Africa. Some of these countries (in particular Singapore) have adopted English even more strongly since becoming independent because they see the economic advantages.

> Valid comment, with an example, but no development.

As the author of Comment 2 writes, *'having more and more people learn English is great for globalization and becoming more interconnected.'* Many global organisations and companies conduct their business in English; and much of what is on the internet is in English. For these reasons, many people living in countries in the Expanding Circle – countries such as China, Russia, Japan, South Korea, Indonesia and Egypt, plus other countries in Europe – also want to learn English, though it played no

> Brings in the ideas of *globalisation*, but development lacking.

part on their historical development. In Europe, many people in the Netherlands and Scandinavia speak English as a Second Language, though in France the Académie française tries to resist the use of English words and expressions.

All three of the comments in Text B mention how the spread of English brings with it the risk that people will abandon their native languages. Comment 3 uses the expression 'heritage language' which makes the danger to native culture more obvious. Damage to indigenous languages can happen in a number of ways. Sometimes young people learn English at school then go on to use it at University or in their careers, finding less and less use for their mother tongue. Although such people are bilingual, they can gradually lose proficiency in their native language as a result of not using it. This is called language attrition, and it can happen to whole groups of people, not just individuals, if their first language does not have social prestige in the way that English does.

Sometimes governments can encourage the process of language attrition, for example by making learning English compulsory in schools or by insisting that signs and notices are in English. On the other hand, governments can provide support for native languages using similar methods, for example by ensuring that all road and traffic signs are bilingual.

At the extreme end of the scale, when language attrition goes on for a long time and over several generations, the number of native speakers of a language can decline to almost nothing. The death or extinction of a language comes when the last native speaker of that language dies; and the most common estimate is that half of the world's current languages will be extinct by the end of this century.

Text A has some different statistics, showing the number of speakers of English as a native language (ENL) in South Africa, divided according to their racial origin. The text does not tell us about what level of social prestige might be carried by each of these divisions, but it does tell us that 'South African English is divided into separate ethnolects and is naturally a continuum ranging from 'standard' to vernacular.' It seems likely that the ethnolect spoken by the 'white' division (1.71 million) would have greater overt prestige than that spoken by the 'Indian' (0.97 million).

The spread of English as a world language is sometimes seen as a force that cannot be resisted, and there are words in Comment 1 ('dominant') and Comment 2 ('over-bearing') which connote something which crushes the alternatives. However, the author of Comment 3 reminds readers that 'The spread of English isn't necessarily forcing people to stop speaking their heritage language ... Some individuals might choose to not pass down their ancestral language to their children, but that is a decision made by the individual, and I don't think that English, or the spread of English is to blame.'

Annotations (left margin):

- Aware that not all countries welcome the spread of English.

- Asserts the link between loss of language and loss of culture. Will _this_ idea be developed?

- Identifies language attrition as an issue/problem, and explains in a general way (without specific examples) how it happens.

- Mentions a relevant concept. Will this be developed?

- Aware that governments can encourage the spread of English or try to support native/indigenous language, but no examples are given.

- The process of language extinction is outlined. No examples are offered, but a broad statistical estimate is referred to.

- Creates a link into this new paragraph by continuing the idea of statistics.

- Mentions _prestige_ again, but doesn't develop the idea.

- Identifies examples of _attitudes_ in the connotative language of two of the Comments in Text B, but doesn't develop this discussion.

- Tries to use a lengthy quotation from Comment 3 to sum up the attitude that the spread of English might pose some risk to other languages, but that people can choose.

The candidate has identified some <u>issues</u> from the texts, and made some connections with concepts from wider study of the topic. But she/he has not been able to identify substantial examples in the texts, nor has she/he been able to draw on specific <u>examples</u> from wider study. Because of the absence of <u>examples</u>, she/he has not been able to construct a developed discussion.

Paper 4, Section B: Language and the self

Remind yourself of how this section of Paper 4 works:

- 5–10 minutes to read the question, and to make sure you understand the 'angle' – the aspect of the topic which is being highlighted – then to write down some relevant ideas and examples from your wider study
- 5–10 minutes to read and annotate the text(s) – picking out the main issues and linking them to <u>concepts</u> from your wider study
- 5 minutes to organise your own ideas and examples, and the ideas and examples from the texts, into groups which will form a paragraph plan
- 45 minutes to write a coherent essay
- 5 minutes to read and correct and add to your essay

     = 65–70 minutes

Link

→ Chapter 7 Introduction to A Level English: How will I be assessed?, page 131.

Link

→ Chapter 11 Language and the self: How to approach an exam-style question on language and the self page 215.

Read the following two texts. **Text A** is a BBC News story from 2010. **Text B** is the introduction to a research paper (2005) from a college of the City University of New York.

Discuss what you feel are the most important issues raised in the texts relating to the ways in which language can shape and reflect social identity. You should refer to specific details from the text as well as to ideas and examples from your wider study of Language and the self.

Text A

Actress Emma Thompson attacks use of sloppy language

Actress Emma Thompson has spoken out against the use of sloppy language.

The 51-year-old Oscar winner said that people who did not speak properly made her feel "insane".

She said: "We have to reinvest, I think, in the idea of articulacy as a form of personal human freedom and power."

Ms Thompson added that on a visit to her old school she told pupils not to use slang words such as "likes" and "innit".

"I told them, 'Just don't do it. Because it makes you sound stupid and you're not stupid.'"

She said: "There is the necessity to have two languages – one that you use with your mates and the other that you need in any official capacity."

'Street speak'

Responding to her comments, English language specialist Prof Clive Upton, from the University of Leeds, said that "street speak" was not necessarily a problem.

He said: "There are certain places where the sort of street speak which a lot of teenagers go in for just doesn't cut the mustard.

"If they do deploy the sort of language they're using on the streets in formal settings then it could well be a disadvantage to them but at other times it's quite clearly the way they get along, the way that they signal they belong in a group, the way that they fit in.

"And we all do that in our professional lives as well. We've got all our acronyms and our little words that we use that send a signal – I'm one of the club."

Mike Clarke from Bideford in Devon contacted the BBC News website to show his support for Ms Thompson's stance. He said: "I entirely agree with her comments. I have been a solicitor for over 25 years and have to communicate and engage with people with widely differing verbal ability and understanding. I despise both extremes – dumbing-down language, just as much as 'poshing' it up. They stem from a desire to set one's self apart from the other party."

Source: www.bbc.co.uk/news/uk-11420737

Text B

Appropriation of African American slang by Asian American youth

African Americans have contributed enormously to American English slang over the past several decades. Many scholars argue that slang terms rooted in African American culture, such as *cool*, *hip* and *gig*, are taken up by mainstream Americans because non-mainstream lifestyle and speech are seen as inventive, exciting and even alluringly dangerous.

The idea that non-African Americans benefit from appropriating the verbal dress of a group that has been the target of much discrimination and racism in the United States is a complex subject that deserves more attention from scholars of language and ethnicity. Eble (2004) notes, 'Adopting the vocabulary of a non-mainstream culture is a way of sharing vicariously in the plusses of that culture without having to experience the minuses associated with it'. While non-African Americans may gain local social prestige through peppering their speech with African American slang terms, they do so without suffering the daily experiences with discrimination that plague the lives of many African Americans.

'Appropriation of African American slang by Asian American youth'
by Angela Reyes from *Journal of Sociolinguistics*

Sample student response

Brief introduction. Just about avoids repeating the question ('ways in which language can shape and reflect social identity') –shows some understanding by using the idea of 'projecting' one's identity.

Clever way of linking the fact that ET is an 'actress' to the theories of acting/performing/roles from wider study of Language and the self.

The two texts – Text A from 2010 and Text B from 2005 – both involve people being aware that choices of language can affect the ways in which a person's identity is projected in society.

Emma Thompson is a well-known actress and therefore likely to be especially aware of how to 'perform'. Some social-linguistic theories (e.g. Goffman's ideas in 'The Presentation of Self in Everyday Life') suggest that we 'perform' all the time in a series of 'roles', and that the kinds of language we use in these roles construct our social identities. Thompson is reported as saying to pupils at her old school that if they use "slang words" then they "sound stupid". She adds that "*you're not stupid*," so she seems to be telling young people that they are in danger of conveying a bad and false impression of themselves.

Text A is a BBC news report, and it is interesting in the way it refers to Emma Thompson. First it twice calls her '<u>Actress</u> Emma Thompson' – once in the headline and then again in the first sentence of the report. 'Actress' is a marked term: it is the feminine form of 'actor', a term which is un-marked for gender, but which for many years <u>implied</u> the masculine gender and not the feminine. In more recent years, it has become less acceptable in many societies to use terms which are marked for gender, and instead to use one un-marked term to cover both male and female. For example, instead of using *policeman/policewoman* as a pair of marked terms, it has become the norm to use the term *police officer*. This is because the important aspect of identity here is the job-role (being in the police force) together with the status and responsibility that come with that job-role. Being male or female should make no difference to these aspects of identity.

Even in the few years since this news report was published (2010), most news outlets have moved to using the un-marked term *actor* for both genders. It would be interesting to hear what Emma Thompson thought about being referred to as an actress. She clearly has strong views about how young people present themselves by their choices of language, seeing *"the idea of articulacy"* as *"a form of personal human freedom and power"*. Although the report is not always quoting her actual words, she is reported as having '*spoken out against the use of <u>sloppy</u> language*', which is contrasted with speaking 'properly'. 'Slang' is equated in the report with '<u>sloppy</u> language', and the examples given are '*likes*' and '*innit*'.

Critics of what the article calls 'street speak' often complain about the use of '*like*' as a filler in spoken language, and also refer to its quotative use, as in "I was, like, 'what are you on about?' and he was, like, 'I've gotta go, innit?'" Language purists (also known as prescriptivists) object to the use of 'innit?' as an all-purpose tag question, pointing out that it's a shortened version of the already-contracted form "isn't it?", which should only be used (speaking 'properly' or 'correctly') in the third person. So the speaker in the example <u>should</u> say "I've got to go, haven't I?" – and by using an 'incorrect' form he/she sounds uneducated. As Emma Thomson says, it "*makes you sound stupid*". However, the English language is not as straightforward as that, because in some dialects and varieties it is the norm to use 'isn't it?' as the accepted tag

---

A not-very-linguistic explanation – but showing an awareness that an 'impression' is a way of shaping-an-identity.

Good awareness that Text A is a news report and that it will therefore be doing some linguistic-construction of its own, whatever ET might have said. This serves as a very clever link to the extremely relevant concepts of <u>marked terms</u> and <u>gendered language</u>.

Simple but effective example of marked-ness.

Clear connection to notions of identity.

Awareness of trends in language. Candidate is careful to keep this fairly short and not drift too far into Paper 3 (Language change) territory.

Careful discussion here; candidate identifies how significant issues are signalled by particular words, and makes precise distinctions between 'sloppy' and 'properly'.

Invents (or has prepared) an example which illustrates exactly the uses of 'like' and 'innit' which in the public imagination exemplify 'sloppy' language. Candidate does very well here to use the general-knowledge view of language use and then to move into much more precise (and well-informed) linguistic discussion.

Aware of the prescriptivist/descriptivist conflict.

Completes a precise-but-simple linguistic explanation.

Adds good understanding from wider study of what happens in other languages and other varieties of English.

question. The French use their third-person equivalent ('n'est-ce pas?') for first- and second-person tag questions. Speakers of English who also speak Welsh do the same, and "isn't it?" is normal in Indian English.

Identifies and explains a point made in Text A.

The problem is that some varieties have low overt prestige in formal situations. An 'English language specialist' (Prof Clive Upton) gives his opinion of 'street speak' in Text A: "If they do deploy the sort of language they're using on the streets in formal settings then it could well be a disadvantage to them" On the other hand, some varieties (such as Afro-American Vernacular English – AAVE) which are 'stigmatised' in formal contexts have high covert prestige in other contexts, especially amongst young speakers. As Text B says, 'slang terms rooted in African American culture, such as *cool*, *hip* and *gig*, are taken up by mainstream Americans because non-mainstream lifestyle and speech are seen as inventive, exciting and even alluringly dangerous.'

Gives an example (from wider study) of a 'stigmatised' variety which has high covert prestige and links this example to Text B.

Here the candidate moves skilfully between giving explanations of relevant concepts from wider study and makes use of the 'expert' opinion from Text A.

People who want to belong to particular social groups often reinforce their in-group identity by using a variety of language with low overt prestige but high covert prestige. Prof Clive Upton explains this in Text A: "... at other times it's quite clearly the way they get along, the way that they signal they belong in a group, the way that they fit in."

Provides an accurate explanation of a complex concept related to Language and the self.

The title of Text B hints at an extreme example of this tendency: 'Appropriation of African American slang by Asian American youth'. Appropriation refers to the way in which one group (often a group based on race or ethnicity) takes something from the culture of another racial or ethnic group, and turns it into something of their own. Some critics see this practice as a compliment to the first group, for example when carnival processions in Britain adopt song and dance from the tradition of Caribbean carnivals. Other critics see *appropriation* in much more negative terms, as a theft of an indigenous group's culture – for example, the naming of American sports teams (e.g. the Washington Redskins) after Native American tribes. Text B goes on to say that 'The idea that non-African Americans benefit from appropriating the verbal dress of a group that has been the target of much discrimination and racism in the United States is a complex subject.' For many years, young white Americans have been using features of AAVE as a way of signalling an identity of rebellion against the values of older generations. And there have been research studies which suggest that young Asian Americans are also using AAVE. Text B points out that is like having your cake and eating it too: 'While non-African Americans may gain local social prestige through peppering their speech with African American slang terms, they do so without suffering the daily experiences with

Good (fairly general) example from wider study.

Good (specific) example from wider study.

Brief reference to a valid and relevant research study. Provides enough to be convincing, but doesn't spend too long exploring what is just one point in a long and developed discussion.

Expresses understanding here in very colloquial terms. This is fine, because the rest of the answer is written in sophisticated style.

discrimination that plague the lives of many African Americans.'

Wanting to belong to an in-group is a very common aspect of most people's social identities. And whenever an in-group is created then there will be an out-group. Young people may deliberately use language and references which their parents or teachers might not understand, or would disapprove of. Individual speech communities develop ways of excluding non-members, which is how the particular features of (for example) text-speak, leet-speak or internet memes developed.

Not everyone is happy about this process. As one contributor to Text A says: "I despise both extremes – dumbing-down language, just as much as 'poshing' it up. They stem from a desire to set one's self apart from the other party."

The language of that comment is very interesting since it draws attention to two crucial concepts in the area of shaping social identity: the notion of the *self* and the idea of *part/apart*. Similarly, when Prof Clive Upton uses the expression 'just doesn't cut the mustard', he is (unconsciously?) giving an example of his own idea that 'we all do that in our professional lives as well. We've got all our acronyms and our little words that we use that send a signal – I'm one of the club.'

> Again, expressing a relevant point in quite general terms. But the in-group/out-group distinction is a proper socio-linguistic concept, and is followed by three examples.

> These are valid examples, though no details are offered. In the context of the whole discussion, there isn't time to go into detail here.

> Showing awareness of different attitudes to the issue: it's not just a linguistic concept – it's something which affects people's feelings and lives.

> A linguistically informed quotation from Text A is used by the candidate to bring the argument back to the topic of this section.

> The candidate is running out of time, so she/he has hit upon an ingenious way of bringing the answer to a close. She/he knows that 'cut the mustard' is an idiom that illustrates what Prof Upton is explaining: the idea of using language to signal belonging (though, for this idiom, there seems to be some disagreement over whether it's British English or American English in origin.

This is a very successful and well-informed answer. It's only about 100 words longer than the 'English in the world' sample response, but it balances the use of examples and ideas from the texts with reference to wider study in a much better way.

Overall examiner comments on the Paper 4 sample responses

1. Neither of the two sample responses offered a long introduction. Both quite soon tackled specific examples from the texts provided.

2. The response to the Section A question struggled to settle down to a line of argument. The candidate tried to identify relevant issues from the texts, and did manage to show some understanding of the topic. But she/he was unable to bring in ideas and examples from wider study to add to the discussion. As a result, points were not developed, and the answer more-or-less had to start again with each new paragraph.

3. The response to the Section B question was very successful in drawing on ideas and examples from wider study to develop the argument. Part of the skill demonstrated was in linking points from one paragraph to the next.

4. Neither of the two sample responses offered a concluding paragraph summing up the answer. The Section A response used a lengthy quotation from the last of the exam texts to try to show awareness of different views, whereas the Section B response went on making good points right to the end.

GLOSSARY

Adjective A word that modifies a noun: the *black* cat.

Adverb A word that modifies a verb: she walked *slowly*.

Agent The person responsible for an action or event. As used in a grammatical sense, the subject of an active verb.

Alliteration The repetition of the same letter or sounds at the beginning of adjacent or closely related words: *she sat silently sewing …*

Allusion Reference to another text, often indirectly.

Anaphora Deliberate repetition of words for rhetorical effect.

Archaic Words that sound old-fashioned and have generally fallen out of common use (*aforementioned* or *thee*, for example).

Audience The receivers of a text, whether spoken, visual or written.

Author The producer of a text.

Autobiography The story of the writer's life told from his or her own point of view.

Backgrounding The choice not to emphasise some aspects of a topic in order perhaps to make the subject more attractive (soda advertisements, for example, don't emphasise that fizzy drinks might make you fat).

Biography An account of someone's life told by a third person narrator.

Borrowing When a word from one language is used in another – for example, English borrowed *bungalow* and *veranda* from Indian.

Clause A unit of grammatical organisation that forms part of a sentence, or can be a sentence on its own as it contains a verb with tense and number: *They went to the beach.*

Co-operative principle The idea that speakers will make whatever contributions are necessary to a conversation in order to make it work.

Co-reference Multiple expressions in a text refer to the same thing: Callum said *he* would help and that *he* would bring *his* tools.

Code switching The adaptation of language levels and/or language variety and/or register to different circumstances and situations.

Cohesion Strategies used by a writer or speaker to ensure that a text is structured and signposted with features that will allow it to be followed by a reader or listener.

Collocation A group (or pair) of words commonly used together; idioms often involve collocation.

Colloquial language Language used in ordinary or familiar conversation; language that is not formal or literary. It is often highly idiomatic and hard for someone to understand if they are not a first language speaker.

Conjunction A linking word in a sentence, often to join two clauses (*and*, *but*, for example).

Connotation The ideas or emotions associated with a word.

Context The situation in which a text is produced, including aspects such as social, cultural and political background; it can also refer to that which precedes or follows a word or text and is essential to its meaning.

Contraction The omission of letters to make things less formal: *I can't come out tonight.*

Convergence The coming together of new and old styles and genres in a text (an email borrowing some of the rules of a letter, for example); also the movement of a speaker's language closer to that of the person they are talking to.

Conversational implicature The things a speaker means but does not say.

Conversational maxims General principles of conversation.

Corpus linguistics The examination of texts (often by computer) to analyse the similarities and differences between texts of the same genre in terms of language, structure, form and style.

Covert prestige Status achieved by being a member of a sub-culture – e.g. a social or racial group that is set apart from the dominant culture.

Deixis A form of Context-dependent language - words or phrases such as *this one* or *over here* that can only be understood from the context of the text or utterance where they are found.

Descriptive linguistics The study of language through its use in practice, rather than through grammatical rules.

Descriptivist An attitude to language which depends on accepting current language usage and trying to describe and explain it in linguistic terms.

Denotation The direct (literal) meaning of a word; the 'dictionary definition'.

Dialogue Interchange between two or more speakers.

Discourse analysis The study of language in use.

Discourse marker A word that signals the link between one piece of text and another in order to create cohesion.

Divergence The movement of a speaker's language away from the language of the person they are talking to.

Dynamics of interaction The way that meaning is created by the shifts in turns and topics in a conversation.

Ellipsis The intentional omission of a word, sentence or section of text for reasons of economy or effect.

Emotive Arousing intense feelings or emotions.

English, standard The generally accepted form of the language in an English speaking country.

Epiphora The repetition of a word at the end of successive clasues or sentences.

Etymology The study of how words originated and the way in which their meanings have changed throughout history.

Euphemism A mild, indirect or vague term used instead of one considered harsh, blunt or offensive. (Put very simply: a nice way of saying a nasty thing.)

Explicit meaning Meaning which is clearly and directly stated.

Figurative Words or phrases used in a non-literal way to create an effect; literary texts often make concentrated use of figurative language such as metaphor, personification and simile.

Foregrounding The emphasis on certain aspects of a topic at the expense of others (the speed of a car, as opposed to its price, for example).

Form The shape/structure of a text.

Formal Language which is of middle/high register, without colloquial/idiomatic expressions.

Framing The presentation of a text producer's attitudes and values in a text.

Genre The types or categories into which texts are grouped.

Genre classification The allocation of a text to a type by examination of the features it shares with similar texts.

Grammar The structure and function of individual words; the arrangement of those words within a sentence.

Ideology The attitudes and values that are either explicitly or implicitly present in a text.

Idiom or idiomatic An expression/phrase that has a particular meaning, different from the meanings of the words understood on their own in a literal fashion (*she's been fired*, for example).

Imagery Figurative, non-literal language, particularly in a literary work.

Imperative Part of the verb used for instruction: *Go away*, for example.

Implicit meaning Something implied by a text but not directly stated: *Sheila drives a Ferrari* (with the implication, therefore, that she is rich).

Infer To deduce from evidence and reasoning.

Infinitive The basic, dictionary form of a verb when not associated with tense: *to go*, *to walk*.

Interjection An interrupting exclamation in speech or writing: *Oh!*, *Dear me!*

Irony A statement that has an underlying meaning different from its surface or literal meaning.

Jargon A special term or expression used by a specific group, often used to exclude other listeners or readers; professional or technical shorthand (RAM with computers, for example).

Language community A group of speakers or writers who demonstrate belonging and identity through their language choices

Lectal continuum The idea that different varieties of English within a society can be placed in order of status and level of formality along a continuum, with the basilect as the least formal/'educated', the acrolect as the most formal/'educated', and the mesolect in the middle. (Not all linguists accept this concept.)

Lexical field A set of words grouped by meaning round a specific subject – law or medicine, for example.

Lexical relationship The way in which a reader/listener understands a word's meaning or grammatical function by considering its use in relation to other words or the syntax of a sentence.

Linguistics The scientific study of human language.

Literal To take words in their usual or most basic sense, without metaphorical implications.

Loanword A word borrowed into a language from another (*pizza*, *bungalow*, for example).

Marginalised Pushed to the edges ('margins') of society; not accepted as societal norm or disapproved of

Metaphor A figure of speech in which a word or phrase is applied to something to which it is not literally applicable: she *ploughed* through the pile of applications.

Metaphor, dead A metaphor so frequently used that it is no longer recognised as metaphorical: to *coin* a phrase, or to *grasp* an idea, for example.

Metaphor, extended An elaboration of one metaphorical significance so that other similarities are seen: *All the world's a stage, And all the men and women merely players; They have their exits and their entrances …*

Metaphor, mixed A confusion of metaphors, usually accidental and with unintentionally comic effect: *to grasp the nettle by the horns, I smell a rat that needs nipping in the bud.*

Mixed medium A text where different genre rules combine to create meaning and significance.

Modifier A word or phrase – particularly an adverb/adverbial phrase or adjective/adjectival phrase – that qualifies or describes, e.g. the *red* sky. This description may come before (pre-modification) or after (post-modification).

Monologue Discourse entirely spoken (or written) by one person.

Mood (definition 1) A term to define different verbal uses, such as infinitive (*to walk*), subjunctive (a state of uncertainty: *If I were younger…*), or indicative – a verb expressing a simple statement of fact (*He is walking*).

Mood (definition 2) The atmosphere or emotion in a written text: *the mood of this text is somewhat subdued because …*

Morpheme The smallest grammatical unit of a language, often only part of a word, such as *breakable*, which can be taken apart as two morphemes, eg *break*, and *able*.

Morphology The study of the structure and form of words in a language, including their derivation and the formation of compounds to create different meanings, such as friend to friend*ly* to *un*friendly.

Motherese/parentese The particular choices of language which parents and other adults make when talking to small children.

Narrative A spoken or written account of connected events.

Narrative voice The voice of the person telling the story.

Narrative, first-person The story is being told by the writer, using the word '*I*'.

Narrative, intrusive The narrator intrudes to shape your opinion of what you are reading or hearing, either by direct comment or implication.

Narrative, restricted The writer, either first or third person, does not know how things will turn out in the end, or has only a partial understanding of the events that are being recounted.

Narrative, third-person Narration recounts what is happening to others, using words like *he*, *she* or *they*.

Narrative, unintrusive You don't get to know what the author thinks about the events being recounted.

Narrative, unrestricted The writer has a seemingly unlimited knowledge regarding events in the text.

Netiquette The evolving conventions for communicating over the internet or social networks.

Netspeak The language of the internet.

Noun A word that identifies people, places or thing.

Novel Prose narrative that tells (in some way) a made up story.

Number Used for analysis of clauses to discuss whether the action is done by one agent (singular) or many (plural).

Objective Not based on personal feelings, tastes or opinions.

Omniscient narrator The person telling the story knows everything (including, probably, how it all turns out).

Overt prestige Status achieved by being part of the dominant group(s) in a culture/society.

Parts of speech Also called *word class* – the grammatical names of the different types of words that combine (nouns, verbs etc) to form units of expression.

Pejoration The opposite process to amelioration, by which a word's meaning gets worse over time as it acquires negative connotations. A pejorative usage is a way of using a word so that it conveys negative associations.

Personification Attributing human characteristics to non-human things: The sun *smiled* on us that day.

Phrase A group of words, a conceptual unit, without a main verb containing tense and number and which therefore can't stand as sentences: *today's weather forecast*, *the little girl next door*.

Point of view A writer or speaker's choices about how to present information, ideology etc.

Pragmatics The branch of linguistics concerned with language in use and the contexts in which it is used. The commmon understandings that allow communication to take place.

Preposition A word governing a noun or pronoun to demonstrate a relationship between it and other elements – *up*, *down*, *in*, *out*, *after*, for example.

Prescriptivist An attitude to language which emphasises 'rules' and criticises anything in current language usage that seems to be a change from the 'correct' forms of the past.

Presupposition An understanding of what a reader or listener already knows about the genre of writing or the situation from which a text emerges.

Prestige The high status accorded to some codes and varieties.

Pronoun A word used to substitute for a noun already mentioned: The students are clever: *they* will pass the examinations.

Prose Ordinary written or spoken language without metrical structure.

Prototype A model or established form for a piece of writing in a genre.

Purpose The author's intention when speaking or writing.

Reference, anaphoric Referring back to a word used earlier to avoid repetition: *Dracula is a vampire; he drinks blood*.

Reference, cataphoric Referring to a word that appears later in the text: *While she was writing her essay, Rosa's phone rang*.

Register The use of different words, style, grammar, pitch and tone in different contexts and situations.

Rhetoric Devices such as pauses, repetitions in order to persuade or convince.

Rhetorical question A question posed by a writer or speaker for emphasis or dramatic effect (*Do you know how lucky you are?*) which doesn't demand an response, as the answer is self-evident.

Semantics The study of meaning.

Semantic amelioration The process by which the meaning of a word 'improves' over time. It might lose negative connotations (or neutral ones) and acquire positive connotations.

Semantic field A group of words related in meaning, but expressing a different degree or shade of that meaning – for example, *alone/ solitary/lonely/isolated*.

Sentence structure How a sentence is composed from different building blocks, ranging from single word classes (types of words) to phrases, to clauses (main and subordinate).

Sentence, complex A sentence with a main clause together with one or more dependent (subordinate) clauses: *The teacher returned the homework after she had marked it*; After she had marked it depends on the first clause with tense and number.

Sentence, compound A sentence containing two independent clauses, joined by a co-ordinator: *The rain continues and we are all bored*.

Sentence, compound-complex A sentence containing at least two independent clauses, with one or more clauses that are subordinate: *The teacher returned the homework after she had marked it, and then she began the lesson* – there are two main clauses here.

Sentence, simple A clause that has a verb with tense and number and can stand as a unit of sense on its own: They *stole* the bicycle.

Setting The time, place and atmosphere in which the action of a piece of writing takes place.

Simile Comparing one thing with another using the words *like* or *as*: *she sings like a strangled parrot, he's as good as gold*.

Situation The location, time, circumstances within a text, or the circumstances in which a text is received.

Slang Informal words or expressions, particularly used in spoken, not written language.

Slogan A short phrase or clause used by advertisers.

Sociolinguistics The descriptive study of the effects of society, cultural norms, expectations and context on the way that language is used and the way language has an effect on society.

Solecism A grammatical mistake.

Stigmatised 'Marked' as not accepted as societal norm; disapproved of because of pejorative associations – e.g. an accent can be stigmatised if its users as stereotyped as inclined to criminal behaviour.

Structure The way in which a text (of whatever length) is organised.

Style A writer's choice of words and strategies to create meaning.

Subjective Based on or influenced by personal feelings, tastes or opinions.

Subordinate clause A series of words, including a verb with tense and number, that form part of a sentence but depend on a main clause (e.g. *when it rang* in *She answered the phone when it rang*).

Symbol Something which stands for or represents something else (an apple in the Bible is used as a symbol for temptation, for example).

Syntax The ways in which words are arranged to form cohesive grammatical structures.

Tense The form of a verb used to describe when something happened.

Tense, past Actions that are definitely finished: *He sold the car*.

Tense, past imperfect Used for actions that happened continuously at some point in the past: The sun was *shining* brightly the day we went on our holidays.

Tense, present continuous Used for things that are currently happening: She *is* walking to the shops.

Tense, simple present He goes to school in the morning.

Text Any spoken, written or visual form of communication.

Tone the quality of the voice (either written or spoken) that conveys the emotional message of the text.

Topic-shift A term from spoken language theory to describe deliberately-caused or naturally-occurring changes of subject.

Tricolon Repetition of a word or phrase three times.

Turn-taking The process of conversation, where speakers allow (or don't allow) others to take over from them.

Verb A word used to describe an action, state or occurrence; the word that tells you what is happening in a sentence: He *walks* to work.

Vernacular The language or dialect spoken by ordinary people.

Voice (definition 1) The persona of a writer or speaker as conveyed through the way that they speak or write.

Voice (definition 2) The form of a verb showing the relation of the subject to the action. The active voice: *The cat chased the dog*. The passive voice: *The dog was chased by the cat*.

Word class Also called parts of speech – the grammatical names of the different types of words that combine (nouns, verbs etc) to form units of expression.

KEY READING LIST

Below is a list of recommended reading material to support your learning and further your study, based on the extracts featured in this book. Use the page numbers to find the relevant extracts within this book.

Collected Poems by William Carlos Williams (page 15)

The Adventures of Huckleberry Finn by Mark Twain (page 18)

The Great Gatsby by F. Scott Fitzgerald (page 19)

A Tale of Two Cities by Charles Dickens (page 20)

Behind the Beautiful Forevers by Katherine Boo (page 21)

Half of a Yellow Sun by Chimamanda Ngozi Adichie (page 23)

In Our Time by Ernest Hemingway (page 31)

The Goldfinch by Donna Tartt (page 31)

The Luminaries by Eleanor Catton (page 32)

The Boy with the Topknot by Sathnam Sanghera (page 39)

Under Milk Wood by Dylan Thomas (page 40)

Wolf Hall by Hilary Mantel (page 45)

Weaving the Web by Tim Berners-Lee (page 51)

The Reluctant Fundamentalist by Mohsin Hamid (page 54)

Autumn by Ali Smith (page 55)

The Diary of Virginia Woolf by Virginia Woolf (page 66)

Why be Happy When You Could be Normal? by Jeanette Winterson (page 67)

To the Is-Land by Janet Frame (page 68)

Wrestling with the Angel: A Life of Janet Frame by Michael King (page 68)

Mirror to Damascus by Colin Thubron (page 76)

Shooting an Elephant by George Orwell (page 85)

David Copperfield by Charles Dickens (page 100)

The Mayor of Casterbridge by Thomas Hardy (page 101)

Cannery Row by John Steinbeck (page 102)

The Hollow Hills by Mary Stewart (page 102)

Mary Poppins by P. L. Travers (page 102)

Moby Dick by Herman Melville (page 102)

The Better Part by Annie S. Swan (page 102)

Cat's Cradle by Kurt Vonnegut (page 102)

The Loud Halo by Lillian Beckwith (page 103)

Lady Chatterley's Lover by D. H. Lawrence (page 103)

To the Lighthouse by Virginia Woolf (page 103)

The General Danced at Dawn by George MacDonald Fraser (page 103)

The Sound and the Fury by William Faulkner (page 103)

The Story of Doctor Dolittle by Hugh Lofting (page 103)

The Handmaid's Tale by Margaret Atwood (page 104)

Will You Please Be Quiet, Please? by Raymond Carver (page 105)

The Big Sleep by Raymond Chandler (page 108)

Americanah by Chimamanda Ngozi Adichie (page 111)

Politics and the English Language by George Orwell (page 125)

Rural Rides by William Cobbett (page 138)

1984 by George Orwell (page 211)

INDEX

INDEX